Palgrave Studies in the History of Finance

The study of the history of financial institutions, markets, instruments and concepts is vital if we are to understand the role played by finance today. At the same time, the methodologies developed by finance academics can provide a new perspective for historical studies. Palgrave Studies in the History of Finance is a multi-disciplinary effort to emphasise the role played by finance in the past, and what lessons historical experiences have for us. It presents original research, in both authored monographs and edited collections, from historians, finance academics and economists, as well as financial practitioners.

Donatella Strangio

The Roman Stock Exchange between the 19th and 20th Centuries

A History of the Italian Stock Market

palgrave
macmillan

Donatella Strangio
Sapienza Università di Roma
Rome, Italy

ISSN 2662-5164 ISSN 2662-5172 (electronic)
Palgrave Studies in the History of Finance
ISBN 978-3-031-00344-8 ISBN 978-3-031-00359-2 (eBook)
https://doi.org/10.1007/978-3-031-00359-2

Cover credit: marco varrone/Alamy Stock Photo

This Palgrave Macmillan imprint is published by the registered company Springer Nature Switzerland AG
The registered company address is: Gewerbestrasse 11, 6330 Cham, Switzerland

This book is dedicated to the memory of Tullio Strangio

Preface I

In his seminal article on the formation of financial centres,[1] Charles Kindleberger observed that in the course of the nineteenth country, in all industrialized countries, a national financial centre emerged, progressively relegating competing ones to a peripheral role. This centre could be the country's political capital, as in the case, for the period covered by the book, of Europe's largest economies—London in the United Kingdom, Paris in France and Berlin in Germany; to which could be added, in less advanced economies, St Petersburg in the Russian empire and Vienna in the Austro-Hungarian empire. But in other countries, the political capital and the financial capital have been two different cities, the obvious case being New York in the United States, but there are others, such as Zurich in Switzerland (though to a certain extent jointly with Geneva and Basel), Montreal in Canada (in competition with Toronto until the latter's eventual predominance) and of course Milan in Italy (though its emergence took place later than that of London, Paris and even Berlin).

Rome has never been a major financial centre nor did it seriously compete with Milan for the position of Italy's financial centre. This is no reason to neglect its financial history. Because of the relationships between state and finance, all political capitals play a role in their country's financial affairs. Moreover, Rome is unique in being Italy's largest city,

[1] Charles Kindleberger, 'The Formation of Financial Centres', *Princeton Studies in International Finance*, 36 (1974), pp. 1–78.

unlike Washington in the United States, Bern in Switzerland or Ottawa in Canada.

It is interesting to look at Rome from this particular viewpoint. Donatella Strangio has aptly entitled her book "Capital City"—and not City of Capital or Capital of Capital, as has been done for London, New York and other leading financial centres.[2] The double meaning of the word "capital" perfectly describes Rome's specific position: a capital city in the political sense of the word, but also a city of some significance as far as financial markets are concerned.

Rather than a history of Rome as a financial centre, Donatella Strangio has written a global history of Rome, seen from the perspective of its Stock Exchange, which was only second to Milan in Italy. Donatella Strangio has taken a *longue durée* approach, going back to the pre-industrial era; she puts Rome in its proper economic, social and political context, and fully integrates its history with that of Italy and she provides a detailed account of the development of its Stock Exchange, in terms of organization and rules, as well as securities quoted, with comparisons with other Italian Stock of Exchanges, primarily Milan.

Donatella Strangio's book thus clearly fills a gap in the literature—not only on Italian history but also on international financial history—in a well-conceived, elegant and scholarly way.

Youssef Cassis
Professor of Economic History
Emeritus
European University Institute
Florence, Italy

[2] Jerry Coakley and Laurence Harris, *The City of Capital. London's role as a Financial Centre* (London, 1983); Steven H. Jaffe and Jessica Lautin, *Capital of Capital. Money, Banking and Power in New York City, 1784–2012* (New York, 2014); Youssef Cassis, *Capitals of Capital. A History of International Financial Centres* (1st ed. Cambridge, 2006).

Preface II

The interest of historiography in the history of Rome, ancient and modern, is certainly a constant in the panorama of Italian and foreign studies. However, as is well known, this interest, full of ideological meanings and teleological readings, has undergone an important and decisive evolution since the publication of the work by Paolo Prodi, (*Il sovrano pontefice. Un corpo e due anime: la monarchia papale nella prima Età moderna* (Bologna, il Mulino, 1982), a watershed in the interpretations of the city's history, for too long and unjustly considered as a static, obsolete, backward city *tout court*.

Obviously, it is not possible here to recall in detail the main researches of the last few decades in the wake of that masterful text—innovative, original and generally solid research from a documentary point of view—, I must limit myself to remembering how, thanks to these works, the paradigm of the fragile *papal immobility* has ended up being completely dismantled, in particular in relation to the early modern age.

Less ploughed, however, is the field of the nineteenth century in Rome, a period still burdened by nationalist and often superficial interpretations due to the ecclesiastical component that conditioned the reality of the papal capital for so long. In fact, while there were those who tried to trace Rome's failure to take off internationally precisely to the conditioning presence of the pontifical see (it was only after its proclamation as the capital of the Kingdom of Italy that the city, finally laicized, began to be a *normal* urban reality), others have instead wanted to underline the links existing between the collapse of the temporal domination (the breach of Porta Pia, 20 September 1870) and the start of Catholicism retreating from the world.

The beautiful volume "Rome Capital City" fills these gaps and far from remaining a prisoner of dichotomous contrasts, traces the difficult history of the city in a balanced way, addressing its complexity and contradictions through a completely new perspective and a herald—I am sure—of new and fruitful interpretative developments.

The goal of the author, Donatella Strangio, consists of a serious and documented analysis of the evolution of the city through a particular observatory, that of the Stock Exchange, considered not so much as an exclusive or absolute protagonist of the financial market, but rather as a subject and object of the history, certainly economic, but also social and political, of Rome and the Papal State. In addition, this singular observatory, despite its atypical nature, seems to be valuable for the purposes of an overall analysis of the behaviour of the local, national and international executive and entrepreneurial classes.

Focussing on six key historical moments, the book starts from the decline in the Pope's temporal power—the aforementioned breach of Porta Pia-: an epochal event, here linked to previous institutional and social transformations as well as to the level of nineteenth–twentieth century internal and external relations. As the subtitle of the work explicitly states (*Structure and activity of the Rome stock market between the nineteenth and twentieth centuries: a history of the Italian stockexchange*), the periodization adopted by the Author is also unconventional.

Starting from 1821—and nevertheless attentive to some important pre-existing joints—Strangio examines the dynamics triggered by the Commerce Regulations to clarify how the Roman stock exchange reacted with respect to the Risorgimento and subsequently to the establishment of the Kingdom of Italy. Embracing both the liberal period and that of the "Belle époque", the study finally reaches the First World War (as the author recalls, it was with the Great War that the "long nineteenth century" ended and a new system of contacts and of exchanges appeared, thanks to which the Eternal City abandoned the *welfare* model that had distinguished it most in previous centuries), and then proceeds to the following decades. This long-term approach allows Donatella Strangio to convincingly demonstrate how, far from confining it to a more restricted space, becoming the Italian capital greatly facilitated the evolution of the urban development trends in Rome, finally released from the nefarious effects of the papal public debt, from which it had suffered for some time, aggravated by the "amputation" of the territory of the Patrimony of St. Peter, after 1861. The rhythms imposed by being the capital influenced all sectors and economic sectors of the city, from industry to the tertiary sector.

Rome Capital City therefore traces the historical evolution of the legislation that is the object of its investigation, the role of financial intermediaries, and the functions of the decision-making and control bodies that were part of the Rome Stock Exchange, in particular in light of the consolidation of the British capitalist model and the Northern European one.

An unusual picture emerges, a picture that portrays the complex financial mechanisms of the nineteenth and twentieth centuries but also the broad world of Roman entrepreneurship, which, moreover, can benefit from the in-depth analysis of stock exchanges between 1860 and 1870, as well as share prices up to the Great War, the Depression and the consolidation of the Fascist period.

Thanks to Donatella Strangio, we can finally take advantage of an innovative and precious contribution to the history of late nineteenth and early twentieth-century Rome; an intelligent contribution, in which we see a dynamic, resilient dimension of the city well integrated into the European political and financial networks, capable of dealing with the rhythms imposed by capital and of perceiving their impact on the various economic sectors, from industry to the tertiary sector.

In the background, we find the peculiar features of a complex and contradictory century—like all centuries—made up of archaisms and tradition, of resistance to the new, but also of unpredictable and radical transformations; a century that invites us to reflect on the elusive aspects of the categories of *modernization*, too often hastily identified as a factor of absolute progress, a "periodizing" generator of contemporaneity.

Marina Formica
Full professor of modern history
University of Tor Vergata - Rome
President of the Italian Society of
XVIII Century Studies
Coordinator of the Rome '800
Research Center

Acknowledgements

The book is the result of a research project stretching over the past years and it benefited from the input and the advice of various colleagues and friends.

I would like to thank Elena Ambrosetti, Giuseppe De Luca, Youssef Cassis, Marina Formica, Luca Mocarelli, Angelo Riva, Stefano Ceccariglia, Marco Dottori, Salvatore Sbriglio and Giuseppe Torneo.

I am grateful to Youssef Cassis, professor of economic history, and Marina Formica, professor of modern history, who kindly gave me their time in reading and writing a preface, as the volume combines aspects related to two disciplines, economic history and modern history.

Of course, the only one responsible for what is written is me.

Introduction

Until a few decades ago, the stock market attracted the interest of few historians and economists. Only recently has it become a subject for historical study.

Nevertheless, "The stock exchange is and remains a precious synthesis observatory that deserves a much broader and more systematic historiographic use than has happened up to now, which deserves, in other words, the opening of a collective work aimed at enhancing the breadth of data offered by the market".[1]

The nineteenth century can be considered as the century that, from an economic and financial viewpoint, officially introduced the stock exchange in Italy as a novel entity. Most likely, even if not formally recognized as such, business centres had already formed in the preceding centuries (even as early as the Middle Ages). These centres included precursors of the subsequent development of the stock market. If we leave aside the medieval era, which was coeval with and linked to the first banking initiatives, the Italian stock exchanges emerged according to the French model following the application in Italy of the Napoleonic Code of Commerce.

In Italy, the first stock exchange was established in Milan on 15 February 1808. In the following years, in chronological order, stock exchanges also opened in Naples, Rome, Florence, Livorno and Genoa.

[1] Baia Curioni, 1995, pp. 37–38.

This book addresses the Rome Stock Exchange, which was established following promulgation of the Trade Regulations of 1 June 1821, according to the following definition:

Stock exchange is the union that takes place under the authority of the government, merchants, ship captains, stockbrokers, and brokers.[2]

It should be noted that until the unification of Italy (1861) and for the subsequent nine years the Rome stock exchange was part of the financial structure of the Papal State.

It was determined to analyse a particular historical period: 1821–1930. During this period, two events occurred that fundamentally marked modern Italian history: (a) the integration of most of the peninsular regions into the new Italian nation and the subsequent end of the Papal State with its more than 1000 year history as a political power; (b) the liberal period and the "belle époque", followed by the outbreak of the Great War.

With the Great War, the "long nineteenth century", as certain scholars have termed it, ends, and following the tragic world war, the liberal period of the early twentieth century and the interwar years commences.[3]

The principle aim of this book is to analyse the transformation of the eternal city, Rome, through an investigation of the historically important establishment of the stock exchange, which is part of the larger financial market, as influenced by critical factors not only from an economic and financial perspective but also from a historical and political one. The book consists of six chapters.

First, several general aspects of the State of the Church and of Rome, its capital, are considered. Historically, the most relevant event of the period was the overthrow of the pope's political power. This event, however, did not occur suddenly but was the conclusion of a process consisting of multiple events, including military battles, interventions by foreign countries, and diplomatic agreements. Economically, following the loss of much of the papal territory in 1860, even the pontifical authorities had come to understand the impossibility of isolating the territory of Lazio within the wide area of the peninsula and thus the need for a form of complementarity if not integration. Therefore, behind a façade of

[2] State Archive of Rome (SAR), Primaria Camera di Commercio, b. 2.

[3] Toniolo, 1990; Hobsbawn, 1995; Cassis, 2006; James and O'Rourke, 2013, pp. 53–96.

resistance, borders began to open, and secretly and progressively a process commenced to establish a new system of relations and exchanges. From a financial perspective, the Papal State had long been pressured to seek new funding to support its increasing budget deficits and combat the decline of its international prestige. In addition, it must be considered that a reduced Papal State was incorporated within the newly born Italy; therefore, it was taken for granted that prior to the capture of Porta Pia on 20 September 1870 interdependencies would be established between the two "countries".

The second chapter is dedicated to the financial and banking situation that will characterize the lists of the Rome Stock Exchange and how the city of Rome reacts to this difficult situation, one that was highly complex because of the failure of the welfare model that made it unique in the centuries prior to the consolidation of the British and Northern European capitalist model. The third chapter is dedicated to the historical evolution of regulations, the role of financial intermediaries and the decision-making and control bodies that were part of the Rome Stock Exchange. Here, topics are addressed (for example, the relationships between stockbrokers and money changers or the prohibitions imposed by supervisory bodies) which at first might seem of marginal importance but are in fact useful to developing a wider understanding of the atmosphere of the Roman business world.

The fourth chapter, which is linked to the previous chapter, is a detailed study of the stock market lists of the decade 1860–1870 and of the transition period up to 20 September 1870. The fifth chapter examines stock prices from 1870 to the outbreak of the Great War, with a specific focus on the most important companies. The final chapter concerns the first postwar period and ends with the Great Depression and the first fascist period.

This work will certainly not exhaust all the aspects, on the contrary I hope that further reflections and questions will emerge, reading it. Histories of stock exchanges are rare and in this case, the effort was to combine the novelty of the Rome Stock Exchange with the transformation of the city before and after the Italian unification, from the capital of the papal state to the capital of Italy.

References

Baia Curioni, Stefano. 1995. *Regolazione e competizione. Storia del mercato azionario in Italia (1808–1938)*, Bologna, Il Mulino.

Cassis, Yousseff. 2006. *Capitals of Capital. A History of International Financial Centres, 1780–2005*, Cambridge: Cambridge University Press (Trad Ita. 2008. *Le Capitali della finanza. Uomini e città protagonisti della storia economica*, Milan: Francesco Brioschi Editore).

Hobsbawn Eric. J. 1995. *Il secolo breve. 1914–1991*, Milan: Rizzoli.

James, Harold and O'Rourke Kevin H. 2013. *La prima globalizzazione e I suoi contraccolpi*, in Gianni Toniolo (ed.) *L'Italia e l'economia mondiale dall'unità a oggi*, Venice: Marsilio Editori: 53–96.

Toniolo, Gianni. 1990. *An Economic History of Liberal Italy, 1850–1918*, London: Routledge.

Contents

List of Figures

List of Tables

CHAPTER 1

Rome and the Papal State: Old Customs and the New Kingdom of Italy

What was the political, economic and financial situation of Rome, the capital of the Papal State, before the Italian Unification? A capital and a state in the heart of Italy, a crossroads of political powers and military armies and, for a long time, a needle in the balance of the political equilibrium of Europe.

The Italian political framework of this historical period was becoming clear enough according to an antagonism that saw the Sardinian Kingdom as the only surviving constitutional, parliamentary and liberal kingdom, in the middle of a peninsula dominated by the Austrian empire. The Papal State entered this constellation of Vienna's satellites without demonstrating any political originality. In fact, more than these satellites, it projected an image of anachronism and substantial weakness, even financial.

1.1 Restoration, Change, Innovation and Tradition

Restoration was defined "as the result of weariness, caused by a long period of daring and innovations in the political and moral field", a withdrawal of forces back upon themselves, a subsequent lively counterattack on rationalist positions and a general movement of reaction

D. Strangio, *The Roman Stock Exchange between the 19th and 20th Centuries*, Palgrave Studies in the History of Finance,
https://doi.org/10.1007/978-3-031-00359-2_1

to the individualism characteristic of the eighteenth century.[1] In the Papal State, the ancient equilibrium was disturbed by new experiences that forced it to seek an intermediary between modern institutions and the old order. Municipal laws, noble privileges, royalties and fishing reserves, hunting, quarries and mines were abolished (although certain exceptions or modifications were made).[2] It has been emphasized how the previous revolutionary-Napoleonic movement provided a stimulus to create more favourable opportunities, which materialized during the age of the Restoration and the Risorgimento.[3] In certain cases, portions of the Napoleonic legislation were maintained. In addition, Napoleon's administrative system, which summarized and concluded a slow development process (but for this no less encouraging to the centralization of power) was preserved in various Italian states in its essential lines[4]; in particular, the process of revision of traditional interpretative models, as noted in the most recent historiography on the period, considered the reality of the Papal State absolutely specific and peculiar.[5]

It is precisely the directives adopted by the ecclesiastical government that reflect both the seriousness of the economic-social crisis experienced by the Papal State in the age of the Restoration and all the backwardness of that government. It is probable that these issues were accentuated by the inadequacy of the response of the class of large landowners to this crisis.[6] However, as Pescosolido observes, in the case of the Borghese, one of the Papal State's most prominent noble families, the level of rent of the estates let according to the traditional system from 1810 to 1838

[1] Petrocchi, 1941, p. 20. Very interesting are the works on Leo XII which highlight the will of the popes to reform and the inevitability of having to modernize the Roman State (Piccinini 2012; Regoli et al. 2019).

[2] Petrocchi, 1941, p. 5.

[3] Caracciolo, 1973, p. 556.

[4] Caracciolo, 1973, p. 6. Regarding the legal historiography of this period, extensive information has been provided by Castracane Mombelli, 1975–1976, pp. 108–156; 1979–1980, pp. 111–240.

[5] For example, see Caffiero, 1997, pp. 137–161; Santoncini, 1994, pp. 158–185.

[6] For example, the Borghese house presents a symptomatic response not only in terms of an attitude of substantial renunciation of any form of productive investment in sectors other than the primary one but also in this context of the renunciation of any attempt to seriously increase production through technical-qualitative modifications (Pescosolido, 1979, p. 199).

experienced a modest increase,[7] while starting in the 1840s, it surged in response to a more pronounced economic dynamism.[8] One can note, therefore, the result of the progressive recovery of noble incomes in an era of normalization and restoration not only at the institutional and political level but also at the level of relations between the classes.[9] The costs generated by a restoration policy that highlighted the power relationship between the state and private finance were high: in fact, the increasing leverage of financing due to ever-increasing government commitments amplified the role of the merchant banker.[10] Under Gregory XVI, there was an unexpected change in terms of protectionism and tax policy.[11] In terms of recourse to debt, it was necessary to issue new tranches of consolidation to cover increasing financial needs, of which a large portion again consisted of interest on public debt.[12] The imbalance in public finances, which was becoming increasingly profound, also made it necessary to resort to increasing international financing.

The financial exploitation of public intervention, which was a response to a real need for reorganization and reaffirmation of papal power, was evident in the reform of the administration of the same sector. This reform was characterized by a reduction of the bureaucratic apparatus (even if this provision established insufficient premises for a genuine recovery), the creation of a discount bank that would aid the government in floating rate transactions, in savings banks[13] and in the reorganization of public debt (to cite only a few examples). The latter represented an ideal blend of old and new; it was an obsolete tool that had to be renewed to achieve new

[7] Pescosolido, 2004, p. 95.

[8] Pescosolido, 1981, p. 397.

[9] Pescosolido, 1981, p. 214. Regarding the strategies of the Roman nobility and patrimonial dynamics, see also La Marca, 2000, vol. 1–3; Palermo, 2008.

[10] Toniolo, 1995. Felisini, 2004, 2016, 2021. See for a general picture of bankers and their networks at the beginning of the Contemporary Age, contributing to the process of social transformation in Italy Gregorini, Romani 2021.

[11] About the general situation of the state during the pontificate of Gregory XVI and its major measures, see Demarco, 1949.

[12] See infra.

[13] Regarding the constitution and the debate on the Banca Romana, see in particular Graziani, 1989, pp. 463–492. The Rome discount bank was established in 1825. It failed five years later because of the immaturity of the Roman credit market. *On* these events, see Graziani, 1993, pp. 83–109. For the subsequent activities of the Banca Romana and its relations with other institutions, see D'Errico, 1993, pp. 111–131; 1999.

and old goals. In this regard, it is evident from a memorandum drawn up by state officials that over the centuries the popes had been able to manage its use and were thus aware of the merits and financial consequences of this type of instrument.[14]

In addition, because for many centuries the use of such a financial instrument could hardly be avoided, restructuring and reorganization were required to restore breath to a market exhausted by the Jacobin events and by the subsequent Napoleonic and Neapolitan political transformations.[15]

The restored government of Pius VII considered it convenient to abandon the now obsolete structure of the *Luoghi di Monte* and to transform those debts that for various reasons had not been liquidated by the preceding government into folders of consolidated debt. The new consolidation differed from the ancient *Luoghi di Monte*. These were specific debts, typical of the papal territories and unconnected to the debts of other states,[16] and the continuous expansion of debt served to finance not only public initiatives but also and above all the pontifical communities, the few industrial initiatives or private families.[17]

With the *Motu Proprio* of 6 July 1816, the provisions on the overall administrative restructuring inherent in the restoration of the Papal State that in June 1815 had regained, with the recovery of the Marche, Romagna and the Duchy of Benevento, its previous territorial outlines, found an organic arrangement. According to the intentions of Cardinal Consalvi, in the *Motu Proprio*, the old and the new had to coexist; that is, all that could be saved from the past government of the popes and all that was new and suited to the needs of the state the French had created.[18] The *Motu Proprio* dictated the rules for the administration of

[14] Strangio, 2001. State Archive of Rome (from now SAR), Camerale II, Debito Pubblico, b.7, fasc.3, Memoria sul debito pubblico dello Stato Pontificio, cc.1–3. SAR, Camerale II, Debito Pubblico b.14, fasc.3, p. 15.

[15] The Neapolitan provisional government, which prepared the resettlement of the papal government, operated from March 29, 1814, to May 10, 1814. See also Strangio, 2001.

[16] SAR, Camerale II, Debito pubblico b.14, fasc.3.

[17] Regarding the institution of "Monti" for private purposes and debt expansion, see Piola Caselli, 1993, pp. 21–55.

[18] SAR, Bandi b.312.

papal public debt.[19] The sphere of intervention ranged from the consolidation of old titles into the fold of the newly consolidated, to the question of those belonging to foreign bodies and private individuals who, by law, during the French domination, had seen their titles revoked, to the thorny questions of whether it was lawful to confirm the transfer of ownership of ecclesiastical assets expropriated by the past government and sold at auction in exchange for public bonds (*Luoghi di Monte*) to be liquidated and of the legitimacy of those assets belonging to French citizens; interest was ordered to start accruing from the first quarter of 1817.[20] The execution of these measures was assigned to a particular congregation *ad referendum*[21]; the direction of the papal public debt was subordinated to this congregation and to the General Treasurer, who effectively managed the entire sector.

Initially, an attempt was made to standardize in all the territories of the State (whether they were first or second "*recupera*")[22] the legal problems that gradually arose, and an attempt was made to resolve the question of the expropriated assets of ecclesiastical entities by paying the latter fair compensation for them.[23]

Leaving aside the arrangement of the post other than the "Luoghi di monte" guarantees but always part of the debt, according to the approach instituted by the French government, it can therefore be stated that for the restored pontifical government the "Luoghi di Monte" not liquidated by the French Liquidation Council were liquidated by article 231 of the previously mentioned *Motu Proprio* but with the capital reduced by 25

[19] By the articles 225–237 and 246 of the *Motu Proprio* of 6 July 1816, the government undertook an initial reorganization of the matter.

[20] SAR, Bandi b. 312, *Motu Proprio* del 6 July 1816, art. 237. Under the old system of financing, *Luoghi di Monte*, interest was paid every two months in arrears.

[21] This congregation consisted of the General Treasurer, the Secretary of the Congregation of Bishops and Regulars, two Auditors of Rota, and a Cleric of the Chamber.

[22] The terms "first and second recover" refer to those parts of the territory that were re-annexed to the Papal State on the basis of the European conventions stipulated in the aftermath of French domination.

[23] Art. 225 del *Motu proprio* del 6 July 1816. Cfr. Cecchi, 1978, pp. 1–50; see Pastura Ruggiero, 1991, pp. 18–19.

scudi for each,[24] while the annual interest was reduced to 1.20 scudi.[25] It is clear that the loss in nominal capital was 76% for those assets liquidated during French domination and 75% for the "Luoghi di Monte" liquidated from 1816 onwards. The annual nominal rate of consolidation was set at 5%[26]; this rate was the nominal interest rate at which Napoleon, as part of the financial reforms, forcibly consolidated the entire French public debt in rentes at 5%.[27] Those who opted for the liquidation of the capital that had been recognized had to prove to the competent bodies that the bond had not been repaid under the previous government.[28]

The riots of 1831 dramatically highlighted the financial problems that had emerged with an expansion of public spending unknown in the previous fifteen years.[29] The official balance sheets for 1814–1827 presented positive balances. However, this circumstance, as underlined in several memoirs of the time, could not lead to errors of evaluation since the results were inflated "by credits whose need was very doubtful"; from 1828, there were continuous deficits.[30]

The causes of these financial difficulties were various,[31] and the same revision congregation established by the pontiff did not hesitate to highlight the excesses of and the damage caused by a government defined as a "false charity system".[32] First, because of recent events, the state could

[24] SAR, Camerale II, Debito Pubblico, B.7, Fasc.3, Memoria, cit., Art. IV De' luoghi di monte non estinti (pp. 82–94).

[25] *Motu Proprio* del 6 July 1816 artt. 232 e 234. See Felloni, 1971, pp. 161–203; Strangio, 2001, pp. 66–74; 2007, pp. 261–266.

[26] *Motu Proprio* del 6 July 1816, art. 237.

[27] Holmer and Sylla, 1995, p. 231.

[28] *Motu Proprio* 6 July 1816 art. 234.

[29] Felisini, 1993, pp. 181–211.

[30] SAR., Tesorierato generale, titolo I, affari generali, b.279, Sullo stato delle finanze pontificie e de' modi di migliorarle—Rapporto di Monsignor Carlo Luigi Morichini Arcivescovo di Nisibi, Protesoriere generale della RCA presentato alla Santità di nostro Signore papa Pio IX, 20 november 1847, p. 2; Pinchera 1961, p. 35; Felisini, 1990, pp. 75–97.

[31] A thorough analysis of the reasons for the annual and increasing financial deficits is presented in Pepoli Napoleone, 1858, pp. 120–125.

[32] Pepoli Napoleone, 1858, p. 121.

no longer count on the financial support of foreign Catholic countries.[33] Furthermore, French domination had not succeeded in eliminating privileges that favoured certain classes or in limiting the extent of inalienable "manomorte", inaccessible to a weak and badly organized tax collection system. Contributing to this deficit were the following: the large and useless military apparatus; contingent factors, such as Asian cholera, which forced the state to face considerable health care costs[34]; the famines of 1816 and 1837; and damage caused by the overflow of rivers and streams in several provinces, such as that caused by the flooding of the Tiber (Tevere) in December 1846.[35]

1.2 The Slow Process of "Italianization"

The Italian political framework of this historical period was becoming clear enough according to an antagonism that saw the Sardinian Kingdom as the only surviving constitutional, parliamentary and liberal kingdom, in the middle of a peninsula dominated by the Austrian empire.[36] The Papal State entered this constellation of Vienna's satellites without demonstrating any political originality. In fact, more than these satellites, it projected an image of anachronism and substantial weakness, which was

[33] At the time of the Counter-Reformation, there had been a reversal of established practice as the Church confronted spreading secularization and the accompanying disinclination to recognize in the pope the religious authority that had previously justified his funding by Christian countries. Although this financial support was lacking, the bodies responsible for managing public finances managed to maintain a positive account balance in the following centuries; Marchetti affirms that nonpapal financial flows recorded throughout the eighteenth century (Marchetti, 1800) equalled approximately 800 thousand scudi. After the last events of the early nineteenth century, these revenues were further reduced.

[34] The bank of Prince Torlonia was initially supposed to lend the State one million scudi (25 March 1837) but later, as a result of the cholera epidemic, this figure was increased by 2 million (Quacquarelli, 1940, p. 7); Moroni, MDCCCLV, p. 334.

[35] Diario di Roma n.23 del 18 March 1847. SAR, Tesorierato generale, titolo I, affari generali, b.279, Sullo stato cit.. Morichini reports a total deficit of approximately 41 million scudi in 1847 (see also Pepoli Napoleone, 1858, p. 125 e Quacquarelli, 1940, p. 2) (It must be considered that the public debt also included, as mentioned, all the pensions and salaries of the administrative bureaucratic apparatus and other debts deriving from loans arranged separately with wealthy families, such as the Leichterberg debt. See Morandi, 1933, p. 503).

[36] Caracciolo and Caravale, 1978, pp. 722–730.

also due to the increasingly widespread suspicion (because of the inherent impossibility that the current chancelleries could survive) of such a strictly theocratic regime in Europe of the second half of the nineteenth century. In addition, the increasingly experienced and powerful Cardinal Antonelli remained head of the Secretariat of State and acted so much in unison with the pope as to disappoint the few who still hoped for a revival, sooner or later, of the liberal face of Pius IX.[37] The "provisional phase" of the new restoration lasted longer than had been foreseen even after the pope's return because of the continuing foreign occupation.[38] In this regard, a certain part of the historiography focuses on the persistent civil delay and "the unsustainable reactionary nature of political action" evident during the 1850s.[39] Certainly, a theocratic and ancien regime kingdom was "anachronistic" at the heart of the Italy that was forming and in the midst of the liberal age. Nevertheless, innovations and initiatives were constrained within a difficult framework from a financial and economic perspective: the reconstitution of the administrative apparatus. "Precisely between 1850 and 1860 in frontal opposition to the ever numerous accusers of bad governance and the archaic nature of the prevailing system" there was no shortage of publicists willing to magnify the reforms introduced and the validity of the administrative system headed by Rome.[40] In the agricultural field, the policy for improvements applied between 1847 and 1860 generally followed that of the premium or regulation and prohibition.[41] The central authorities adopted customs measures that while aiming to favour the employment of the working class contributed to the slowdown in commercial traffic in 1847[42]; this resulted in a decrease in exports of agricultural products in

[37] Caracciolo and Caravale, 1978, p. 673. Giovanni Maria Mastai Ferretti was born in Senigallia on May 13, 1792, to a family of medium-level nobility (Caracciolo and Caravale, 1978, p. 26).

[38] Caracciolo and Caravale, 1978, p. 679.

[39] See the new research lines represented by Caffiero, 2001; Monsagrati, 2001, pp. 217–262; De Longis, 2001, pp. 263–284; Riall, 2001, pp. 285–306; Castracane Mombelli, 2001, 1998, pp. 9–63.

[40] Caracciolo and Caravale, 1978, p. 684.

[41] Caracciolo and Caravale, 1978, p. 690.

[42] For a description of the contents of previous and subsequent provisions regarding the freedom of imports or export bans, see Raccolta delle leggi e disposizioni di pubblica amministrazione dello stato pontificio, Roma 1934–1870, vol. I, decree 3 January and 20

the face of a significant increase that did not translate into the increase in profits hoped for by the traders, who for their part had engaged in speculation and were clamouring for the restoration of free trade.[43] In fact, the greater imports combined with the good harvests of that year disappointed the expectations of the traders and the communities of the state who had taken steps to create stocks, which then remained unsold, with serious repercussions for their owners and the contracting communities.[44] This critical commercial situation resembled the one that affected other European countries in 1847.[45] The deficit caused by the greater imports of cereals resulted in a need to find money abroad and in a slowdown in monetary circulation; to these difficulties, we can add the outflow of capital to service loans contracted in Paris and Genoa.[46] Furthermore, the capital's money market was in trouble due to the activity of the Treasury, which was begging for money from the Roman Bank or from wealthy citizens[47]; the decrease in customs revenue and the increase in public debt

Febraury 1847, pp. 115–116 e 126–128 and vol. II, in particular the decree of 14 April 1848, p. 109; SAR, Consulta di Stato, b. 2, Rapporto della Consulta di stato intorno alle istanze di parecchie province che chiedevano la revoca del divieto di estrazione dei cereali, 31 January 1848. On 17 April 1847, the State Council was established, which was to represent all the provinces of the State, and with the subsequent *Motu Proprio* of 12 June 1847, it was determined to create a Council of Ministers composed exclusively of ecclesiastics (*Raccolta delle leggi e disposizion*, 1849, pp. 167–183). Furthermore, among the innovations introduced by Pius IX, on 5 July of the same year, it was determined to establish a civic guard, which represented a means to protect public order.

[43] For the accounting data, see Bonelli, 1961, p. 74; SAR, Camerlengato, parte II, Annona e Grascia b. 766, letter of A. Braga, segretario della Camera di Commercio di Ancona al camerlengo Riario Sforza, 7 july 1847.

[44] SAR, Consulta di stato, b. 2, Rapporto, cit. The prices of basic necessities, in particular, potatoes, cereals and olive oil, increased by approximately 30% (Pinchera, 1857).

[45] In particular, England was experiencing a critical period, primarily with respect to railway stock investments Deane, 1990; Gourvish Terence, 1980; Collins, 1995; "Il Commercio", roman periodical, 1847.

[46] Morichini, 1847, in particular the attached 5; see also Felisini, 1990, pp. 122–123. Another consequence was a sharp increase in requests for reimbursement of deposits at the Cassa di Risparmio di Roma, which generated, especially in the second half of 1847, a greater number of withdrawals (which increased by 188%) and for the first time a negative balance in the area of collection operations (D'Errico, 1999, p. 110). The lower inflow of deposits may have been due to a crisis of mistrust but also to the fact that there were more profitable investment opportunities for depositors, who had been relying on cash as their main source of liquidity.

[47] Farini, 1853, vol. II, p. 48.

burdens had more than doubled the state deficit compared to previous years. Among the various measures taken by the treasurer was that of resorting to credit by opening current accounts.[48] Following the involvement in the war against Austria, the financing needs of the Treasury increased, adding a large expenditure on arms to the papal deficit.[49] In particular, the use of credit from the Roman Bank, renewed and increased in the summer of 1847, caused a reduction in the metal reserves the Treasury held to cover the notes issued, which worsened its liquidity[50]; Ludovico Potenziani denounced this policy. Potenziani[51] was the bank's administrator while trying to lighten its position and rescue its management from the discredit into which it fell, a "violation that is all the more reprehensible since the Government was made to obtain from the Bank leftovers of money that it could not provide without placing the violating hand on the reserve chest".[52] Government intervention in support of banking institutions matured in the context of financial conduct, which, putting aside the extraordinary finance projects, caused it to conclude it had no other way to ensure the coverage of expenses than by creating liquidity through the printing of securities, backed by fiat, to ensure that they were held by the public. The decree of April 1848 marked not only

[48] Morichini, 1847, p. 16. In this regard, the loan request that remained unanswered by the treasurer at the Cassa di Risparmio di Roma is emblematic; see D'Errico, 1999. With the approval of the fundamental statute of the temporal government of church states, signed by the pope and published on March 14, 1848, two deliberative chambers for the formation of laws were established: the High Council of Sovereign Appointment and the Council of Sovereign Appointment and the Council of Deputies, elected by census suffrage, which deliberated on budgetary matters and political economic-financial matters (see "Appendice al giornale del foro", 1848, vol. 1).

[49] SAR, Ministero delle finanze, b. 551, Rapporto delle sezioni delle Armi e delle Finanze alla Consulta di Stato.

[50] Pius IX considered a hypothetical negotiation with the French Catholic bank De la Hante, from which he had procured a loan of one million scudi, but because of a serious financial failure by the bank, this loan was only 90 thousand scudi a month as opposed to the initially agreed 150 thousand (Felisini, 1990, p. 122). Regarding the Banca Romana, see Graziani, Roma 1995, p. 465.

[51] Marquis and wealthy owner of Rieti estates (1784–1854).

[52] Le assemblee del Risorgimento, Roma 1911, 4 voll, I, pp. 227–228. SAR Camerale II, Debito pubblico, b. 14, Rapporto del tesoriere per l'udienza di Sua Santità, 14 august 1847. See Raccolta delle leggi, cit., vol. II, decree 29 april 1848, pp. 115–120; SAR Ministero dell'Interno, Commercio b. 319, Agostino Feoli, amministratore generale della Banca Romana ai componenti della Consulta di Stato, 14 april 1848; Farini, 1853, II, p. 48.

the first issue of government bonds but also the beginning of a monetary policy in which subsequent issues of bonds and notes influenced the increase in paper inflation.[53] The policy and financial conduct of the provisional government from 25 November 1848 to 9 February 1849 and of the republican government from February 1849 to the following 3 July did not differ from that of the papal government[54]; in fact, during the brief period of the Roman Republic,[55] fiat bonds in circulation increased together with the notes printed by the Banca Romana on the orders of the republican authorities.[56]

With the defeat of the Roman Republic by the French (allies of the Roman state) in the summer of 1849, an interlude that had lasted a few months ended. Pope Pius IX was forced into exile and to temporarily transfer control of the capital. However, on 17 July 1849, Pius IX appointed a state government commission for the reorganization of the papal government, and on September 12 of the same year, the pope issued a *Motu Proprio* with which he reorganized the absolutist structure of the state after the short republican period. For Europe, the 1850s represented a phase of not only nearly ubiquitous peace but also one of development in the economy, technology and social values. It was precisely in this

[53] SAR, Ministero delle finanze, b, 551; six projects aimed at providing for the urgent needs of finance, sd, April 1848, and the Report of the Finance and Arms Sections to the State Council regarding these projects presented by the Ministry of Finance, sd, April 1848. During the compulsory course quarter, bank notes could be exchanged for newly issued treasury bills; the bonds, with an annual interest of 3.60%, were considered a novelty in the offer of papal bonds and constituted a portion of the short-term state debt (Pinchera, 1957, p. 19; D'Errico, 1999, p. 89).

[54] In September 1848, the government was entrusted to the economist Pellegrino Rossi, who was reputed to favour a constitutional regime of the French type; through him, Pope Pius IX hoped to resolve the Papal State's most urgent financial problems. Unfortunately, his hopes were misplaced because Rossi adopted behaviour defined as "dictatorial", and on November 15, he was assassinated at the entrance of parliament, just as he was to present his reform program. These events led to the pope's siege of his Quirinal palace to obtain a Constituent Assembly and to the subsequent flight of Pius IX to Gaeta on November 25, 1848, putting an end to the constitutional phase in the State of the Church (Aubert, 1964; Caracciolo and Caravale, 1978, p. 659).

[55] Caffiero, 2001; Bollettino delle leggi, 1849; Bartoccini, 1993, p. 243.

[56] The 3.6% yield enjoyed by all government issues up to January 1849 was abolished in March, thus equating public debt securities with bank notes (Bollettino delle leggi, Decree del 26 march 1849, pp. 211–213; subsequent ordinances of 21 febbraio, 5–11-17–28 april, 5 may, 6 e 15 june 1849; decreti del 21 february e del 17 april 1849, pp. 38–39, 211–213, 383–384, 524–528).

climate of dynamism and orderly progress that the State of the Church projected, even more than before, a particularly static and narrow self-image. "The structure of society in this country is rotten from top to bottom", Michelangelo Caetani confessed in 1851 to a foreign visitor; the absence of a consistent and authoritative bourgeois class contributed to the lack of development of the state, in contrast to the general trend, clearly expansive, and on an international scale.[57]

The 1860s commenced with an important event that marked the penultimate step of the journey that would end ten years later with the end of the temporal power established and maintained by the Church for approximately a millennium. On 18 September 1860, in Castelfidardo, papal troops suffered a major defeat by the Piedmontese army, led by General Cialdini. The plebiscites of 4 and 5 November sanctioned the annexation of the Marche and Umbria to Piedmont and the reduction of the Papal State. The ecclesiastical kingdom thus lost territorial power within the Italian peninsula and was reduced to a territory delimited by the borders of Lazio (with the exception of Rieti, which was officially annexed to the Italian state on 14 November 1860); additionally, it saw its political weight weakened within Europe despite the initial support of Austria and then of France.[58]

Vittorio Emanuele II was about to complete the project of the Kingdom of Italy, and the dominion of the Church decreased from 41,000 to 12,000 square km. Ten years later, that dominion would be reduced to the territory of the Vatican alone.

The first years of the new-dimensioned Papal State were difficult: Rome was a city that enjoyed worldwide ideological and spiritual influence. However, the city was inept when it came to integrating into the historical reality of a rapidly evolving world.

Pius IX opposed the course of events in every way: on 18 June 1859, he issued the "Encyclical Qui Nuper", in which he reiterated the need for a "Civil Principality" and referred to the Italian Risorgimento as "that movement of sedition that just broke out in Italy".[59]

[57] So stated Nassau, Senior, referring to an interview on March 5, 1851 during his stay in Rome, 1937, p. 189.

[58] Caracciolo, 1991, pp. 5–6. See also Bartoccini and Strangio, 1997; Pastura Ruggiero, 1991, p. 35.

[59] Jemolo, 1963, p. 158.

1.2.1 *Rome and United Italy*

By now, however, circumstances were well defined, and for the pope and the Secretary of State Cardinal Antonelli, having lost the weapon of French diplomatic support, the reorganization of the army was not enough to avoid defeat. The new military contingent, which increased from 16,000 to approximately 21,000 men but did not attain the intended size of 28,000, was characterized by improvisation and unpreparedness, and the judgement expressed by many contemporaries was harsh in this regard: "In the presence of Italian outlaws and bandits, to whom he had been granted forgiveness by His Holiness as long as they became part of his army".[60]

On 26 March 1860, Pius IX issued a major ex-communication without a precise addressee. The pontiff's angry words applied to most Italians, starting with the House of Savoy and extending to public officials, the army and all those who contributed, with their labour or will, to the fulfilment of the new decisions. The Papal State existed for another decade without making significant changes to its institutional arrangement or its administrative and judicial organization. On 17 February 1861, according to a law issued by the new parliament of the Italian state, the Kingdom of Italy became a political and legal reality, against which the Papal State opposed its temporal power. In the first five years following the unification of Italy, a desire to reach conciliation, or a "modus vivendi", with the Church was manifested within the Italian ruling class. On 25 March 1861, Cavour explained to the Chamber of Deputies the moral reasons why Rome should become the capital of Italy, while repudiating any violent means to achieving this goal.[61]

In the first months of 1864, news regarding the health of Pius IX, who claimed to be afflicted by a dangerous illness, suddenly spread in Italy and across Europe. This period was one of intense diplomatic activity between the Italian and French governments. However, the eventuality of Pius IX's death might facilitate easier solutions. The Italian leaders,

[60] Ragionieri, 1978, p. 100. De Cesare, 1907, p. 392. Federico Francesco Saverio de Mérode (Brussels, 26 March 1820–Rome, 12 July 1874) was the son of Count Félix de Mérode, minister of Leopold I of Belgium. A Belgian Catholic archbishop, he was the protagonist of the first phase of the urbanization of the city of Rome following its proclamation as Italy's capital.

[61] Cavour's speech of March 25, 1861, in Parliamentary Acts, Chamber of Deputies of March 27, 1861.

hoping for the advent to the papal throne of a cardinal less rigid than the current pope, began to seek detailed information on the high hierarchy of the Church. Another possibility was that of an agreement with France, both regarding a preliminary accord on a cardinal who could change his view of the hostile Roman attitude and regarding the end of the French diplomatic-military policy in defence of Rome. Another approach might be to leverage the transition period on the basis of the "vacant seat" to reach an agreement directly with the Roman people. All these assumptions remained potential strategies as in August of the same year Pius IX overcame his illness and returned to the leadership of the Papal State, a position he would occupy for another 14 years.

Interrupted by Cavour's death,[62] negotiations resumed in June 1864 aimed at putting an end to the French occupation of Rome and placing the papal territory under the guarantee of the Italian government. Napoleon III wanted the occupation, which represented a permanent source of expense and danger, to end. However, he did not want to lose the conservative and Catholic consensus deriving from support for the pope. In September 1864, the negotiations culminated in the Convention between Italy and France, which marked an important step towards the dissolution of the Papal State. This document established that in two years France would evacuate its army from the Roman state and that at the same time the Papal State would reorganize its military. In return for the latter, Italy would peacefully accept the new papal army.

Failure to recognize the Holy See's right to speak immediately provoked a papal response. On 8 December 1864, Pius IX published the encyclical "Quanta Cura" and the "Syllabus", with which he refused any form of agreement, preferring to act on a purely spiritual rather than political level. The Syllabus was a collection of 80 propositions denouncing the main errors of modern civilization, directly extracted from encyclicals, apostolic letters, speeches and briefs of Pius IX from 1846 onwards[63] and reiterating his opposition to communism and socialism.[64]

The papal documents provoked a harsh reaction from the entire liberal milieu, which perceived in them the radical opposition of the Church and

[62] Camillo Benso Conte di Cavour, was born in Turin on 10 August 1810 and died on 6 June 1861.

[63] Encyclical "Quanta Cura", 8 dicembre 1864 e "Sillabo", in Momigliano and Casolari, 1979, pp. 262–280.

[64] Encyclical "Quanta Cura", cit. See also Caracciolo and Caravale, 1978, pp. 718–720.

Catholicism to progress and modern civilization. Even the Italian and foreign press raised a cry of protest against the pontiff's "rash and insane" gesture. In its 28 December 1864, issue, the English Times stated that even if the pope, cardinals and bishops truly believed they could stop the path of progress their efforts to this end would be in vain because the achievements of civilization were permanent and the great political lines of modern society were absolutely impregnable to such impotent assaults.[65]

In the second half of the 1860s, the "Italianization" process was introduced, which shortly thereafter would result in the unification of Lazio as well. As Bartoccini wrote,

> The process was greatly accelerated when, behind the screen of official declarations, on a level different from that of diplomatic activity, which is so often full of smoke, a realistic policy of the papal government began to be outlined after 1865, that, behind the rigidity of the proclamation of the principles hid the renunciation of claims and the acceptance of small things, in the hope of maintaining the status quo, a policy that found not a small consents on the Italian side within some groups of the majority power, inclined to religious peace and compromise with the pontiff.[66]

The fate of the Papal State was marked by several events: the withdrawal of the French troops that garrisoned Rome and Civitavecchia, the victories of Prussia and the fall of the Second Empire, which increasingly aggravated the status of the small papal territory. On the Italian side, the ultimate goal remained that of annexing Rome and conquering the capital, even if the Italian government was divided between a group advocating patience and a diplomatic solution and a group desiring direct military intervention. Certain individuals also hoped for an internal insurrection, in response to which a military intervention could commence under the excuse of maintaining order. All doubts and uncertainties were swept away on 12 September 1870, when Italian troops entered the papal territory.[67]

[65] Bartoccini, 1971, p. 19.

[66] Ibidem.

[67] SAR Ministero dell'nterno, b. 1168 (1870), where both the Proclamation and the Notification of General Kanzler, commander of the papal troops, are held.

Despite the reassurances, at dawn on September 20, the bombardment of the walls of Rome began. A few hours later, the Italian troops entered through the breach opened near Porta Pia, putting a final end to the temporal power of the popes. The pontiff, although resigned, was hostile and averse to conciliation; he shut himself up in the Vatican, rejecting any relationship with the "usurping regime" and forbidding any form of military defence.[68]

In the face of the progressive position of the rationalist bourgeoisie, Pius IX showed "insuperable distrust" towards every novelty and diplomatic relationship, and with an essentially religious and universal concept of his mission, he addressed the people directly to remind them of the meaning of Christian brotherhood as opposed to the selfishness of the new ruling classes. It was precisely this total disinclination to cooperate, one not reflected in Antonelli's greater political sense, that offended the residual sympathies of the great European powers and resulted in the pope's definitive isolation.

The legislative and administrative integration of the Lazio territories into united Italy occurred with the appointment in the five provinces of provisional councils that were intended to provide government and administration. The Giunta in Rome was chosen directly by Italian general Cadorna from among the representatives of high society and the bourgeoisie with moderate political ideas, thus avoiding a free election.

An important affirmation of the people's will occurred with the plebiscite of 2 October 1870 regarding the annexation of Rome and Lazio to Italy. Of 167,548 registered voters, 135,188 voted. There were 133,681 votes in favour and 1,507 opposed. In Rome, there were 40,785 votes in favour of the measure and 46 opposed.

On 9 October 1870, Rome and the entire papal territory were annexed by royal decree to the Kingdom of Italy.[69]

The annexation of the Papal State to the Kingdom of Italy occurred abruptly. The insufficiently prepared Lazio population struggled to establish a balanced position within national life. It remains to be clarified whether the façade of policy, expressed above all by formal actions, was

[68] "Dichiarazione al Governo Pontificio dei motivi che lo inducevano ad occupare quel territorio militarmente"; the declaration, which was not presented to the pontifical government, bore the signature of Deputy Minister Lanza; it is undated but evidently from September 1870; the document is included in Mori, 1967, p. 598.

[69] Caracciolo, 1991, p. 6.

accompanied by a mood of resignation regarding the process referred to as "Italianization" and consisting of economic reforms, trade agreements and even the replacement of the papal currency by the Italian lira. In reality, economic progress represented the only instrument the Holy See possessed with which to strengthen its state. Until the end, it tried to implement reform programmes that would support new productive activities. Despite its economic leverage and the introduction of reform legislation in the administrative field, the state retained an absolutist and theocratic structure.

It was a state that unlike other modern countries did not provide for the separation of powers on the basis of Montesquieu's theory but relied solely on the institutions of the pontiff-sovereign and the secretariat of state.[70] The uselessness of the dense administrative structure was evident, as only the pope and the secretary of state were entitled to make final decisions on provisions no matter what their type.

The only elected bodies were the municipal councils, two-thirds of whose members were drawn from the landowning class. Thus, the councils could hardly harbour subversive tendencies. Nevertheless, they guaranteed good political, moral and religious conduct. It should be noted that the election of council members still required confirmation by the sovereign.

The two tendencies of government, i.e., the centralization of power and the formal but fictitious granting of local autonomy that resulted from certain reforms, revealed only an apparent contradiction. In reality, behind the "mask" of a government system and a bureaucratic and administrative structure that evolved towards more advanced state models was a global political project that foreshadowed the creation and consolidation of a police state.

The "taking" of Rome had immense moral and historical significance: it sanctioned the autonomy and independence of the Italian state sphere with respect to the religious position of the Holy See. Although, in the

[70] Regarding the role and major interpretations of the sovereign-pontiff, see in particular Prodi, 1986, pp. 198–216. The idea of the tripartite division of the fundamental functions of the state (i.e., the legislative, executive, judicial functions) is already found in Aristotele. The idea of the separation of powers can be traced to Montesquieu, who emphasized the need to entrust the three functions to different bodies in positions of mutual independence so as to avoid any threat to freedom. In the Spirit of the Laws (1748), the French philosopher founds his theory on the idea that "Whoever has power is led to abuse it; he goes as far as he finds no limits [...]".

unification of 1861, a large part of the peninsula had been annexed, only with the annexation of Rome was the ancient condition put to an end characterized by the presence of a Church dominion in the heart of the country. Only now does the Italian state acquire internal political emancipation and, above all, full acknowledgement from the rest of Europe.

1.3 Territorial and Demographic Structure of the State

The events of 1859–1860 caused the Papal State to close in on itself within a territorial context that was only apparently inhomogeneous. In fact, the limits constituted to the north by the Volsini Mountains, to the east by the course of the Tiber, to the south by the course of the Liri and the Aurunci and to the west by the Tyrrhenian Sea included a highly structured geographical area from the perspective of the physical substrate. Nearly all of the space coincided with a geomorphic unit represented by a set of structures originating in volcanic activity and connected by a blanket of deposits of pyroclastic material. We can also note substantial homogeneity at the level of the anthropic use of this space: a similar style of life distinguished the settled communities, a consequence of their similar historical paths and despite local differentiations.

In terms of size, the new Papal State (Fig. 1.1) took its place among the other European states, both with reference to area (just under a third of that of Belgium, the smallest European state) and population (less than half of that of Denmark or Norway, the least populous states of the continent).

The low territorial density of the population (approximately 60 inhabitants per km^2) resulted in a negative constraint on the state's growth and development.

The transition from a premodern territorial organization to one marked by the urban-industrial revolution occurred substantially more slowly in Lazio than the peninsula overall and particularly the rest of Europe and was less evident. The reasons for this retarded pace of change were due both to the difficulty of modernizing the Lazio territorial system and the excessive predominance of Rome. The shadow effect, which Rome traditionally exerted on the surrounding area, expanded to include all of Lazio, starting a process of urban desertification that would lead to

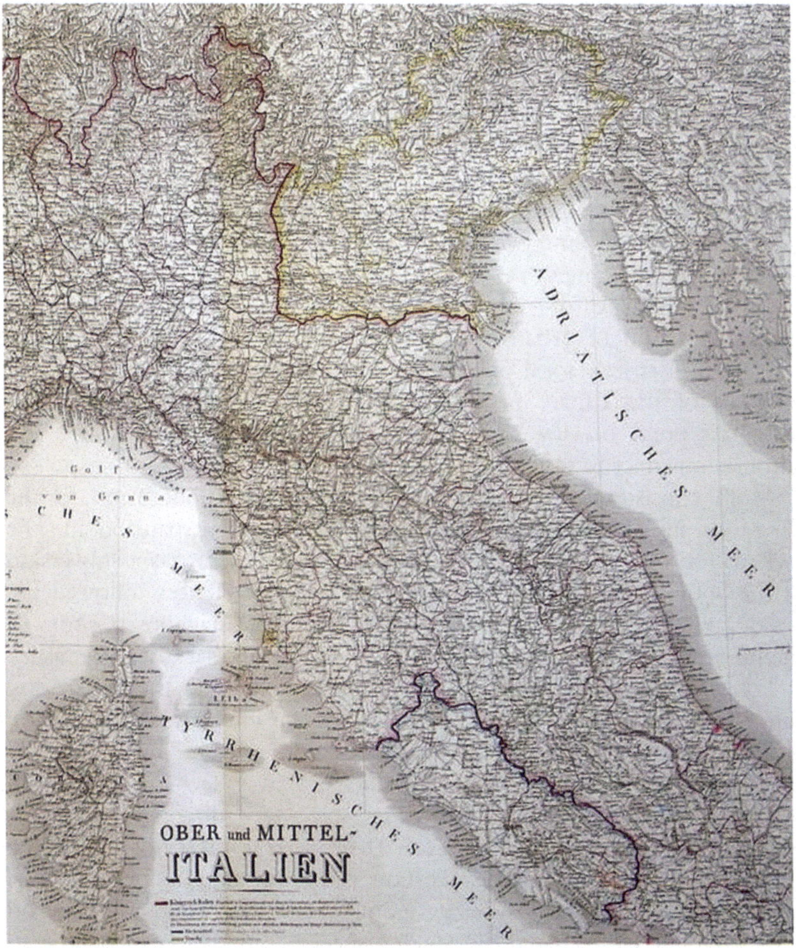

Fig. 1.1 The Papal State in 1861 (*Source* Heinrich Kiepert, 1860, Public domain, via Wikimedia Commons [https://commons.wikimedia.org/wiki/File:Northern_and_central_Italy_in_1860.jpg])

the emergence of a purely rural area outside Rome proper. The close presence of a world city such as Rome certainly slowed the process towards greater local articulation. In 1860, Rome, with 195,000 inhabitants, was defined as "too large and too little functional to have any positive future in that geopolitical order".[71]

Although dependent on Rome in general manner, the Lazio urban system often consisted of small, substantially self-sufficient elements based on the classic city-countryside relationship, with little or no propensity for supra-local interchange.

An important feature was the near absence of regional relations, and the proliferation of urban centres had the sole objective of providing services to a strictly local population. Therefore, the contraction of the territory of the Papal State in 1860 did not produce major effects from this point of view as it represented a curtailment of single and autonomous microsystems.

More consistent consequences appear following annexation to the Kingdom, initially, particularly in Rome, the building expansion and the reclamation of the Agro. However, subsequently, there was a subversion of the entire local settlement system. Other consequences followed the development of the railway and the related disadvantageous position of the port cities due to their increasing marginality and lack of dynamism.

For a demographic analysis, it is important to note the population census ordered by Gregory XVI in 1833, which estimated the population of the Papal State to be 2,732,436 inhabitants.[72]

At the end of Gregory XVI's pontificate, it was deemed appropriate to compile a demographic survey, which was attached to the documents published by the census presidency of 1847, even if it was not considered an official act, to address the question of railway development. In this regard, Pius IX, among his first economic measures, issued a circular on 17 September 1846, based on which a special commission was chose to establish five railway lines.[73]

In 1844, the Papal State had a population of 2,929,807, with a density of 71 inhabitants per km^2 (in eleven years, the population had increased by 197,371 with an annual increase of 17,943). After returning

[71] Almagià, 1976, p. 40.

[72] Raccolta delle leggi, vol. I, Rome 1835, pp. 145–428.

[73] Negri, 1967.

from Gaeta, Pope Pius IX, after taking out various loans, issued several measures that concerned the imposition and increase of taxes, in particular on mortgages and the register, and increased duties on imports, exports and consumption.[74] In 1853, he had the last census taken, entrusting the task to the ecclesiastical and municipal authorities of the state. This census recorded 3,124,668 inhabitants and a density of 76 per km^2. Nine years after the last survey, although this assessment was not formal, there were an additional 194,861 inhabitants, representing an average annual increase of 21,651 (non-Catholic foreigners were not considered). Of this total, 1,009,145 were farmers, 206,558 were property owners, 9,062 soldiers, 14,576 magistrates, 38,320 churchmen, 258,872 artisans, 99,571 traders, 7,049 doctors, 4,440 lawyers, 5,309 professors, 1,474 engineers and 37,015 were destitute. A total of 608,280 families resided in the state. A total of 9,237 were Jews in addition to 263 other non-Catholics; 49,089 were foreigners, of whom 15,525 resided in Rome. There were 1,599,729 males and 1,524,449 females, with a surplus of the former of 75,280. The average age for men was 50 years, while for women, it was a few years older. There was a fair distribution of the population between the urban districts compared to the countryside (1,585,715 and 1,538,953, respectively; this distribution was likely due to the inveterate use of sharecropping).[75]

For the decade 1860–1870, it is necessary to consider the population statistics of the Papal State for 1853 and to relate them to the last ecclesiastical census and the data from the 1871 census of the Kingdom of Italy.

On the basis of the average annual increase, it can be calculated that the demographic size of "Papal Lazio" in 1860 was 735,000. In a territory that constituted over 4% of the Italian peninsula, the Lazio population comprised approximately 3% of the overall Italian population, with a

[74] Corridore, 1906.

[75] For these data, see Corridore, 1906, p. 23 and chapter II, in particular the conclusion. It should be emphasized that the territory of the Papal State was that established by the Treaty of Vienna of 1814 and that it had not undergone any subsequent changes. This territory included the provinces of Bologna, Ferrara, Forlì and Ravenna, the Marche, Umbria, Lazio and the territories of Benevento and Pontecorvo, a total extent of 41,958 km^2. In the following years, prior to 1860, there were important changes that concerned the town of Ancarano in the province of Ascoli, which passed to the Kingdom of the two Sicilies, and the territories of Benevento and Pontecorvo, sold in 1859 (Rossi Ragazzi, 1956, pp. 3–4).

Table 1.1 Estimate of the absolute and relative populations in 1860 and 1870

Province	*Surface*	*Population 1860*		*Population 1870*		*Increase (%)*
	km²	*Inhabitants*	*Inhab./km²*	*Inhabitants*	*Inhab./km²*	
Civitavecchia	1.114	24.250	12.8	29.300	26.3	+20.8
Frosinone	1.823	148.900	81.7	154.600	84.8	+3.8
Rome	4.626	356.200	77.0	398.650	86.2	11.9
Without the city and the suburbs	4.602	161.200	35.0	174.650	38.0	+9.3
Velletri	1.492	66.300	44.4	72.450	48.6	+9.3
Viterbo	3.023	139.800	46.2	156.150	51.7	+11.7
Lazio	12.078	732.450	60.9	811.150	67.2	+10.3

Source Salvatori et al., 1997, p. 76

density of just under 61 inhabitants per km^2, much lower than that of wider Italy, whose density was 87 inhabitants per km^2.

Other important demographic characteristics were a high birth rate and a low life expectancy caused by high mortality, particularly among infants. In addition to in Rome, the population density was high in the major agricultural and commercial centres as a result of superior hygienic-sanitary conditions, a lower risk of malarial contagion and better protection from banditry.[76]

Over the course of the decade, certain demographic dynamics, such as the depopulation of the mountain and hill areas towards the coast (with a view to improving their economic conditions) and the close correlation between the development of communication routes (particularly railways) and human settlement, changed the population distribution. From 1857 onwards, the territories serviced by a good railway network display a significant demographic increase and greater economic development. In contrast, the areas with poor communications (particularly the provinces of Frosinone and Viterbo) encountered greater difficulties in economic and demographic growth.

During the decade 1860–1870, the average annual increase in the Lazio population (Table 1.1) was approximately 75,000 individuals; the

[76] Regarding banditry, see Bartolini, 2010, pp. 3–15.

years of greatest immigration were the two years 1860–1861 and 1866–1867; in the latter period, the migratory flow was a consequence of the suppression of religious orders, which occurred with the law of 7 July 1866.[77]

The prelude to the advent of Rome as capital was Cavour's solemn and unforgotten albeit purely formal, proclamation before parliament in March 1861. However, the new political structure was concretely applied only after the Italian military occupation. With the law of 3 February 1871, Rome was declared the capital of the Kingdom by a large majority. From this moment on, the words Rome and capital would sound like synonyms for Roman residents and for all Italian citizens generally.

After 20 September and unification with the Kingdom, the population of the former Roman state reached approximately 811,150 inhabitants, with a density of over 67 per km^2, less than that of the entire peninsula, which was 93 inhabitants per km^2. However, it would be simplistic to link these variations entirely to political change. The effects of infrastructural progress, which had already begun, would have occurred even without institutional change. It is the arrival of modernity that stimulates the start of a reorganization, albeit partial and the means of this reorganization are much more economic than political.[78]

1.4 Economic Conditions

Between 1860 and 1870, the Papal State could no longer count on the most productive and economically developed regions of the centre-north, reduced as it was to a narrow strip of territory, which was, moreover, Italy's poorest, that is, Lazio.[79]

Therefore, greater development of all of Lazio was necessary. However, the scarcity of capital (raised primarily with public debt) left little room for public and private productive investments. The failure to expand production and the slowness of the accumulation of capital kept Rome and Lazio from participating fully in the birth of modern capitalism.

The events of September–October 1860 resulted in the abolition of the pontifical customs of the Marche, Umbria and the Kingdom of Naples

[77] See Falco, 1910.

[78] See Salvatori et al., 1997, p. 96.

[79] Almagià, 1976, p. 40.

and the establishment of a customs frontier between the new Kingdom and the remaining part of the Papal State, which in the administrative subdivision included the Presidency of Rome and Comarca and the Delegations of Viterbo, Civitavecchia, Velletri and Frosinone.

The beginning of the decade saw a sharp decrease in maritime activity, with the loss of the major ports on the Adriatic, while Civitavecchia, Fiumicino, Terracina and Porto d'Anzio on the Tyrrhenian coast remained part of the Papal State. The most important role was played by the port of Civitavecchia[80]; however, even here, the failure to construct facilities and introduce new port equipment constrained commercial shipping. The port also suffered a major restriction of merchant traffic after the opening in April 1859 of the Rome-Civitavecchia railway line. Other minor landing places were reserved for the shelter of small fishing boats and of purely local importance. Pressed by political and financial circumstances, the government reduced its intervention to protect "… a tiny and inefficient navy".[81]

The clear evidence of the minimal governmental role in the maritime sphere is highlighted by the low incidence of extraordinary interventions, in this decade, compared to those of the ordinary type. Expenses were mainly focused on maintenance although renewal was likely necessary compared to the past.[82] Poor economic organization and the lack of steamships and other large ships prevented foreign competition from being challenged on international routes. However, until the mid-nineteenth century, the volume of business with England and the other European industrial countries of the ecclesiastical state was higher than that of Italy.

Another reason for this regression was the lack of development of the shipping and shipbuilding industry. In fact, as Palermo writes, "the events of growth or decline are therefore in principle linked to the overall model of economic evolution of the city, regional or state structure in which it is organically inserted".[83]

[80] Negrisoli, 1857, p. 86. Regarding the port of Civitavecchia, see Calisse, 1936 (ed. orig. 1898); Attuoni, 1958; Strangio, 2006, pp. 761–776; Strangio and Vaquero Piñeiro, 2009, pp. 405–430.

[81] Gabriele, 1961, p. 41.

[82] Strangio, 1997, p. 160.

[83] Palermo, 1994, p. 84.

Government policy in the late 1860s was limited to the application of old provisions, and on the eve of September 20, the state had come to grant private individuals the right to construct and exploit several new ports. The advent of the unitary state and the cessation of the bonus system, which had been the basis of papal shipbuilding policy, resulted in a severe recession in the shipbuilding sector. In contrast, the positive development of railway networks contributed to making the state more accessible and less isolated from the rest of the peninsula.[84]

However, soon all doubts were dispelled, and the growth of the exploitation of the railway for commercial traffic initiated the decline of the papal merchant navy, as is also demonstrated by the Tiberine River liquidation, once a flourishing transport route.[85]

At first, primarily because of the inconvenience for travellers (the stations were located too far from the towns), the railway companies did not achieve the hoped for profits.

The railway network developed independently of political events, accelerating integration with the Kingdom of Italy while neglecting to connect Lazio's urban centres, such as Viterbo and Frosinone. Two-thirds of the railway network was constructed between 1860 and 1870, during which period the 3 existing lines (Rome-Frascati, Rome-Albano, Rome-Civitavecchia) extended 113 km. Other lines were added, extending the network to approximately 220 km.

The time required for a train journey was not yet competitive. Imagine that the stretch from Rome to Naples required 7 and a half hours. However, rail travel was beginning to be the preferred means of transport because it was safer and less stressful than carriage travel.

The layout of the road network was substantially extended following the road system of ancient Rome. The poor maintenance of the roads caused difficulties. Comparing the expenses for the national roads of the period 1860–1867 (Table 1.2 and Fig. 1.2) with those 1852–1859, we can note a decrease in major repairs and new works.

The state's economic structure was based on agriculture, with low productivity due to the use of ancient exploitation techniques (see Table 1.3 on the distribution of the population by economic sectors).

[84] Momo, 1845, pp. 6, 9.

[85] Gabriele, 1961, p. 44 and 1963; Manca, 1986, pp. 73–93.

Table 1.2 Average incidence per km of expenses for the national roads (1860–1867)

Average incidence	*1860*	*1861*	*1862*	*1863*	*1864*	*1865*	*1866*	*1867*
Ordinary maintenance	83.0	160.5	160.9	168.8	154.4	148.7	156.3	140.3
Major repairs	6·6	26.9	34.4	19.6	7.6	12.5	2.1	7.9
New works	3.1	2.1	26.2	28.8	13.6	28	18.2	21.2
Assistance to the works and campaign expenses	4.4	6.1	8.1	7	6.2	6.8	6.7	6.9
Removal of snow and frost	0.2	–	0.7	–	0.4	–	–	–
Total	97.3	195.6	230.3	224.2	182.2	196	183.3	176.3

Source Data processing by Friz, 1967

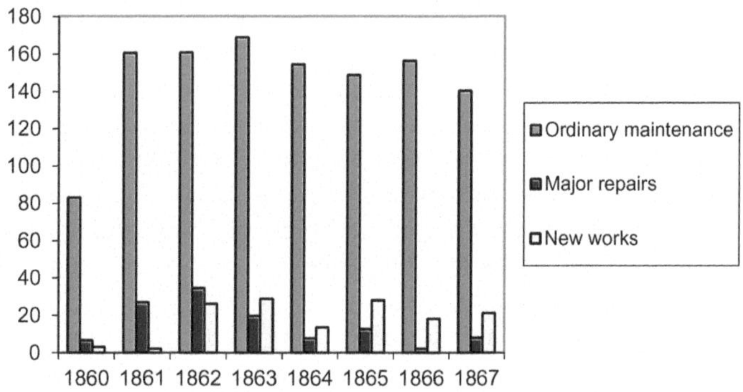

Fig. 1.2 Subdivision of the works (*Source* Data processing by Friz, 1967)

Table 1.3 Active population by economic sector according to the censuses of 1853 and 1871

	Agriculture		*Industry*		*Service*	
	1853 (%)	*1871 (%)*	*1853 (%)*	*1871 (%)*	*1853 (%)*	*1871 (%)*
Civitavecchia	17.9	49.9	9.8	15.6	72.3	34.5
Frosinone	68.7	78.4	9.1	10.8	22.2	10.8
Roma	26.7	40.0	24.4	23.1	48.9	36.9
Velletri	45.0	68.9	6.3	10.7	48.7	15.9
Viterbo	61.8	62.0	11.2	12.8	27.0	24.4
Lazio	49.8	54.7	15.6	17.3	15.6	28.0

Source Salvatori et al., 1997, p. 80

Only towards the end of the 1860s was there greater interest in innovation, as underlined by a document drawn up on 14 October 1868 by the General Treasury.[86] In addition, the ministry emphasized cost reduction and better workmanship and consistency of industrial products.[87]

Because of a decrease in cereal production (from 68,044 Rubbia of wheat produced in 1855 to 52,000 in 1858 and 42,052 in 1859), an edict of 11 September 1861 established a general ban on wheat exports and duty exemption for imports of grain and other foodstuffs, with the aim of protecting domestic supplies. In 1864, the government tried to introduce the cultivation of cotton although the results were not too satisfactory.[88] The cotton industry of the period was characterized by technical obsolescence and scarcity of capital.[89]

The greatest production effort was made in spinning and weaving the main raw material supplied by the nearby countryside: wool. Until 1860, Roman textile products had benefited from protectionist measures, including heavy duties on foreign products. Subsequently, due to the pontiff's "indulgence", products from the former ecclesiastical territories were still considered duty-free. Therefore, Tuscan, Lombard or Piedmontese manufacturers were supplied with smuggled counterfeit products so they too could enjoy the advantages granted to the factories of the new provinces annexed. To counter the northern industries, the Roman manufacturers required fabrics from the Marche and the territories of the former Legations to carry certificates of origin. After 1860, the government no longer sent silks and wools to international exhibitions, demonstrating that even in terms of quality, Roman products were no longer competitive.[90]

The prizes and protections that the Papal State granted over time had the result of rewarding producers in the short term, but after many years,

86 SAR., Ministero delle Finanze, b. 605.

87 Ibidem.

88 SAR., Ministero del Commercio, Belle Arti, Industria, Agricoltura e Lavori Pubblici, b. 573, "Notificazione sull'incoraggiamento per la coltivazione del cotone", Rome 4 March 1864.

89 Negrisoli, 1857, pp. 71, 86 e 97.

90 Parisi, 1993, pp. 17–46, pp. 41–42.

they caused a loss of competitiveness of Roman products, which was also attributable to obsolete production techniques.[91]

The removal of all limitations on the free movement of goods after 20 September would produce the definitive collapse of the textile industry; it is significant, however, that even in difficult conditions, traders tried to maintain a supportive and cohesive vision of their business.[92]

In 1864, the Chamber of Commerce of Rome was commissioned by the Minister of Commerce to analyse the entire economy of the state, with the aim of determining whether a protective or a free trade regime was more appropriate.[93] The Chamber conducted an investigation of major traders, including country merchants,[94] and found these merchants favoured a protective system, while other categories of merchants favoured free trade; the Chamber sided openly with the latter group.[95]

Among the few new industrial investments were the establishment in 1865 of the *Pia Antica Marcia Water Company* (Società Acqua Pia Antica Marcia) and in 1869 of the *Manifattura dei Tabacchi* in Trastevere. The use of capital in the real-estate sector turned out to be more in keeping with the short-term investment capacity of the Roman state. Here, the role played by Monsignor De Merode was important. After being dismissed from the post of pro-minister of arms following the defeat of Castelfidardo, De Merode undertook the arrangement in Rome of Piazza Pia and the design of new neighbourhoods on the Quirinale, Viminale and Esquilino hills.[96] De Merode's initiatives attracted the capital of an emerging Roman business class, even after 1870.

[91] Ellena, 1882, p. 94.

[92] SAR, Ministero del commercio, belle arti, industria, agricoltura e lavori pubblici, b. 573, "Rapporto del Consiglio del Nobile Collegio de' Commercianti di Roma, letto nell'adunanza generale 30 may 1862".

[93] See infra chap. 2 par. 2.3.

[94] Regarding the views and role of country merchants, see Piscitelli, 1958, pp. 119–173; 1968, pp. 446–457. De Tournon, 1855, pp. 309–324; Girelli, 1998, pp. 211–250; 1999, pp. 504–532; Sansa, 2009, pp. 1008–1024; Sanfilippo, 2009, pp. 73–85, in particular pp.74–80; Brice, 2020.

[95] Astraldi, 1956, p. 46.

[96] Cuccia, 1991; Della Seta, 1954, pp. 78–83; Della Seta and Della Seta, 1988; Insolera, 1976; Piacentini and Giudi, 1952. For a financial and banking perspective on these events, see Palermo, 2006.

During this period, numerous real-estate companies dedicated to the construction of public housing emerged. An example is the *Società Anonima Immobiliare*, which was established in 1868 to provide healthy and comfortable housing for the poorest social classes at a modest price.[97]

Combining welfare purposes and production activities, large factories were located in numerous hospices, particularly in the textile and paper sector (the factory at the convent of S. Rosa in Viterbo was important).[98]

Mining, which was required for the development of the construction industry, provided peperino (Albano, Frosinone, Genazzano), travertine (Tivoli, Viterbo, Civitavecchia), tuff (Agro Romano, Rome, Velletri, Frosinone, Viterbo, Comarca), alabaster (Civitavecchia), alum (Allumiere), vitriol (Viterbo, Civitavecchia, Montefiascone) and metals (Tolfa, Viterbo).

The vast Roman bureaucratic apparatus remained intact and in fact expanded by absorbing employees of the former provinces while decreasing services related to the functions of the city capital. The cost of living increased in the face of decreasing wages. Misery and discontent increased, particularly when circumstances were compared to the different conditions that could be glimpsed beyond the borders. An attempt was made to appease popular unease with price controls and speculation. In addition, social assistance was increased in the areas of health and food, and the construction of public housing began. The pontifical authorities, realizing the impossibility of an economic isolation of the Lazio territory within the broad framework of the peninsula, sought to strengthen relations with the more developed Kingdom of Italy. However, the greatest impulse to the "Italianization" process came from emigration, particularly that of un- and underemployed individuals, who departed in the hope of finding jobs and a better future. The children of the nobles were sent to join elite groups and the young bourgeois who started studying in Italian universities also emigrated, with the aim of greater social affirmation.[99] On the eve of unification, the Lazio economy consisted of

[97] Bocci, 1998, pp. 169–199.

[98] SAR, Camerale II, Commercio e industria, b. 4, Memoria indirizzata Alla Commissione deputata per la qualità delle manifatture.

[99] For a synthetic depiction of the migratory movement towards and within "Rome as capital", see the contribution by Bonifazi and Crisci (2016). http://www.dirittoestoria.it/16/memorie/romaterzaroma/Bonifazi-Crisci-Le-migrazioni-nella-storia-di-Roma-Capitale-[2016].htm.

a slowly evolving agricultural sector, a decaying industrial sector and a service sector that did not offer better administrative services. Lazio was annexed to the Kingdom of Italy nearly ten years after the latter's proclamation. The region was incorporated into a state entity that now had several years of experience. For local elites, annexation to the new state probably represented much more an acquisition of resources than a loss of autonomy or ancient rights and privileges (which were not lacking, particularly in certain productive sectors suddenly deprived of pre-unification customs protection). The pontifical institutional structure, for example, had always left little room for the financial autonomy of local administrations. The 1870 annexation to the Kingdom offered more freedom to the local ruling classes in managing municipal finances.

Inclusion in Italy was difficult, particularly given the weakness of the Italian economy compared to that of other European nations. It was hard to find employment, especially for the unskilled unless one resigned oneself to road, railway and port construction work.

References

Almagià, Roberto. 1976. *Il Lazio*. Turin: Utet.

Astraldi, Romolo. 1956. *La Camera di Commercio di Roma nei centoventicinque anni di vita. (1831–1956)*, Rome: Fratelli Palombi Editori.

Attuoni, Pietro. 1958. *Civitavecchia, il porto e la città*. Rome: Società Geografica Italiana.

Aubert, Roger. 1964. *Storia della Chiesa. Pontificato di Pio IX. 1846–1878*, Turin: Saie.

Bartoccini, Fiorella. 1971. *La Roma dei romani*. Rome: Istituto per la Storia del Risorgimento Italiano.

Bartoccini, Fiorella. 1993. L'aristocrazia romana nel tramonto del potere temporale. *Dimensione problemi della ricerca storica* 2: 240–255.

Bartoccini, Fiorella and Donatella Strangio, eds. 1997. *Lo Stato del Lazio 1860–1870*. Rome: Istituto Nazionale di Studi Romani.

Bartolini, Carlo. 2010 (anastic reprint 1897). *Il brigantaggio nello Stato Pontificio*, Bologna: Arnaldo Forni Editore.

Bocci, Marco. 1998. Costruttori di città: le società per azioni immobiliari nell'Italia post-unitaria (1861–1894). *Studi Storici Luigi Simeoni*, XLVIII: 169–199.

Bonelli, Franco. 1961. *Il commercio estero dello Stato Pontificio nel secolo XIX*, Rome: Archivio Economico dell'Unificazione Italiana", S.I, Vol. XI.

Bonifazi, Corrado and Massimiliano Crisci. 2016. *Le Migrazioni di Roma Capitale* in *Da Roma alla Terza Roma*, XXXVI seminario internazionale di studi storici, Campidoglio, 21–22 aprile (http://www.dirittoestoria.it/16/memorie/romaterzaroma/Bonifazi-Crisci-Le-migrazioni-nella-storia-di-Roma-Capitale-[2016].htm).

Brice, Catherine. 2020. Les «mercanti di campagna» romains. Profils et trajectoires d'une modernisation paradoxale (1789–1849). *Annales historiques de la Révolution française*, 3(n° 401): 159–182

Caffiero, Marina. 1997. L'agricoltura nello Stato Pontifico tra età della Restaurazione e Rivoluzione (1815–1848), in Ilaria Zilli (ed.) *Lo Stato e l'economia tra Restaurazione e Rivoluzione (1815–1848).* Naples: Edizioni Scientifiche Italiane.

Caffiero, Marina. 2001. Roma Repubblicana 1798–99, 1849. *Roma moderna e contemporanea*, IX(1–3): 9–28.

Calisse, Carlo. 1936 (or. ed. 1898). *Storia di Civitavecchia*, Florence: Barbera.

Caracciolo, Alberto and Mario Caravale. 1978. *Lo Stato Pontificio da Martino V a Pio IX*, in Giuseppe Galasso (ed.) *Storia d'Italia*, Turin: Utet.

Caracciolo, Alberto. 1973. *La storia economica, in Storia d'Italia*, vol. III Dal primo Settcento all'Unità, 511–693. Turin: Einaudi.

Caracciolo, Alberto. 1991. *La regione storica e reale*, in "*Storia d'Italia. Le regioni dall'Unità a oggi. Il Lazio*", Turin: Utet.

Castracane Mombelli Mirella. 1975–1976. *Per una storia dei tentativi di codificazione sullo Stato pontificio nel se. XIX. La fase consalviana (Parte I)*, in «Annali della scuola speciale per archivisti e bibliotecai dell'Università di Roma» XV–XVI, Turin, 108–156.

Castracane-Mombelli, Mirella. 1979–1980. *Per una storia dei tentativi di codificazione sullo Stato pontificio nel se. XIX. La fase consalviana (Parte II)*, in «Annali della scuola speciale per archivisti e bibliotecai dell'Università di Roma» XIX–XX, Turin, 111–240.

Castracane Mombelli, Mirella. 1997. Governo, legislazione, amministrazione centrale e locale dello Stato romano tra il 1860 e il 1870, in Fiorella Bartoccini and Donatella Strangio (eds.) *Lo Stato del Lazio 1860–1870*, Rome: Istituto Nazionale di Studi Romani, 9–63.

Cecchi, Dante. 1978. *L'amministrazione pontificia nella seconda Restaurazione (1814–1823)*, Macerata: Tip. Bi. Emmegraf.

Corridore, Francesco. 1906. *La popolazione dello Stato romano dal 1656 al 1901*, Rome: E. Loescher ed.

Cuccia, Giuseppe. 1991. *Urbanistica, edilizia, infrastrutture di Roma capitale, 1870–1990*, Rome-Bari: Laterza.

D'Errico, Rita. 1993. La *Cassa di Risparmio di Roma*. Un episodio di modernizzazione finanziaria nell'Ottocento. *Roma Moderna e Contemporanea*, I(2): 111–131.

D'Errico, Rita. 1999. Una gestione bancaria ottocentesca. La *Cassa di risparmio di Roma* dal 1836 al 1890, Naples: Edizioni Scientifiche Italiane.

De Cesare, Raffaele. 1907. *Roma e lo Stato del Papa dal ritorno di Pio IX al XX settembre*, vol. 2, Rome: Forzani *e* C. Tipografi-Editori.

De Longis, Rosanna. 2001. Tra sfera pubblica e difesa dell'onore. Donne nella Roma del 1849. *Roma moderna e contemporanea*, IX(1–3): 263–284.

Deane, Phillys. 1990. *La prima rivoluzione industriale*. Bologna: Il Mulino.

Della Seta, Piero. 1954. Un problema tipico della capitale: la speculazione edilizia. *Critica economica*, 4: 78–83.

Della Seta, Piero, and Roberto Della Seta. 1988. *I suoli di Roma*, Rome: Editori Riuniti.

Demarco, Domenico. 1949. *Il tramonto dello stato pontificio. Il papato di Gregorio XVI*, Turin: Giulio Einaudi editore.

Ellena, Vittorio. 1882. *Le industrie della provincia di Roma, Annali di statistica*, III, II, Rome: Ministero dell'Agricoltura, Industria e Commercio.

Falco, Mirio. 1910. *Il riordinamento della proprietà ecclesiastica*. Turin: Fratelli Bocca editori.

Farini, Luigi Carlo. 1853. *Lo Stato romano dal 1815 al 1850*, Firenze: Felice Le Monnier, vol. II.

Felisini, Daniela. 1990. *Le finanze pontificie e i Rothschild (1830–1870)*, Naples: Edizione Sscientifiche Italiane.

Felisini, Daniela. 1993. Le finanze pontificie nell'ottocento tra inquietudine politico-sociale e crisi economica, in Antonio Di Vittorio (ed.) *La finanza in età di crisi*, Bari: Cacucci, 181–211.

Felisini, Daniela. 1997. Il denaro di S. Pietro. Finanze pubbliche e finanze private nello Stato pontificio dell'ultimo decennio, in Fiorella Bartoccini and Donatella Strangio (eds.) *Lo Stato del Lazio. 1860–1870*, Rome: Istituto Nazionale di Studi Romani, 189–229.

Felisini, Daniela. 2004. *Quel capitalista per ricchezza principalissimo. Alessandro Torlonia principe banchiere, imprenditore nell'Ottocento romano*, Soveria Mannelli (CZ): Rubbettino editor.

Felisini, Daniela. 2016. *Alessandro Torlonia. The Pope's Banker*, London: Palgrave Studies in the History of Finance.

Felisini Daniela. 2021. Il Principe e le Grand Baron: modelli e contesti operative a confronto, in Giovanni Gregorini, Marina Romani (eds) *Borghesie nazionali, borghesie cosmopolite. Banca private, finanza, reti* (Italia, secoli XVIII–XX), Milan: FrancoAngeli, 143–158.

Felloni, Giuseppe. 1971. *Gli investimenti finanziari genovesi in Europa tra il Settecento e la Restaurazione*. Milan: Giuffrè.

Gabriele, Mariano. 1961, *L'industria delle costruzioni navali nei territori dello Stato Pontificio dal 1815 al 1880*, in "Archivio Economico dell'Unificazione Italiana", s. I, vol. XI, fasc. 4, Turin: Ilte.

Gabriele, Mariano. 1963. "*I porti dello Stato Pontificio dal 1835 al 1880*", in "Archivio Economico dell'Unificazione Italiana", s. I, vol. XII, fasc. 2.

Girelli, Angela Maria. 1998. Per la storia del mercante di campagna. Attività agricola e formazione di patrimoni privati nella Roma del primo Ottocento, in Tommaso Fanfani (ed.) *Saggi di storia economica in onore di Amelio Tagliaferro*, Pisa: Pacini, 209–250.

Girelli, Angela Maria. 1999. Alla ricerca del mercante di campagna. Una figura del lavoro romano nel primo Ottocento, in Alberto Guenzi, Paola, Massa, Anglo, Moioli (eds.) *Corporazioni e gruppi professionali nell'Italia moderna*, Milan: FrancoAngeli, 504–532.

Gourvish Terence, Richard. 1980. *Railways and the British Economy 1830–1914*, London: Macmillan.

Graziani, Ersilia. 1993. Sugli «stabilimenti di sussidio commerciale e pubblico» nello Stato pontificio. *Roma Moderna e Contemporanea*, I(2): 83–109.

Graziani, Ersilia. 1995. *La Banca Romana (1834-1870)*, in *Gli Archivi degli Istituti di Credito e le fonti d'archivio per la storia delle banche*, Rome: Ministero per I beni culturali e ambientali. Ufficio centrale per i beni archivistici, 463–492.

Holmer, Sidney, and Sylla Richard. 1995. *Storia dei tassi di interesse.* Rome: Cariplo-Laterza.

Insolera, Italo. 1976. *Roma moderna.* Turin: Einaudi.

Jemolo, Arturo Carlo. 1963. *Chiesa e Stato negli ultimi cento anni*, Turin: Einaudi.

La Marca, Nicola. 2000. *La nobiltà romana e i suoi strumenti di perpetuazione del potere*, Rome: Bulzoni editor, vols. 1–3.

Le assemblee del Risorgimento, Rome 1911, 4 vols.

Manca, Ciro. 1986. La storiografia marittima sullo Stato della Chiesa, in Antonio Di Vittorio (ed.) *Tendenze e orientamenti nella storiografia marittima contemporanea*, Naples: Edizioni Scientifiche Italiane, 73–93.

Momigliano, Eucardio and Gabriele M. Casolari. 1979 (5 ed.). *Tutte* le *encicliche dei sommi pontefici, raccolte e annotate da E. Momigliano e G.M. Casolari*, Milan: DallìOglio.

Monsagrati, Giuseppe. 2001. L'arte in guerra. Monumenti e politica a Roma al tempo dell'assedio del 1849. *Roma moderna e contemporanea, IX* 1–3: 217–262.

Morandi, Mario. 1933. Le condizioni economiche dello Stato pontificio al tempo della Repubblica Romana (1848–1849). *Rivista italiana di statistica, economia e finanza*, V (3), XI: 490–545.

Mori, Renato. 1967. *Il tramonto del potere temporale 1866–1870.* Rome: Edizioni di storia e letteratura.

Morichini, Carlo Luigi. 1847. *Sullo stato delle finanze pontificie e de' modi per migliorarle*, Roma.

Negri, Pietro. 1967. *Le ferrovie nello Stato Pontificio (1844-1870)*, Archivio Economico dell'Unificazione Italiana, s. I, vol. XVI, fasc. 2, Turin: Ilte.

Palermo, Luciano. 1994. I porti dello Stato della Chiesa in età moderna, infrastrutture e politica degli investimenti, in Giorgio Simoncini (ed.) *Sopra i porti di mare, IV, Lo Stato Pontificio*, Florence: Le Monnier, 81–150.

Palermo, Stefano. 2006. *La Banca Tiberina. Finanza ed edilizia tra Roma, Napoli e Torino 1869–1895*, Naples: Editoriale Scientifica Italian.

Palermo, Stefano. 2008. *Terra, città, finanza. I Boncompagni Ludovisi di Roma (1841–1896)*, Milan: FrancoAngeli.

Parisi, Emanuela. 1993. *Tentativi di innovazione dell'industria laniera nella Roma dell'Ottocento*, in Daniela Brignone (ed.) *Innovazione tecnologica ed industria in Italia. Cinque realtà emblematiche 1860–1940*, Rome: Bulzoni, 17–46.

Pepoli Napoleone, Gioacchino. 1858. Il debito pubblico pontificio. Lettera al Conte Costa della Torre. *Rivista contemporanea*, XIV(6): 120–125.

Pescosolido, Guido. 1979. *Terra e nobiltà. I Borghese (secoli XVIII e XIX)*, Rome: Jouvence.

Pescosolido, Guido. 1981. Baronaggio e usi civici nell'Ottocento romano, in Renato Lefevre (ed.) *Ottocento nel Lazio*, Rome: F.lli Palombi, 385–403.

Pescosolido, Guido. 2004, *Agricoltura e industria nell'Italia unita*, Rome-Bari: Ed. Laterza.

Petrocchi, Massimo. 1941. *La restaurazione il Cardinal Consalvi e la Riforma del 1816*, Florence: Le Monnier.

Piacentini, Marcello and Francesco Giudi. 1952. *Le vicende edilizie di Roma dal 1870 ad oggi*, Rome: F.lli Palombi Editore.

Piccinini, Gilberto. 2012. *Il Pontificato di leone XII. Restaurazione e riforme nel governo della Chiesa e nello Stato, Quaderni del Consiglio regionale delle Marche, 116*, Ancona: Centro stampa digitale dell'Assemblea legislativa.

Pinchera, Stefano. 1957. *Corso dei cambi sulla piazza di Roma dal 1838 al 1870*, "Archivio dell'Unificazione Italiana", fasc. III, vol.VI, Rome: Ilte.

Pinchera, Stefano. 1961. *Le spese effettive e il bilancio dello Stato pontificio dal 1827 al 1867*, Turin: Ilte, Archivio Economico dell'Unificazione Italiana, I, vol. IX, fasc. 5.

Piola Caselli, Fausto. 1993. Una montagna di debiti. I monti baronali dell'aristocrazia romana del Seicento. *Roma moderna e contemporanea*, I(2): 21–55.

Piscitelli, Enzo. 1958. Una famiglia di mercanti di campagna. I Merolli. Cenni genealogici. *Archivio della società romana di storia patria*, LXXXI: 119–173.

Piscitelli, Enzo. 1968. Un ceto scomparso nello Stato della Chiesa. *I mercanti di campagna, Studi romani, XVI* 4: 446–457.

Prodi, Paolo. 1986. *Il Sovrano Pontefice*, in *Storia d'Italia*, in Annali vol. 9, Giorgio Chittolini and Giovanni Miccoli (eds.) *La Chiesa e il potere politico dal Medioevo all'Età Contemporanea*, Turin: Einaudi, 198–216.

Quacquarelli, Antonio. 1940. La crisi economica dello Stato pontificio nell'età della Restaurazione, *Rivista italiana di scienze economiche*, XII(8), XVIII: 1–9

Ragionieri, Ernesto. 1978. *Italia giudicata 1861–1945 ovvero la storia degli italiani scritta dagli altri*, vol. I. Turin: Einaudi.

Regoli, Roberto, Fiumi Sermattei Ilaria and Maria Rosa Di Simone. 2019. *Governo della Chiesa governo dello Stato. Il tempo di leone XII, Quaderni del Consiglio regionale delle Marche, 291,* Ancona: Centro stampa digitale dell'Assemblea legislativa.

Relazione della Commissione parlamentare d'inchiesta sul corso forzoso dei biglietti di banca deliberata nella tornata del 10 marzo 1868, sess. 1867–1868, in Atti Parlamentari, Camera dei Deputati, Legislazione X, vol III Deposizioni.

Riall, Lucy. 2001. Rivoluzione, repubblicanesimo e Risorgimento: Roma e i suoi storici, 1789–99 e 1849. *Roma moderna e contemporanea*, IX(1–3): 285–306.

Rossi Ragazzi, Bruno. 1956. *Le entrate dello Stato pontificio dal 1827 al 1867*, Archivio economico dell'Unificazione italiana, vol. I, fasc. 4, Turin: Ilte.

Ruggiero, Pastura, and Maria Grazia. 1991. *L'amministrazione del debito pubblico nelle province romane*. Rome: Archivio di Stato di Roma.

Salvatori, Franco, Marcello Ricci, Claudio Cerreti and Maurizio Simoncelli. 1997. *Lo Stato pontificio 1860-1870: tra implosione territoriale e integrazione spaziale*, in Fiorella Bartoccini and Donatella Strangio (eds.) *Lo Stato del Lazio 1860-1870*, Rome: Istituto Nazionale di Studi Romani, 66–112.

Sanfilippo, Mario. 2009. L'Agro Romano tra Ottocento e Duemila, in Vittorio Emiliani (ed.) *Il riscatto dell'Agro. L'agricoltura a difesa del paesaggio*, Bologna: Minerva edizioni, 73–85.

Sansa, Renato. 2009. Un imprenditore anomalo? Achille Gori Mazzoleni da mercante di campagna a possidente innovatore (sec. XIX), in Franco Amatori and Andrea Colli (eds.) *Imprenditorialità e sviluppo economico. Il caso italiano (secc. XIII-XX)*, Milan: Egea, 1008–1024.

Santoncini, Gabriella. 1994. Appunti per una bibliografia critica nella seconda restaurazione pontificia. *Proposte e Ricerche, XVII* 32: 158–185.

Strangio, Donatella and Manuel Vaquero Piñeiro. 2009. Il porto di Civitavecchia alla vigilia del Regno d'Italia: tra politica doganale e traffici nel Mediterraneo, in Raffaella Salvemini (ed.) *Istituzioni e traffici nel Mediterraneo tra età antica e crescita moderna*, Naples: Cnr-Istituto di Studi sulle Società del Mediterraneo, 405–430.

Strangio, Donatella. 1997. *L'economia dello Stato pontificio tra il 1860–1870*, in Fiorella Bartoccini and Donatella Strangio (eds.), *Lo Stato del Lazio. 1860–1870*, Rome: Istituto Nazionale di Studi Romani, 147–187.

Strangio, Donatella. 2001, *Il debito pubblico pontificio. Cambiamento e continuità nella finanza pontificia dal periodo francese alla restaurazione romana. 1798–1820*, Padova: Cedam.

Strangio, Donatella. 2006. *Il porto di Civitavecchia (secc. XVI-XVIII): investimenti e sviluppo economico*, in Simonetta Cavaciocchi (ed.) Atti delle "Settimane di Studi", 37, *Ricchezza del mare Ricchezza dal mare. Secc. XIII-XVIII,* Istituto Internazionale di Storia Economica "F. Datini" di Prato (11–15 aprile 2005), Florence: Le Monnier, pp. 761–772.

Strangio, Donatella. 2007. *Debito pubblico e mercato finanziario a Roma e nello stato pontificio tra XVIII e XIX secolo: l'istituzione della Borsa di Roma*, in Giuseppe De Luca and Angelo Moioli (eds.) *Debito pubblico e mercati finanziari in Italia. Secoli XIII-XX*, Milan: FrancoAngeli, 251–270.

William, Nassau Senior. 1937. *L'Italia dopo il 1848*, Bari: Laterza.

Toniolo, Gianni. 1995. *Sull'arte del banchiere centrale in Italia: fatti stilizzati e congetture (1861–1947)*, Temi di discussione del servizio studi di Banca d'Italia, 255, September, pp. 1–65.

Sources

State Archive of Rome (from now SAR).

Bandi b.312.

Camerale II, Debito Pubblico, b.7, fasc.3; b.14, fasc.3.

Camerale II, Commercio e industria, b. 4.

Camera di Commercio, bb. 1,12,14, 29 and bb.40–44

Consulta di Stato, b. 1, 2.

Camerlengato, parte II, Annona e Grascia b. 319 and 766.

Commissariato generale per le ferrovie pontificie, bb.1.

Ministero delle finanze, b. 551.

Ministero dell'Interno, Commercio b. 319, 1168.

Ministero delle finanze, b, 551, 605.

Ministero del Commercio, Belle Arti, Industria, Agricoltura e Lavori Pubblici, b. 573.

Tesorierato generale, titolo I, affari generali, b.279.

Edited Sources

"Appendice al giornale del foro", Leggi ordinanze, regolamenti e circolari d'interesse generale per lo stato pontificio, 14 march 1848, vol. 1.

Bollettino delle leggi, proclami, regolamenti e altre disposizioni della Repubblica Romana, Rome 1849.

Giornale di Roma (July 1849–december 1860).

Il Commercio". 1847. Roman periodical newspaper.

«Civiltà Cattolica» 6 January 872.

«Frusta», Roman periodical newspaper 3/01/ 1871, n. 1

Diario di Roma n. 23, 18 March 1847.

Il Commercio (periodico romano) Year 1, n. 49, 20 November 1847.

Monitore Romano (Febraury 1849–July 1849).

Marchetti, Giovanni. 1800. *Calcolo ragionato del denaro straniero che viene a Roma e che se ne va per cause ecclesiastiche.* Rome: S.N.L.

Momo Giovanni (cardinal). 1845. "Quali vantaggi ha conseguiti e conseguirà la civile società. Dalle Macchine a Vapore, dalle Strade Ferrate e dalle Casse di Risparmio? Riflessioni interessantissime del C. Giovanni Momo.", Florence: s.n. 6, 9.

Moroni Gaetano, 1855. *Dizionario d'erudizione storico–ecclesiastica*, Venice: Tipografia Emiliana, vol. LXXIV.

Negrisoli, Gaetano. 1857. *Rivista dei più importanti prodotti naturali e manifatturieri dello Stato Pontificio*, Ferrara: Tipografia governativa Taddei.

Raccolta di leggi e disposizioni di pubblica amministrazione dello Stato pontificio, Roma 1834–1870, 23 vols.

Raccolta delle leggi e disposizioni di pubblica amministrazione dello stato pontificio, Roma 1834–1870, vols. I, II.

Raccolta delle leggi e disposizioni di pubblica amministrazione nello stato pontificio 1846–1847, Roma 1849

Raccolta delle leggi e disposizioni di pubblica amministrazione, vol. I, Rome 1835.

De Tournon, Camille Comte. 1855. *Etudes statistiques sur Rome et la partie occidentale des ètats romaines*, Paris: Firmin Didot Frères.

CHAPTER 2

Finance and Banking

In the various parts of pre-unification Italy the diffusion of institutions such as discount and issue banks and savings banks was widespread, which is configured as one of the aspects that offer the measure of the financial modernization process underway in the various central decades of the nineteenth century.

The year 1866 brought about a profound change in the attitude of the Roman government, as evidenced by the agreement with the Italian administration on the division of the debt and the transformation of the monetary system. The resistance of the pope in the first part of the decade gave way to an increasing willingness to collaborate with the Kingdom of Italy. Reinforcing the view that the taking of Porta Pia was not a true watershed, there is evidence of the transformation of the territory, above all through railway construction and urban planning works, already started before 1870. Ultimately, in the aftermath of the unification, there were no major upheavals in Lazio; in contrast, strong elements of continuity with the pontifical structures were maintained.

D. Strangio, *The Roman Stock Exchange between the 19th and 20th Centuries*, Palgrave Studies in the History of Finance, https://doi.org/10.1007/978-3-031-00359-2_2

2.1 Institutions and Financial Market

The last forty years of the Papal State (1830–1870) were characterized by a progressive worsening of its financial condition. The causes of the difficulty varied. However, at the bottom, there was a profound inability to accept the new economic and social demands and constitutional political principles, which would inevitably undermine papal absolutism. At the institutional level, there was great inefficiency and corruption, and the administrative apparatus was dysfunctional, primarily due to the difficulty of ascertaining and collecting taxes.[1]

The extreme political and military precariousness of 1860 had a negative impact on Papal State finances, characterized by a large imbalance between income and expenditure.

The loss of the central-eastern regions had major financial effects: tax revenues were halved compared to those of 1850–1860, with a volume for the entire decade between 5 and 7 million scudi per year.[2] There was a decline in both direct taxes, due to the loss of large amounts of taxable income, and indirect taxes, consisting mainly of consumer and customs duties, whose collection became increasingly difficult due to the phenomenon of smuggling. Tax receipts from transfers (e.g., registration, stamp duty and mortgages) also decreased. The new structure of the Papal State was defined by Cardinal Antonelli as "a small body with a disproportionate, very large head that absorbs resources".[3]

> In the first months of the year, an appeal was made to European Catholics "... to contribute money and men to the defence of the Pope's temporal domains"; however, only 300,000 scudi were collected.[4]

[1] SAR. Ministero delle finanze, b. 671, "Cenni di ciò che all'epoca presente (september 1849) potrebbe facilitare una buona riorganizzazione nelle finanze dello Stato Pontificio".

[2] The monetary unit used in the Papal State from 1835 to 1866 was the shield, which was divided into decimal submultiples: 1 shield = 10 paoli; 1 paolo = 10 baiocchi.

Following the reform of the monetary order, decreed by the edict of June 18, 1866, the shield was replaced by the papal lira, equivalent to the Italian lira and divided, like the lira, into lire and cents, its decimal sub-multiples. In the same edict, the parity between the shield and the papal lira was fixed according to the following ratio: 1 scudo = 5.375 lire; 1 lira = 0.1865 scudi (Balbi De Caro, Londei, 1984).

[3] Felisini, 1997, p. 193.

[4] Felisini, 1997, p. 193.

Despite the limitations, the costs of the new army and military spending in general weighed heavily on state budgets.[5] In 1860, the expenses for the armed forces had more than doubled compared to previous years, to the point of comprising 32% of total expenditure. The reduction of the army in the years 1861–1865 was not enough to engender a significant decrease in military spending, which remained high throughout the decade, both in the state budgets and the finances of local authorities.[6]

The papal treasury continued to incur substantial expenses for public administration resulting from the maintenance of employees, officials and members of the clergy of the lost provinces, with the aim of maintaining their fidelity.

Another significant portion of state spending consisted of the resources allocated to public assistance. Charity, very common in the state, was provided both directly and through religious orders, parishes and the twelve "legionary congregations of subsidies".[7] It was estimated that in 1870, the Apostolic Chamber, the central government body, paid approximately 3.5 million lire (600,000 scudi) into the coffers of hospitals and other welfare organizations, a gesture aimed at compensating for the waste and inefficiency of a poor administration.[8]

The welfare structures, in addition to addressing strictly medical tasks, were also committed to coping with unemployment and phenomena related to social disintegration, such as wandering.

The limited public expenditure to support certain productive sectors, both agricultural and industrial (in the entire decade, this expenditure represented on average only 2.5–3% of total state expenditure), contributed to the closure of numerous factories, particularly in the wool and tanning sector. The decrease in expenditure related to public works was an inevitable consequence of the scarcity of financial resources available to the state, which severely limited active intervention in the area. This scarcity had greater consequences for the Lazio provinces, increasing

[5] Manetti, 2009, pp. 192–193 underlines how military expenditures underwent considerable expansion, particularly for the defence and maintenance of French and then Austrian troops, the latter starting in 1831 (the Austrian garrison allocation), on the Papal State's territory. See Felisini, 1997; Della Torre, 1941, pp. 45–99.

[6] Felisini, 1997, p. 205.

[7] Rossi, 1848, p. 320. Regarding charity in the Papal State, see Piccialuti Caprioli, 1994.

[8] Piccialuti Caprioli, 1991, pp. 368–369.

the isolation in which they found themselves and which would last at least through the first postunification decade.

Ultimately, the expenditures required to maintain the political control apparatus for social consensus and the financial burden of the public debt were too much higher than those for infrastructure construction and the incentives necessary to boost the economy. A static economic model emerged, in which the deficit, once an extraordinary financial phenomenon, became a structural feature of the public budget.

To cover the deficit of 1860, it was necessary to find the most effective tools. In fact, neither an increase in the tax burden nor increased stimulus to invest in the internal financial market were conceivable: both were already widely used. The only remaining option was foreign lending. However, the idea of a loan from the Rothschilds was impractical for several reasons. First, the Austrian Maison perceived the serious financial conditions the Roman state was facing and foresaw its imminent definitive crisis. In addition, it was necessary to consider that the Austrian family was one of the major financiers of Cavour's economic and military policy. Therefore, it would have been difficult for it to take a position against the Kingdom of Italy.

As a result, together with Belgian and French Catholic bankers, the launch of a "Catholic loan" was planned, with the issuance at par of consolidated notes for 50 million francs (equal to approximately 9.3 million scudi according to the exchange rate set at 5.37 francs for one scudo) with an annual interest of 5%. For the placement of the new titles, committees were established in various European states with the participation of eminent personalities suggested by local bishops. Subscriptions were opened on 1 May 1860 in Rome, Naples, Paris, Brussels, Amsterdam, London, Dublin, Frankfurt, Vienna, Munich, Berlin, Lucerne, Madrid and Lisbon. The possibility was offered to buy the securities in instalments "… to allow a greater number of Catholics to rush to the relief of the pressure in which the Papal Treasury finds itself due to the present difficult circumstances".[9] The phrasing of this statement shows that more than a financial transaction was involved; rather, the plan was

[9] "Chirografo della Santità di Nostro Signore Pio Papa IX sulla emissione e vendita di un prestito fruttifero per pubblica sottoscrizione", 18 april 1860, in Raccolta delle leggi, n. 42, 1860.

an appeal to the religious sentiment of European Catholics. After a hesitant start, the loan programme found a good reception. Approximately 6.75 million scudi were signed, especially in France, Belgium and Spain.

The problems of the papal treasury remained numerous. Therefore, additional measures were adopted, such as a loan of 800,000 scudi from Francesco II, King of Naples. In addition, the ancient institution of the "Obolo" of St. Peter was strengthened.[10] These measures resulted in an increase in the budget deficit because to cover the new consolidation greater financing charges were added to the already substantial public debt. The loss of the Legations, Marche and Umbria, and therefore of a large part of the assets and income that constituted the guarantee of the debts, exacerbated the distrust and insecurity of potential creditors towards the papal government. The attitude of the French government also became more critical, urging Rome to a greater spirit of compromise with Italy and to grant important and necessary reforms.

The loss of credibility of the Papal State is also evidenced by the loss of nearly sixteen points of the papal bonds, which had decreased from 88 scudi in the first half of 1859 to 72.6 scudi in the same period of 1861. Starting in 1861, the papal accounts presented substantial negative balances, approximately 5 million scudi, and beginning in 1866, they surpassed 6 million. In 1863, in addition to completing the sale of the bonds of the Catholic loan of 1860, 5% Treasury certificates were issued, worth 100 scudi each for a value of 4 million scudi. Given the moderate success of the previous loan of 1860, in March 1864, the Roman Treasury authorized a second loan with the issue of 5% securities for a value of 9.3 million scudi. The modalities of the operation mirrored those of the previous loan, with the exception of the placement, which, instead of resorting to the dioceses was entrusted to the Belgian banker Langrand-Dumonceau. Subscriptions were rather scarce; the second Catholic loan did not win the market's favour, collecting just over 3.7 million scudi at par and only 200,000 scudi at 75%.

[10] The "Obolo" of San Peter originated in the eighth century as an annual tribute by the rulers to the pope. The tradition weakened during the Reformation, and was transformed into offerings by the faithful for specific initiatives and events. After the institution of the Opera in 1860, the Obolo was initially managed separately from the finances of the State, then merged directly into the Apostolic Treasury and, from 1926, into the general administration of the assets of the Holy See, until it came to represent, in recent decades, the main financial resource of the Vatican budget.

The budget deficit of 1865, which stood at approximately 5.3 million scudi, required new financial sources. The Roman Treasury turned to Maison Blont in Paris. A contract was signed for the issue of 60 million francs (equal to just over 11 million scudi) of bearer bonds of 500 francs each, with an annual interest of 5% payable every six months and an amortization of 1% per annum starting from 1870.

During the decade 1860–1870, several meetings were held to determine the transfer of the papal public debt to be borne by the Italian government but without the papal government ever entering into negotiations. The pope rejected every proposal, considering the debt not as a commitment of the state but as an "indivisible and personal" obligation contracted by the sovereign. It was observed that with the acceptance of the transfer of part of the obligations to the Kingdom of Italy, one would be tacitly consenting to the new geopolitical structure of the Peninsula. The French, who played a primary role in this period, did not share this position, arguing that the state debt did not represent an obligation of the sovereign but of the community and the resources that are part of the state itself.

The Convention signed by Italy and France in Paris on 15 September 1864, established that in exchange for the evacuation of French troops and the guarantee not to attack the Papal State, Italy would negotiate with Rome the assumption of a portion of the papal public debt proportional to the annexed provinces in 1859–1860. Despite the pressing difficulties of the Roman treasury, reaching an agreement for the division was long and difficult as the papal government did not consider the Convention favourably. The entry into force in the Kingdom of Italy of the new civil code and the law of 7 July on religious corporations generated fears of even greater resistance from the Holy See. However, in reality, the delays in the negotiations were due to other issues.

The report on the public debt, dated 1866 and signed by Cardinal Antonelli, reported the parameters and data according to which it was necessary to carry out the division of the debt between the two administrations. The report noted that, in the 1864 Convention between "the French Government and the Court of Turin", contained in Article 4, the Court of Turin intended to prepare to enter into negotiations to assume a proportional part of the debt "of the ancient States of the Church". The French government, in stipulating this Convention, knew that the pontifical government would not be willing to execute the part that concerned it. Therefore, it reserved for itself the responsibility to establish the amount of the public debt referable to the usurped provinces, proposing to receive annually from the government of King Vittorio Emanuele II the corresponding sum to make it available to the papal government, and at the same time officially declared to the legislative body, that the regulation of the portion of the papal public debt that he had in mind to establish with the aforementioned government should not in any way prejudice the rights of the Holy See over the usurped provinces, and that this operation was only to be considered as a bank transaction aimed at passing a sum determined by the Piedmontese government to that of France, a sum that the latter proposed to make over to the Rothschild house to be employed to pay by them for the consolidation of the Papal State guaranteed by the revenues of the State of the Holy See. Under these conditions, the papal government did not perceive "any inconvenience that the Imperial government put its good will into effect", and, in this regard, in 1865, it arranged for the French Ambassador in Rome to have "two sheets", of which the first (Table 2.1) reported the situation of the public debt of the Papal State in the fall of 1860 and the other (Table 2.2) the debts incurred from 1861 through the end of 1865 "to make up for the annual deficit deriving from the payment of the public debt and the imbalance of the general expenses of the State". Another sheet was added (Table 2.3) to show that the papal government debt related to the invaded provinces "should have been for approximately 27 million francs".[11]

It was determined that the allotment would be calculated from 30 June 1859 for the Romagne and from 30 September 1860 for the Marche and Umbria in proportion to the number of inhabitants of the annexed provinces and those remaining under papal sovereignty, as recorded in the survey of 1857. The financial data contained in the Great Book of the papal public debt would be used, and it was determined that the calculation should be made specifically for each category of debt, without making the distribution of the general total, as requested by the pope.

Another important decision was that according to which Italy agreed to pay the arrears from the moment of annexation, excluding, however, the payment of interest, as requested by the French. On 7 December

[11] SAR. Archivio Antonelli, b. 31, "Relazione sul debito pubblico gravante le province invase". Regarding the role of the Monte di Pietà in Rome, see Tamilia, 1900; Tosi, 1937; Travaglini, 1988, pp. 463–482; 1991, pp. 619–639; 2001; De Rita, 2011; Procaccia, 1994–1997; Arcelli, 1999, 2004.

Table 2.1 Situation of the public debt of the Papal State in the fall of 1860

TITLE I	
Permanent debt	*Roman Scudi*
Consolidated annuities recorded	1,628,319
Enrollable annuities	637
Census and other annuities from different sources	102,224
Grants for worship, charity, public education and various other parameters	216,909
Checks in favour of individuals with reversibility to the State	2,232
Annuities substituted for canons franked by virtue of the law of March 9, 1848	19,494
Amortization fund in "*Luoghi di Monte*" of the annuality resulting from the amortized folders in the form of Art. 7 of the Notification of 20 December 1835	68,048
TOTAL TITLE I	2,037,864
TITLE II	
Redeemable Debt	*Roman Scudi*
Annual interest and repurchase fund for the bonds of loans contracted abroad	1,702,500
Fee for the annual payment of interest and the repurchase fund (commissions and possible exchange losses not included)	10,095
Annuities established for the freeing of De'Canoni, levels by virtue of the sovereign Chirografo of 28 July 1832	24,999
Annuities established for the extinction of receivables from the Treasury in June 1849 in the form of the Edict of the Secretariat of State of June 20, 1855	9,193
Interest on the securities of the unsecured loan authorized April 18, 1860	465,000
Interest on the fund of one million divided into 5,000 shares, requested with the Notification of October 3, 1854 for the new Ammin. Government of the Regia de'Sali e Tabacchi	50,000
TOTAL TITLE II	2,261,787
TITLE III	
Life-long debt	*Roman Scudi*
Jubilation payments and pensions for civilian employees and their families in the form of the *Motu Proprio* dl 1 May 1828	505,998
Jubilation payments to the customs guards in the form of the Regulations of 24 October 1827	41,827
Jubilation payments and military pensions in the form of the *Motu Proprio* of 30 June 1822	353,465
Ecclesiastical pensions to individuals of unrestored religious houses	4,644

(continued)

Table 2.1 (continued)

Pensions and checks assumed with the Conventions for the Provinces already joined to the former Kingdom of Italy	10,312
So-called Chamber and Reform pensions, and others of different origins	155,730
Checks and subsidies payable on the main anniversaries of the year	9,089
TOTAL TITLE III	1,081067
SYNTHESIS	
Title I Permanent Debt	2,037,864
Title II Redeemable Debt	2,261,787
Title III Lifetime Debt	1,081067
TOTAL annual debt in the fall of 1860	5,380,720

Source SAR. Archivio Antonelli, b. 31, "Relazione sul debito pubblico gravante le province invase" del 1866

Table 2.2 Debts created from 1861 through the end of 1865 to make up for the annual deficit deriving from the payment of the Public Debt and from the imbalance of the general expenses of the State

TITLE I	
Permanent debt	*Roman Scudi*
Consolidated annuity created by Sovereign rescript of January 16, 1861	100,000
Consolidated annuity created by Sovereign rescript of November 20, 1861	350,000
Consolidated annuity created by Sovereign rescript of 12 July 1865	450,000
INCREASES ON TITLE I	900,000
TITLE II	
Redeemable Debt	*Roman Scudi*
Interest on 40,000 certificates of 100 shields each issued under the Edict of the Secretariat of State of January 28, 1863	200,000
Amortization fund for the aforementioned certificates	266,666
Interest on the securities of the loan authorized with the Sovrano Chirografo of 26 March 1864	465,000
Amortization fund established with the aforementioned unsecured loan for both this loan and the similar loan from 1860	186,000
INCREASES ON TITLE II	1,117,666
SYNTHESIS	*Roman Scudi*
Title I Increases	900,000
Title II Increases	1,117,666
TOTAL DEBTS CREATED FROM 1861 THROUGH THE END OF 1865	2,017,666

Source SAR Archivio Antonelli, b. 31, "Relazione sul debito pubblico gravante le province invase" del 1866

Table 2.3 Debt of the invaded pontifical provinces

From the amount of the annual debt existing in the fall of 1860	5,380720
Deduct the share corresponding to the population of the capital and the remaining provinces derived from the statistics published by the Ministry of the Interior	1,186,448
They remain for the invaded provinces annually	4,194,271
From which sum deducted the amount of the items that were paid in the same provinces	760,381
One has the part remaining in the weight of the Pontifical Government	3,433,889
The Pontifical Government must provide for the entire deficit produced by the usurpation of the Provinces with the creation of new debts, which realize on average approximately 75%, that have increased the public debt by a large sum, consequently burdening the Treasury with interest payments. The aforementioned share of 3,433,889 corresponds to a debt created through the end of 1865 of approximately 27 million scudi, deemed realizable at 75% and the only interest of 5% to be added to the aforementioned amount of interest over 27 million and the amortization fund due to the 1%, which represents in total	1,620,000
the annuity from which the Papal Government should be discharged	5,053,889
Equal to francs	27,171,446

Source SAR, Archivio Antonelli, b. 31, "Relazione sul debito pubblico gravante le province invase" del 1866.

1866, the Convention and the annexed protocol for the division of the papal debt were signed in Paris: an annual quota of 7,892,984 lire for perpetual debt and 7,337,160 lire for redeemable debt passed to the Italian Treasury. As far as the life debt was concerned, the Italian government would pay all the pensions to the holders belonging to the former papal provinces and now residing in the Kingdom.

The Convention was favourably accepted by the French and, from a certain perspective, also by the pontifical governing bodies that were trying to relieve the budget of heavy financial burdens. Despite several discussions, the Italian Parliament first approved law no. 3745 of 27 May 1867, and then, on 31 July 1868, the Final Protocol for the execution of the Convention of December 1866 was signed.

The absence of fundamental structural change and the difficult relationship with the Italian economy resulted in a financial crisis of the "Lazio" state in the same year of the treaty, with a public debt that reached 20 million and a "pontifical" currency (the shield) that had problems finding acceptance in the international foreign exchange market. On

Table 2.4 Roman bond prices 5% Paris stock exchange—1859–1869[a]

Year	*Semester I*	*Semester II*
1859	84.7	85.4
1860	81.9	77.9
1861	72.7	70.7
1862	71.1	73.7
1863	76.0	76.7
1864	76.0	74.2
1865	74.0	73.5
1866	64.7	60.3
1867	62.4	61.9
1868	64.7	67.2
1869	67.0	66.0

[a] Six-monthly arithmetic averages
Source "Le Moniteur Universel"

18 June 1866, an edict of the secretary of state established a new monetary system; a papal lira linked to the value of the Italian lira was created; this step was motivated by a desire for alignment with "other states, with which we have greater and more direct commercial relations"[12] (without the Kingdom of Italy being named).

Foreign stock exchanges also reflect the sharp decline in the financial depth of the state (see Table 2.4 relating to the prices of Roman bonds on the Paris stock exchange).

In addition, in the Bank of the Papal State, the state did not have valid support capable of encouraging economic development; more than anything, the bank had become a centre of easy speculation for credit adventures.[13] The years immediately following the events of 1859–1860 were characterized by the growth of the fiduciary circulation of the issuing institute as a result of an expansive credit policy (the amount of the notes registered among the liabilities of the Bank of the Papal State, which in the 1850s only exceptionally exceeded 2,500,000 scudi, increased progressively starting in the following decade from 3.07 million scudi in 1863 to over 6.2 million in 1870).

[12] Edict of the Secretary of State of 18 june 1866, "Nuovo sistema di moneta pontificia in lire e centesimi".

[13] Caracciolo, 1954, p. 203.

Until the summer of 1865, the Bank managed to maintain the liquidity ratio between its metal reserve and the notes in circulation at 1 to 3, as provided for by its regulations. Subsequently, however, an increase in the trade deficit, low yields in the agricultural sector and political instability at the state borders contributed to increased hoarding and export of metal species, increasing the requests for the conversion of bank notes. Provisions were adopted regarding the exchange of the various types of papal currency.[14]

Following the halving of the gold reserves, in December 1865, a notification was prepared (never published) in which for six months the Bank was exempted from the obligation to convert its tickets, limiting the daily exchange rate to 8,000 scudi. The government also offered its guarantee for the institute's paper circulation. However, the measure was only implemented during the following year following the worsening of the Bank's liquidity, particularly following the proclamation of a fiat tender in the neighbouring Kingdom of Italy.[15]

In the provision of 18 June 1866 by the Minister of Finance, Monsignor Giuseppe Ferrari, any reference to the duration was excluded, while the limit on the exchange of tickets was reduced from 8,000 to 6,000 scudi, and no mention was made of the government guarantee on the tickets, which would be granted the following October.[16] However, these extraordinary measures did nothing but temporarily assuage the by now chronic bank inflation, for which the government had its share of the blame. Since 1860–1861, the share of paper currency in Rome was approximately 18 lire per lira of metal currency, while in the other Italian provinces, even in the most advanced ones, it barely reached 14 lire.[17]

[14] "Disposizioni sul cambio delle diverse specie di moneta pontificia" del Ministro del Commercio, Lavori Pubblici, Industria e Agricoltura Costantini Baldini, 6 december 1865, in "Raccolta delle leggi e disposizioni", cit., Rome 1865, vol. n. 47.

[15] SAR, Camera di Commercio, b. 28, Notificazione del Tesoriere Generale Ministro delle Finanze G. Ferrari, 18 june 1866.

[16] SAR, Camera di Commercio, b. 28, Notificazione del Tesoriere Generale Ministro delle Finanze G. Ferrari, 4 october 1866.

[17] De Mattia, 1959, p. 25.

Starting in May 1866, according to the "governor" of the Bank of the Papal State, Filippo Antonelli, there were many requests for the exchange of paper money.[18]

The conditions of the Bank had become very serious, and not even the adopted measures brought the desired results, as demonstrated by a report on the monetary crisis and measures to be taken with respect to the Bank of the Papal State by the treasurer of the Ministry of Finance. Overwhelmed by the monetary crisis, the Bank was already in difficult conditions and had no possibility by ordinary means of meeting its commitments. The "metal currency" contained in its coffers to guarantee the fiduciary notes in circulation, already reduced by the exchange rate, would have run out if the notification of 18 June 1865 had not limited exchanges to six thousand scudi daily (see above).[19]

The competition from the new Bank of the Four Legations, the restriction of the papal economic context of the last decade, together with structural weaknesses, including the incomplete payment of the share capital, and a management approach that was never completely clear often brought the Bank close to liquidation or absorption. This irregular activity always found government approval precisely because the government used it to support the treasury and put paper money into circulation without coverage.[20]

The adoption of the fiat course (i.e., the inconvertibility of paper money) by the Roman state beginning in the second half of 1866 was another indication of the difficulties of the Bank of the Papal State.

In the capital, there were also private banks, and among these (as explained in other parts of this book) the activity of the *Cassa di Risparmio di Roma* was important.[21] The leader of the local banking system since its foundation in 1836, this bank was set up on the initiative of several exponents of the noble and entrepreneurial classes. It established itself both as a large deposit collection institution and to serve the interests of the economic and financial elite. As highlighted in a report of

[18] Report of the governor of the Bank of the Papal State for the general meeting 7 march 1867.

[19] SAR, Ministero delle Finanze, b. 605, "Rapporto sulla crisi monetaria e provvedimenti da prendersi rispetto alla Banca dello Stato Pontificio", 21 september 1866.

[20] Porisini, 1969, p. 22.

[21] D'Errico, 1999.

1859, the activities of the pontifical savings bank included several important functions. One was that of receiving weekly and in certain amounts small sums from artisans and farmers, in short, individuals who used thrift saved to create a small, useful income that could be drawn on to confront unexpected adversity.[22]

The institutes, paying a fair interest on the sums received on deposit, to be claimed within established deadlines, invested the received sums, of which they were custodians, in duly guaranteed assets.[23]

In this way, on the one hand, "the less wealthy" were provided an opportunity to save and make their savings bear fruit, while, on the other, sums were made available to small traders, who thus could avoid resorting to usurers.[24]

During the decade 1860–1870, the activity of the Roman Cassa was affected not only by the economic and financial events of the Papal State but also by extra economic factors. In the bank's collection operations, the use of bank notes was accepted more frequently because of the increased circulation of paper currency, a consequence of the lack of metal species. Deposits in paper money yielded 4% interest to the customer.

The first part of the decade was characterized by an increase in deposits and the difficulty of investing these sums as a result of the absence of credit requests from the small clientele of the Roman institute.

The success of the savings banks is symptomatic of the presence in Rome of considerable accumulations of capital which, however, found few and simple investment opportunities and were channelled above all into purchases of real estate and land, short-term speculation, grain trading and loans.[25]

The excessive positive balances that characterized the collection in the early 1860s were interpreted as a not very reassuring signal from the

[22] SAR, Ministero delle Finanze, b. 607, "Relazione rassegnata alla Santità di Nostro Signore Papa Pio IX da Monsignor Ministro dell'interno, 20 april 1859, Andrea Pila. Sulla istituzione delle Casse di Risparmio nello Stato Pontificio sul progresso delle medesime a tutto il 31 dicembre 1857".

[23] Ibidem.

[24] Ibidem.

[25] Graziani, 1995, p. 466. Archival sources testify to a series of observations made by contemporary experts in the field to the minister of commerce: SAR, Camera di Commercio, b. 28, "Osservazioni di Giuseppe Spada sul progetto della società romana per l'industria fondiaria", 6 july 1866.

market and related to "the abundance of idle money in the capital", which could have heralded "a progressive increase in deposits".[26]

The Cassa initiated various investments: it sought to expand its clientele, financed private companies and religious entities and explored the foreign securities market. The first result was an enlargement of the beneficiaries of Cassa credit. The number of its debtors increased from 112 in 1861 to 171 in 1865. In 1865–1870, there was a decrease in deposits and consequently in investment as a corollary of monetary and political-military events. The inversion of the deposit trend and the climate of political instability were determined by the higher effective yield on securities issued by the neighbouring Kingdom of Italy (9.9% in 1867 and 9.54% in 1868) and by the fact that the interest on behalf of underwriters resident abroad was paid in metal species.

On the eve of 1870, the capital of the *Cassa di Risparmio di Roma* exceeded 2 million lire, with 28,000 booklets and 20 million deposits. The political-military events determined the conditions for changes, the effects of which also affected the banking system of the Roman square. Starting in 1871, new financial intermediaries were introduced, and the changes in the city's economy created new opportunities regarding both collection and loans. The climate of speculative euphoria, then dominant in Italy and Europe and particularly in Germany and Austria, favoured the entry of new operators into the market. Two large credit institutions were founded with foreign capital: the General Bank and the Italian German Bank. In just over a year, the financial boom brought to Rome a dozen banks and resulted in the opening of numerous branches of institutes based in other Italian cities. The increase in competition did not cause the *Cassa di Risparmio di Roma* to lose many customers, and it managed to maintain a "loyal", albeit niche, clientele.[27]

The year 1866 brought about a profound change in the attitude of the Roman government, as evidenced by the agreement with the Italian administration on the division of the debt and the transformation of the monetary system. The resistance of the pope in the first part of the decade gave way to an increasing willingness to collaborate with the Kingdom of Italy. Reinforcing the view that the breach of Porta Pia was

[26] D'Errico, 1999, pp. 134–135.

[27] D'Errico, 1999, p. 165.

not a true watershed, there is evidence of the transformation of the territory, above all through railway construction and urban planning works, already started before 1870. Ultimately, in the aftermath of the unification, there were no major upheavals in Lazio; in contrast, strong elements of continuity with the pontifical structures were maintained.[28]

2.2 Rome: From the Capital of "State of Lazio" to the Capital of Italy

In Rome, after restrictions were placed on the borders of the Papal State in 1860, the reasons why the pontiff felt "robbed and threatened" were clear, a thesis also supported by the "Giornale di Roma" (the main Roman newspaper). In the 1860s, the capital was described as "a head without a body": it was the capital of a state that had lost more than 71% of its territory and approximately 77% of its population. As we have observed, over the decade, the ties between Rome and the Kingdom of Italy increased, albeit slowly; the worsening internal conditions and encirclement by the Italian state initiated an adjustment process that ended on that famous 20 September.[29]

When the Roman question began to impose itself on the conscience of Europeans and began affecting the international equilibrium of various states, many foreign travellers came to Rome to more closely observe its political, economic, social and religious activity, as Fiorella Bartoccini notes.[30]

Most visitors came to Rome for a religious reason, which then also became a political one: in the last years of the papal temporal power, the faithful sought to manifest their devotion to Pius IX by assuming positions in defence of the papal claims.

Rome did not witness the economic and civil transformations that have marked the rise of new societies elsewhere.[31]

Thus, the city was not subject to the convulsive and frenetic social rhythms that characterized the industrial expansion of the modern world. Although the city did not enjoy the advantages of progress, in Rome,

[28] Bartoccini, 1997, p. 7.

[29] Formica, 2019, pp. 232–236.

[30] Bartoccini, 1971, p. 55.

[31] Castellani, 1881, p. 395.

thanks to public and private charity, no one was starving; however, "while the number of inhabitants increases, production is static or in decline".[32]

The Italianization process, which officially commenced in 1870, had in fact already started earlier. As we have observed, Rome began to become "Italian" in a legitimate conservative manner: the ancient face of the pontifical city began to change when exiles from the other regions of the Papal State annexed to Piedmont or from the Italian states arrived, when new words or ideas resounded in conversation, when different languages were heard echoing, when the quiet city was transformed into a besieged fortress and the usual spectacle of the tourist with guidebook in hand was replaced by that of the volunteer in arms, when the ancient rhythm of life and customs began to disintegrate. The "Italianization" of the city continued, transforming it in Italian and national terms as the Romans became aware of and interested in what was occurring beyond the now very close border and as they began to discover the reality of the new Italy.[33]

The rigid border control does not suffice to explain the inertia and unreceptiveness of Rome's citizens in the new liberal society. The crystallized political-administrative, economic-social structure reflected the closed Roman mentality, which remained far from accepting towards new life and work experiences and above all towards assuming greater political and civil responsibilities (and because the best-qualified personnel had traditionally been directed into ecclesiastical service). However, one cannot speak of Rome as a lifeless city. Its population raised barriers to external stimuli not only because it found them extraneous to the rhythm of existence but above all because it felt satisfied by its ideals, the result of a centuries-old history.

To implement his reforms, Pius IX called on individuals from other regions of the state in search of a greater wealth of ideas and external experience. Among the most evident characteristics of the Romans was a deep sense of realism: they remained attached to the concrete and reluctant to consider difficult and complex ideas or far-reaching programmes they did not understand.[34]

[32] Friz, 1980, pp. 220, 221. SAR, Ministero del commercio, belle arti, industria, agricoltura e lavori pubblici, b. 573, "Rapporto del Consiglio del Nobile Collegio de' Commercianti di Roma, letto nell'adunanza generale, 30 may 1862".

[33] Bartoccini, 1971, p. 18; Caracciolo, 1984, p. 35.

[34] Bartoccini, 1971, pp. 153–154.

On a social level, there were three major classes: the nobility, the bourgeoisie and the petits bourgeois, which in turn were divided into smaller groups. Although social distinctions were clear, social limits impassable and interclass relationships nearly absent, it cannot be said there was hatred and antagonism, rather only tacit acceptance. In fact, clerical dominance, which rejected common ambitions, was often a valid element of unity in the struggle against any other dominant power. Alongside the clergy, who held power in all its forms, the aristocracy was the only group that could be termed "free" since it was protected from the pressure that suffocated the other classes thanks to the financial security and social prestige it enjoyed.

The high nobility had a rather passive role, contenting itself with small advantages, such as the granting of governmental offices or facilitating the careers of relatives who had entered ecclesiastical life. The bourgeois class enjoyed a standard of living far below that of the ruling classes (i.e., the high clergy and aristocracy). However, it lived in a certain degree of security, and certain of its members, such as landowners, small industrialists and contractors, were wealthy.

On the other end of the social spectrum, large masses of people inhabited the crowded local neighbourhoods, living precariously from day to day under miserable conditions and clinging to the few sources of employment and income.

On the eve of unification in Rome, most production was linked to the market offered by the vast ecclesiastical apparatus, to tourism and, but only partially, to consumption by the landed nobility and the sparse and poor lower class. The increasing imbalance between the agricultural backwardness of the Roman Province and the agricultural progress in other regions and nations determined a progressive decline in land rent. In addition, the greater economic development of certain regions as opposed to others positively influenced the economic system, making the latter more competitive in the area of prices.[35]

[35] Methodologically, albeit with due caution, as Pescosolido recommends, a possible use for the Pollard model has also been found for Italy, "whose energetic reference to the factors of spontaneous and therefore regionalistic diffusion of the industrialization process of Europe" provides a way to re-read the dominant characters at least for the initial stages of the transformation of our local economy in "a more restricted perspective to the individual regional areas" (Pescosolido, 1985, p. 183). See Pollard, 1989. Furthermore, comparisons between the views of historians and those of other social scientists (whose

In Rome and throughout the state, the raw materials that were produced, instead of becoming a determining factor in the location of processing industries, were exported to be processed elsewhere and then repurchased as finished products[36]; production relations were backward.

In the Roman economy, the tertiary sector play the predominant role (unlike the rest of the state, which was purely agricultural), whereby the papal presence was added to the city's function as state capital and characterized by consuming a large amount and producing little.[37] These two elements (i.e., clerical centre and administrative bureaucracy) developed multiple cultural centres to a greater extent than elsewhere. They preferred to defend the religious function and an ideal size of the city, and they were concerned regarding assisting the weakest or unemployment resulting from the introduction of new technologies. The suffocating and inert protection of the authorities was combined with a lack of qualifications with respect to entrepreneurial strength and an unprepared workforce.

The immense real-estate assets of the nobles did not produce income or facilitate the circulation of capital. Their only function was to ensure their owners a luxurious life.

The investments that were made came from two groups of capitalists. On the one hand, there was a small group of local bourgeois, mostly from the country merchant class, who, taking advantage of the economic situation, attempted investments and speculations that would enable them to strengthen their position. On the other hand, foreign capital played a decisive role, particularly in the late 1860s, by introducing elements of novelty into a backward economic setting and generating good profits.

In the final decade of the Papal State, however, certain new elements appeared. At the banking level, there was a significant increase in the number of credit institutions, which contributed to lowering interest rates. In addition, several joint-stock companies were founded in various commercial sectors, a new phenomenon unknown only a few decades previously.

interventions are noted in Mocarelli, 1996) have been fruitful; they have enlivened interdisciplinary exchange on the theme of economic development on the regional scale and generated food for thought.

[36] Ellena, 1882, p. 92.

[37] Garrigos, 1881, vol. II, p. 3.

After 1870, for a certain period, it was as if two cities existed side by side: Papal Rome and the new Italian capital. There was no integration, and both "aimed at oppression". The process of transformation into the true capital of Italy occurred slowly.[38]

For the Romans, the upheaval also led to an economic crisis that caused unemployment, a decrease in assistance and an increase in prices and taxes.[39]

Excessive tax pressure was one reason for the emergence of a Roman protest against the new kingdom. In addition to being incapable of understanding the meaning of taxation by a state and its place in citizen–nation relations, the people found themselves receiving poor services, certainly worse than those provided by the pope, in exchange for onerous taxes.[40]

The financial records of the Municipality of Rome for the period 1851 to 1870 show an overall balance of the accounts according to the budget balance values. However, starting in 1851, the municipal representatives had to address a new phenomenon: in certain years, there were budget deficits. To cope with these deficits, the finances of the *Campidoglio* resorted to mortgages with the *Cassa di Risparmio di Roma* in 1857, 1862, 1864 and 1865 in the amounts of 40,000, 55,000, 40,000 and again 40,000 scudi, respectively, for a total of 175,000 scudi.

In the last years of papal government, the Capitoline finance records show a numerical increase in budget values. Revenues increased from 482,000 scudi in 1860 to 634,000 scudi in 1870, whereas expenditures increased from 497,000 to 754,000 scudi for the same period. Between 1851 and 1870, the increase in revenues was 54%, while expenses increased 117%, with a more consistent rate of growth after 1860 as political and institutional conditions changed.

After the loss of more than two-thirds of its territory, the papal government tried to oppose the new-born Kingdom of Italy, maintaining and increasing the political consensus in the capital. The competences, number of employees and revenues of the Municipality of Rome increased

[38] *Civiltà Cattolica* (roman newspaper) 6 january 1872.

[39] De Cesare, 1907, p. 379.

[40] An example of this discontent is provided by a poem entitled "Strenne to the Romans", published in *Frusta*, roman periodical of the time: 3 january 1871, n. 1.

under a situation of crisis in the state budgets (between 1858 and 1861, state revenues increased from 14.567557 to 5.766.780 scudi).[41]

The Municipality of Rome was able to take advantage of a historical situation in which the Roman State, showing a strong organic weakness, was forced to increase the concessions of the municipality while maintaining control of the most important decisions regarding the city.

In 1870, Rome was a capital still to be built, both from an urban perspective and in relation to the new Kingdom. In the decision to establish Rome as Italy's capital, there was no intention of establishing the political and economic centre of the nation there, as had occurred in Paris or London. The "city of Lazio" was chosen not to catalyse the nation's economic development but because of its central location and millenary historical tradition. Parliament determined to transfer to the new capital in February 1871. However, only in the mid-1870s were the last offices transferred from Florence (the former capital). During this period, Rome played the role of capital in a provisional way. From a formal viewpoint, a significant moment was the transfer of Parliament (September 1871), which was located at the heart of the city: the Chamber of Deputies in Montecitorio and the Senate in the Madama palace.

The economic and social events of Rome in the early seventies were linked to two opposite phenomena: the loss of the functions of the city as the capital of the Papal State and the assumption of those of the capital of Italy.[42]

In the years directly following the breach of Porta Pia, the capital of northern Italy often indicated that it considered Rome purely as a market for its products. The distrust in Rome's development as a manufacturing centre is highlighted by the views of a northern capitalist who affirmed that the city of Rome had an absorbing function rather than that of a manufacturing city, and its potential for the latter would always remain an unknown factor.[43]

Others indicated, however, that the technical conditions favourable to industrial development were not lacking in Rome.[44]

[41] Colzi, 1996, p. 452; Torri, 1954.

[42] Bartoccini, 1995, p. 513.

[43] Giordano, 1871, p. 197.

[44] Guzzoni, 1872; Ellena, 1882, p. 129.

The reality was that the existence of raw materials and a local driving force was not enough for the Roman wool industry to withstand the fierce external competition.[45]

Ultimately, even after 1870, the capital did not find a way to transform itself into an industrial city. The data show that a year after annexation approximately 45,000 industrial workers had been registered, that is, 13% of the total population. Ten years later, in 1881, the percentage remained the same, with an absolute figure of 63,000 workers. In the following decades, the gap between the industrial development of cities such as Milan or Turin and Rome would widen.[46]

The Roman urban phenomenon of this period was not accompanied by a parallel process of industrial development. Therefore, only a portion of the thousands of Italians who after 1870 arrived to settle in the city found employment with the state. The rest created a mass of labourers dependent on occasional work if not forced to join the ranks of that part of the population compelled to live day to day.

However, in addition to such important factors as economic backwardness and excessive bureaucracy, there were two major factors, which were linked, that prevented modern industrial development from occurring in Rome. The fundamental factor was the lack of capital, which had the immediate effect of weakening industry, which in turn hindered the application of new technologies in factories and their subsequent physical transformation by virtue of the incessant development of technology.[47] Second, because of the insufficiency of credit capital, banks were often reluctant to grant financial advances necessary for investment. Additionally, it was not in the interest of the large capitalists of northern Italy to deprive themselves of a convenient and safe outlet market, such as the Roman market, and to install in its place a new, potentially competing industrial plant. In this regard, Caracciolo writes of "a substantial continuity of the economic and social structure" of Rome in the years following the unification with respect to the last decades of the Papal State.[48]

[45] Garrigos, 1881, p. 4.

[46] Insolera, 1995, p. 368.

[47] Garrigos, 1881, p. 3.

[48] Caracciolo, 1954, p. 347.

The increasing cost of living in Europe and Italy due to the general increase in prices underwent a major surge in Rome as a result of an increase in demand and trade speculation, at a time when authorizations and controls remained lacking.

However, the concrete implementation of certain positive aspects deriving from the new conditions of the capital did not take long. The sources reveal a demographic increase (Rome had 183,000 registered inhabitants in 1860, 213,633 in 1871, and 267,872 in 1880) determined by the presence of immigrants of working age able to earn an income, to spend it or to set it aside.

The major economic activities that developed in Rome after 1870 were state production (e.g., the tobacco monopoly, the mint), public services (e.g., railways, urban transport, water, gas and subsequently electric lighting, telephone service), printing and paper-related activity (in connection with Rome's function as a political and administrative centre and thus its hosting of, for example, important newspapers, offices) and the manufacture of construction materials.

However, two investment sectors were more significant than the others: the construction sector and the public service procurement sector.

2.3 The Economy Outside the Borders of the Ecclesiastical State

The first part of the decade 1860–1870 falls within the broader period of the early second half of the nineteenth century, which was characterized by the prevalence of a strongly expansive trend on an international scale. At the international level, the repercussions on trade with major European countries (e.g., price increases) resulting from the Civil War in North America and fears regarding worsening relations between Austria and Prussia had negative repercussions on the prices of raw materials.

Inside Italy, in addition to uncertainties caused by institutional innovations, concern arose from the wine and silkworm crises, the events involved with the transfer of the capital from Turin to Florence, the repression of southern brigandage and the "question" of the pontifical state.[49]

[49] Fumi, 1993, p. 239.

The realization of the political unity of Italy did not correspond to a radical renewal of the pre-existing legal structure in either the civil or commercial fields. This was mainly due to the convulsive political situation of the years immediately following unification, which suggested a simple revision of the legislative system in force, one essentially based on the French codification.

As far as the legislation of commercial companies was concerned, the new commercial code, which entered into force in 1866, recognized three types of company: general, limited partnership and anonymous. It also allowed joint ventures and mutual associations, thus including all the ways in which companies could be constituted.[50]

The free trade policy adopted by the government in the first years after 1861 (then attenuated in the following decades) drastically restricted leeway for the development of new production systems and the growth of manufacturing activity generally.[51] However, it should be noted that the scholarly debate regarding the results achieved by the economic and financial policy implemented at the time remains heated. On a strictly financial level, the 1860s were a period of heavy debt for the nation; in particular, high military spending, in relation to the other expenditure items, contributed significantly to the state budget deficit. Another important expenditure concerned investment in public works, particularly the construction of roads and railways, primarily in southern Italy.[52]

The unfavourable conditions of public finances did not allow the state to take charge of the country's economic growth; private initiative, still latent, made the establishment and development of solid companies difficult.[53]

The abolition of intermediate customs borders between one state and another, which enlarged the internal market and made international

[50] Maestri, 1870, pp. 270–271.

[51] Regarding these issues, see Toniolo, 1988; Fenoaltea, 2006; Zamagni, 1990 e 1993 II ed., pp. 67–263; Cohen, Federico, 2001, pp. 25–41.

[52] Nitti, 1900, pp. 284–288. See the report on the administration of public works from 1860 to 1867 presented to Parliament on January 31, 1867, by the Minister of Public Works in office, Jacini, which explains the activity of his department (Jacini, 1867, pp. 1, 74, 75).

[53] Maestri, 1869, p. 337. See De Cecco, Pedone, 2005, pp. 253–299.

trade relations easier, considerably diminished the source of income from duties, without any substitute revenue.[54]

With the impossibility of finding relief in the increase in tax revenues and given the already high taxation, the government resorted to the sale of public assets: railways and state property, including those belonging to the Ecclesiastical Fund as a consequence of the suppression of religious entities and confiscation of their assets.[55]

Excessive public debt was created, out of all proportion with the country's resources.[56] Budget deficits were caused by the failure of financial recovery programmes, sudden political events and the modest economic growth of those years.[57] There was a significant decrease in the prices of the national rent on the main European stock exchanges and in particular on the Paris stock exchange, according to the detached analysis of the Rothschilds' representative to the government of Florence.[58]

Given the importance of the Paris stock exchange and national rent levels, the growing mistrust in other public and private funds also occurred inside Italy. With the country on the eve of a new war with Austria, public credit in ruins, fiduciary circulation in full crisis and

[54] Regarding duty policy, see De Cecco, Pedone, 2005, pp. 274–291.

[55] Regarding the liquidation of the Ecclesiastical Axis, see Sereni, 1966; Sereni, 1971; Villani, 1966, 7, 3, pp. 471–514; Placanica, 1979; Villani, 1964. In 1862, with the law of 21 August, the transfer to state property of the assets of the Ecclesiastical Fund was ordered for the sale of the properties received from the religious corporations and other ecclesiastical moral bodies suppressed by the laws of 29 May 1855, 11 December 1860, 3 January and 17 February 1861. The government was authorized to register in the Grand Book of public debt in the name of the Ecclesiastical Fund an income at 5% in consideration of the real estate of the same passed to state ownership. The laws of 1866 and 1867 regarding the suppression of religious corporations and the liquidation of ecclesiastical assets, which followed the Piedmontese pre-unification legislation on the subject, affected the entire territory with the exception of Rome and Lazio, for which there was a decree, after 20 September 1870, of March 4, 1871 (see Fiorentino, 1966; regarding sources, see Ciccozzi, 2005, pp. 222–232).

[56] Maestri, 1869, p. 334.

[57] Izzo, 1962, p. 59.

[58] "Relazione della Commissione parlamentare d'inchiesta sul corso forzoso dei biglietti di banca deliberata nella tornata del 10 marzo 1868", in Atti Parlamentari, Camera dei Deputati, Legislazione X, sess. 1867–1868, vol III Deposizioni, p. 317.

coinage disappearing because of hoarding or being sent abroad, an important decision was made (on 1 May 1866).[59]

> The Treasury turned to the major issuing bank to obtain the necessary credit while exempting itself from the obligation to change its notes into metal currency, that is, by financing its expenses through the monetary system, giving the impossibility of continuing to do so on the basis of taxes and debt alone.[60]

Approximately fifteen years later, with law no. 133 of 7 April 1881, the compulsory tender was abolished.[61]

The weakness of the Italian export trade in the context of international transactions required important interventions. An examination of the trends of foreign exchanges according to the categories of goods provided for by the customs tariff for the period 1862–1866 reveals the most deficient exports in the following order: grains and flours, cotton and related yarns and fabrics and colonial goods, while the prevalence of the following exports was identified, also in order of importance: wines and oils, silk products and minerals. In trade with the new Kingdom, both regarding imports and exports, France was most significant, followed by Great Britain, Austria and Switzerland. As previously noted, Italian trade suffered strong repercussions following the abolition of the "tariff dams" between states. As a result of political and financial unification, certain production centres, which emerged from the previous conditions, ceased to function as such, while others favoured by the new state of affairs were established.

In the early 1860s, manufacturing suffered from the political and economic changes that took place, aggravating the already difficult circumstances.[62]

[59] "Relazione della Commissione parlamentare d'inchiesta…", cit. vol. III Deposizioni, p. 311.

[60] "Legge che autorizza il Governo del Re ad ordinare le spese necessarie alla difesa dello Stato ed a provvedere con mezzi straordinari ai bisogni del Tesoro", n. 2872, Firenze 1 maggio 1866.

[61] Atti Parlamentari, Camera dei Deputati, Legislazione XIV, sessione 1880, p. 343 e seg. Atti Magliani; see Cessi, de Stefani, 1925.

[62] Rossi, 1861, p. 183.

Various international industrial exhibitions revealed a gap between the continuous rapid growth of foreign industrial expansion and Italy's internal stasis.[63] The sector most in decline was textiles, mainly due to obstacles arising in the international market following the closure, due to the war, of North American outlets and increased French competition.[64]

The negative circumstances of the textile sector are offset by better conditions in the other most important sectors, from the exploitation of minerals to the steel industry to machinery.

The shipbuilding industry, which was among the most developed sectors and which employed local raw materials and workers, prompted improvement in the transport sector.

At the end of 1868, the country had only 303 trading companies, of which 287 were national. The total share capital amounted to 1,430,271,898 lire. The anonymous company was the most widespread company form, representing approximately 99% of nominal capital.

The severe conditions for agricultural activity originated in the years immediately preceding the change in the political structure of the Italian Peninsula, and simple institutional change could not combat factors that were difficult to change in the short term.

Overall, the picture offered by the cereal, wine and sericulture sector[65] (albeit with various differences) was characterized by the persistence of the difficulties that arose in the previous decade and consequently by the worsening of the land-ownership situation.

The increase in difficulties as well as the mobility of the peasant population expanded the possibility of making use of a workforce willing to accept strenuous work for low wages. This possibility, however, hindered the introduction of machines and new production techniques and created performance problems in many factories and considering the lack of technical and cultural training of the workers.

In the 1860s, we can speak of a late commercial integration of the peninsula with respect to its political unification, which significantly slowed the region's economic rise in the European context. Regional divisions emerged, above all between northern and southern Italy.[66]

[63] On the role of exhibitions for Italy, see Bigatti, Onger, 2007; Onger, 2010.

[64] Maestri, 1870, p. 87.

[65] Regarding the role of sericulture in Italy, see Federico, 2005, pp. 134–154; 1994; 1995, pp. 45–75; 1992, pp. 183–222; Capalbo, 1988, pp. 73–96; Girelli Bocci, 1997, pp. 683–719; Vaquero Piñeiro, 2010.

[66] Fumi, 1993, p. 230.

The banking events of the 1860s were characterized by a tendency towards instability of the system. This instability manifested itself during the crisis of 1866, which questioned the viability of the Italian market and the main securities institutions of the time. Starting in the mid-1870s, a spiral of financial investments was triggered, which mainly involved the central-northern Italian market. The arrival of new foreign capital in Italy was important. From 1870 to 1873, foreign capital experienced an increase and a simultaneous change in its traditional composition, prompted by international events linked to the Franco-Prussian war and the influx of French war indemnities.

Foreign capital interventions occurred in various sectors, especially the railway sector and the large securities companies. As Fenoaltea highlighted,[67] growth and fluctuations in Italy were closely linked with the cycle of foreign investments. Thus, the fluctuations in Italian construction and other sectors reflected variations in the world supply of capital, which reveals a strong link between domestic economic activity and international capital flows. In a previous study, Fenoaltea attributed industrial investments to fluctuations in government policy, which were highly active, particularly in the periods 1876–1887 and 1896–1914, while the hostility and indifference of government action in 1861–1876 and 1887–1896 discouraged such investments.[68] These themes are addressed and enhanced with new statistical data in recent research[69] in which Fenoaltea reiterates his view that overall production increases without particular discontinuities but in large cyclical movements whose alternating phases depend precisely on the international financial markets; thus, the Italian economy thrived when the capital of central-northern Europe poured into peripheral countries and stagnated or receded when it was withdrawn.

In this regard, Luzzatto[70] previously identified the factors of the recovery of the period 1868–1873 as the improvement of the trade balance, the completion of a first part of the main railway network and the opening of the Suez Canal and the Frejus Tunnel. Thus, in his analysis of the banking cycle of the early 1870s, Polsi wrote that it was "impossible to give a unitary explanation of the phenomenon due to

[67] Fenoaltea, 1988, pp. 605–637.

[68] Fenoaltea, 1973, pp. 121–156.

[69] Fenoaltea, 2006.

[70] Luzzatto, 1968, p. 73.

the complexity and heterogeneity of the forces that are intertwined in the whirlwind of those years, nor can the sparse macroeconomic evidence exhaust their complexity, underlining that contemporaries were in agreement in tracing the origins of banking expansion in the state of grace experienced by national trade for almost two years, freed, thanks to the war, from overwhelming French competition, and favoured by a period of good agricultural harvests and abundant silk production".[71]

The contribution of foreign capital to banks and real-estate companies during the nineteenth century is examined in various studies; for example, in a recent essay, Bocci uses several estimates to calculate the overall contribution of foreign financiers in institutions linked to real-estate investments in the first twenty years after unification: approximately 50 million lire, that is, 20% of total investments in this sector. The most significant contribution was made by French investors in the period 1861–1881 (concentrated in 14 of the 45 largest real-estate companies).[72]

Between 1861 and 1936, the Italian banking system was characterized by the long maturation of the central bank, which culminated in 1926, the adoption of models (first French and later German) adapted to Italian circumstances and the use of operating methods tending to despecialization as well as an extensive presence of medium and small credit institutions attentive to the social dimension of the markets (with local provincial and occasional regional operations, such as savings banks, cooperative banks and rural banks).[73] It was therefore a highly mobile, rapidly evolving scenario. The well-known thesis of Gerschenkron, i.e., that in the backward countries the banks are oriented to assume a much more active role in the industrialization process by more direct and stimulating activity than in countries such as England, is in certain respects well-founded but in the Italian case only partially applicable.[74] The composite structure of the Italian credit system was affected by accentuated territorial dualism. Until the 1930s, two different ways of offering financial support to businesses can be identified: on the one hand, banks and private bankers

[71] Polsi, 1993; Palermo, 2006 p. 96.

[72] Bocci, 1998.

[73] Guarino and Toniolo, 1993.

[74] Coehn, Federico, 2001; Da Crema, 1997, pp. 23–26; La Francesca, 2004, pp. 71–82. See Gerschenkron, 1962 and 1968.

(characterized by credit planning and centralization and public interventions) and on the other, smaller and local banks, characterized by network logic.

The shortcomings and structural problems of the credit system did not prevent the Italian banking system, albeit within the limits of the economic context and the specific context of financial intermediation, from focusing on a financing model. This model, from which banks would draw inspiration for the entire thirty years following Italian unification, was that of movable credit. Piedmont's capital, Turin, was the "laboratory" of the first experiments in movable credit. During the 1860s, the securities institutions that accompanied the credit market began forming in a process that lasted until the end of the century.

In Turin, there was a substantial nucleus of private and industrial bankers. In addition, as the capital of the Kingdom of Sardinia and the headquarters of the National Bank, the city was linked to the new Italian ruling class. Even after the national capital was moved, first to Florence and then to Rome, Turin's financial class could count on a series of relationships that helped subalpine bankers assume a more significant role in the urban planning investments of the 1880s, one beyond the volume of resources actually raised.

The names of Ulrico Geisser, a Swiss financier transplanted to Turin, and Giacomo Servadio, a Florentine landowner banker, often appear within the most active companies of the time, and they are included among that group of 450 individuals described by the historian Polsi as representing the highest levels of the financial system of the time. Both men sensed the importance of urban investment in the capital city of Rome. They belonged to a composite elite, "not necessarily compromised from a legal or moral point of view, whose analysis cannot be ignored in order to understand the events of those years".

In the second half of the seventies, with the aim of enhancing the real-estate properties of Italo-German Bank, Tiberina Bank also fully entered into the changes underway in the Roman market and in the eighties entered the building and financial market by increasing sales and purchase activities and supporting banking operations for builders. The favourable economic context, characterized by the government's monetary policy, by the new forms of public intervention of the Magliani decrees[75] and by

[75] In certain respects, these decrees facilitated the important function of deficit spending (Di Taranto, 1997, pp. 809–831).

the operational strategies of the main issuing banks with a resumption of discounts and direct loans to companies engaged in building speculation, positively influenced corporate expansion.

Ulrico Geisser played a significant role in liaising with *Compagnia Fondiaria* (in which the Swiss financier had invested) and Esquilino Enterprise, financially linked to the Bank of Turin, which were among the most important companies operating in the construction sector. A connection with the Turin banking world, which in many respects was the centre of national finance in those years, guaranteed an important series of relations between Rome and the national ruling class, especially the Savoy.

The building market came to be considered particularly profitable by the banks after certain events occurred, such as the promulgation of the second law for the Roman Capital. The difficulties faced by the Turin square as a whole and the Italian credit system generally were at the basis of government pressure for an intervention by the National Bank of the Kingdom and the *Banco di Napoli*.[76] The banking crises of those decades were the consequence of the particular "morphology of Italian capitalism"[77]; underlying everything was a structure that conditioned the new sectors that had to address technological backwardness and constraints in the procurement of raw materials. "It is then that the capital needs of Italian companies are presented to a national market in formation... In addition, it is then that the difficulties of a fragile banking system are perceived, having on the one hand an unconsolidated monetary structure and on the other a real developing economy".[78] These developments reveal a financial market characterized by private relations between the bank and the political and entrepreneurial class typical of a banking-oriented economy, such as that of Italy in recent years, as opposed to a market-oriented economy in which efficiency is calculated by the stock exchanges, typical of Anglo-Saxon societies.[79]

[76] Confalonieri, 1974, pp. 149–163; De Rosa, 1983, pp. 113–112. La Francesca, 2001.

[77] Pecorari, 2006.

[78] La Francesca, 2001, pp. 43–44.

[79] Regarding the distinctive features of Italian central banking and the main events of its evolutionary process between 1861 and 1947, see Toniolo, 1995, pp. 1–65.

References

Arcelli, Federico. 1999. *Gli Statuti del 1581 del Sacro Monte di Pietà di Roma*, Soveria Mannelli (CZ): Rubbettino.

Arcelli, Federico. 2004. *Il Sacro Monte di Pietà di Roma nel XVI secolo (1539–1584) dalla costituzione del Monte all'assegnazione del Banco dei Depositi*, Naples: Edizioni Scientifiche Italiane.

Balbi De Caro, Silvana and Londei Luigi. 1984. *Moneta pontificia: da Innocenzo XI a Gregorio XVI*, Rome: Edizioni Quasar.

Bartoccini, Fiorella. 1971. *La Roma dei romani*, Rome: Istituto per la Storia del Risorgimento Italiano.

Bartoccini, Fiorella. 1972. Il problema di Roma capitale e i romani, in *La fine del potere temporale e il ricongiungimento di Roma all'Italia.* Atti del XLV Congresso di Storia del Risorgimento Italiano (Rome, 21–25 september 1970), Rome: Istituto per la Storia del Risorgimento Italiano, 593–613.

Bartoccini, Fiorella. 1995. *Roma nell'Ottocento*, Bologna: Cappelli Editore.

Bartoccini, Fiorella. 1997. Introduzione, in Fiorella Bartoccini and Donatella Strangio (eds.) *Lo Stato del Lazio 1860–1870*, Rome: Istituto Nazionale di Studi Romani, 7.

Bigatti, Giorgio and Onger Sergio (eds.). 2007. *Arti, tecnologia progetto. Le esposizioni d'industria in Italia prima dell'Unità*, Milan: FrancoAngeli.

Bocci, Marco. 1998. Costruttori di città: le società per azioni immobiliari nell'Italia post-unitaria (1861–1894). *Studi Storici Luigi Simeoni*, XLVIII: 169–199.

Capalbo, Cinzia. 1988. Mercato esterno e tradizione di mestiere. La produzione della seta a Cosenza tra sette e ottocento. *Meridiana*, 3: 73–96.

Caracciolo, Alberto. 1954. Continuità della struttura economica di Roma. *Nuova Rivista Storica*, XXXVIII(1): 182–206.

Caracciolo, Alberto. 1984 (1956 I ed.). *Roma Capitale. Dal Risorgimento alla crisi dello Stato liberale*, Rome: Editori Riuniti.

Castellani, Augusto. 1881. L'arte nell'Industria, in *Monografia della città di Roma e della Campagna Romana*, vol. II, Rome: Tipografia Elzeviriana, 395–420.

Cessi Roberto, de Stefani Alberto. 1925. *L'azione dello Stato italiano per le opera pubbliche (1862–1924)*, Rome: Libreria dello Stato.

Ciccozzi, Erminia. 2005. L'archivio della liquidazione dell'asse ecclesiastico. Un nuovo versamento all'Archivio centrale dello Stato (1866–1933). *Rassegna degli Archivi di stato*, nuova serie, I(1–2): 222–232.

Cohen, Jon and Federico Giovanni. 2001. *Lo sviluppo economico italiano 1820–1960*, Bologna: Il Mulino.

Colzi, Francesco. 1996. Il Campidoglio e le sue finanze in anni di trasformazione (1851-1881). *Roma Moderna e contemporanea*, IV(2): 441–469.

Confalonieri, Antonio. 1974. *Banca e industria in Italia. 1894–1906, vol. I, Le premesse: dall'abolizione del corso forzoso alla caduta del Credito mobiliare*, Milan: BCI, 149–163.

D'Errico, Rita. 1999. *Una gestione bancaria ottocentesca. La Cassa di risparmio di Roma dal 1836 al 1890*, Naples: Edizioni Scientifiche Italiane.

Da Crema, Pierangelo. 1997. *L'evoluzione della banca in Italia, Profili storici e tecnici*, Milan: EGEA.

De Cecco, Marcello and Pedone Antonio. 2005. Le istituzioni dell'economia, in Raffaele Romanelli (ed.) *Storia dello Stato italiano. Dall'Unità a oggi*, Rome: Donzelli editore, 253–299.

De Cesare, Raffaele. 1907. *Roma e lo Stato del Papa dal ritorno di Pio IX al XX settembre*, vol. 2, Rome: Forzani *e* C. Tipografi-Editori.

De Mattia, Renato. 1959. *L'unificazione monetaria italiana*, Archivio Economico dell'Unificazione Italiana, Turin: ILTE, serie II, vol. II.

De Rita, Rossella. 2011. *Il Monte di Pietà di Roma. Credito e beneficienza alla fine dell'Ottocento*, Rome: Edito Progetto Cultura.

De Rosa, Luigi. 1983. Istituto di emissione nell'Italia unita (1863–1926), Tomo II: La crisi (1883–1896), in Direzione Generale in occasione del IV centenario (ed.) *Storia del Banco di Napoli*, Naples: Banco Di Napoli, 113–112.

Della Torre, Paolo. 1941. Materiali per una storia dell'esercito pontificio. *Rassegna Storica del Risorgimento*, XXVIII(I): 45–99.

Di Taranto, Giuseppe. 1997. Economia sociale e finanza pubblica in un inedito di Agostino Magliani del 1849, in Alberto Guenzi and Diomede Ivone (eds.) *Politica economica, amministrazione e finanza nell'opera di Agostino Magliani*, Atti del Convegno di studi Salerno-Laurino, 11–13 october 1995, Naples: Editoriale Scientifica Italiana, 809–831.

Ellena, Vittorio. 1882. *Le industrie della provincia di Roma*, Rome: Ministero dell'Agricoltura, Industria e Commercio, Annali di statistica, III, I.

Federico, Giovanni. 1992. Il baco e la filanda. Il mercato dei bozzoli in Italia (secoli XIX e XX). *Meridiana*, 15: 183–222.

Federico, Giovanni. 1994. *Il filo d'oro. L'industria mondiale della seta dalla restaurazione alla grande crisi*, Venice: Marsilio

Federico, Giovanni. 1995. Politica industriale, stato e lobbies nello stato liberale: un settore perdente, l'industria serica (1877–1912). *Società e Storia*, XVII(67): 45–75.

Federico, Giovanni. 2005. Seta agricoltura e sviluppo economico in Italia. *Rivista di storia economica*, XXI(2): 134–154.

Fenoaltea, Stefano. 1973. Riflessioni sull'esperienza industriale italiana dal Risorgimento alla prima Guerra Mondiale, in Gianni Toniolo (ed.) *Lo sviluppo economico italiano 1861–1940*, Bari: Laterza: 121–156.

Fenoaltea, Stefano. 1988. International Resource Flows and Construction Movements in the Atlantic Economy: The Kuznets Cycle in Italy. *Journal of Economic History*, 48: 605–637.

Fenoaltea, Stefano. 2006. *L'economia italiana dall'Unità alla Grande guerra*, Rome-Bari: Laterza.

Fiorentino, Carlo M. 1966. *Chiesa e Stato a Roma negli anni della Destra storica, 1870–1876. Il trasferimento della Capitale e la soppressione delle Corporazioni religiose*, Rome: Istituto per la Storia del Risorgimento italiano.

Formica, Marina. 2019. *Roma, Romae. Una capitale in Età moderna*, Rome-Bari: Laterza.

Friz, Giuliano. 1980. *Consumi, tenore di vita e prezzi a Roma dal 1770 al 1900*, Rome: Edindustria.

Fumi, Gianpiero. 1993. L'integrazione economica e i suoi limiti nei decenni dell'unificazione politica (1848–1878), in Sergio Zaninelli (ed.) *L'Ottocento economico italiano*, Bologna: Monduzzi editore.

Gerschenkron, Alexandre. 1962. *Economic Backwardness in Historical Perspectives: A Book of Essays*, Cambridge, MA: Belknap Press of Harvard University Press.

Gerschenkron, Alexandre. 1968. *Continuity in History and Other Essay*, Cambridge, MA: Belknap Press of Harvard University Press.

Girelli Bocci, Angela Maria. 1997. La vittoria del bozzolo: la seta a Verona tra Sette e Ottocento, in Giovanni Luigi Fontana (ed.) *Le vie dell'industrializzazione europea. Sistemi a confronto*, Bologna: Il Mulino: 683–719.

Graziani, Ersilia. 1995. La Banca Romana (1834–1870), in *Gli Archivi degli Istituti di Credito e le fonti d'archivio per la storia delle banche*, Rome: Ministero per I beni culturali e ambientali. Ufficio centrale per i beni archivistici, 463–492.

Guarino, Sergio and Gianni Toniolo (ed.). 1993. *La banca d'Italia e il Sistema bancario. 1919–1936*, Rome-Bari: Editore Laterza.

Insolera, Italo. 1995. *Le città nella Storia d'Italia: Roma*, Rome-Bari: Laterza.

Izzo, Luigi. 1962. *La finanza pubblica nel primo decennio dell'unità italiana*, Milan: Giuffrè Editore.

La Francesca, Salvatore. 2001. *Credito e finanza tra continuità e trasformazioni istituzionali (1861–1993)*, in Giuseppe Conti and Salvatore La Francesca (eds.) *Banche e reti di banche nell'Italia postunitaria*, Bologna: Il Mulino.

La Francesca, Salvatore. 2004. *Storia del sistema bancario italiano*, Bologna: Il Mulino.

Luzzatto, Gino. 1968. *L'economia italiana dal 1861 al 1894*, Turin: Einaudi.

Manetti, Daniela. 2009. *La «civil difesa». Economia, finanza e sistema militare nel Granducato di toscana (1814–1859)*, Florence: Leo S. Olschki Editore.

Mocarelli, Luca (ed.). 1996. *Lo sviluppo economico regionale in prospettiva storica, Atti dell'incontro interdisciplinare* Milano 18–19 maggio 1995, Quaderni del

Dipartimento di storia della Società e delle Istituzioni Facoltà di Scienze Politiche Università degli Studi di Milano, Milan.

Nitti, F. Saverio. 1900. *Il bilancio dello Stato dal 1862 al 1896–97*, Naples: Società Anonima Cooperativa Letteraria.

Onger, Sergio. 2010. *Verso la modernità. I bresciani e le esposizioni industriali 1800–1915*, Milan: FrancoAngeli.

Palermo, Stefano. 2006. *La Banca Tiberina. Finanza ed edilizia tra Roma, Napoli e Torino 1869–1895*, Naples: Editoriale scientifica Italiana.

Pecorari, Paolo (ed.). 2006. *Crisi e scandali bancari nella storia d'Italia*, Venice: Ist. Veneto di Scienze, Lettere ed Arti.

Pescosolido, Guido. 1985. Lo sviluppo industriale di Roma e del Lazio dal 1870 alla seconda guerra mondiale nelle riflessioni storiografiche, in Lucio Avagliano (ed.) *L'Italia industriale nelle sue regioni. Bilancio storiografico*, Naples: Edizioni scientifiche italiane.

Piccialuti Caprioli, Maura. 1991. Amministrazione pubblica ed istituzioni assistenziali dal 1871 al 1911, in Alberto Caracciolo (ed.) *Storia d'Italia. Le regioni, Il Lazio*, Turin: Utet, 368–369.

Piccialuti Caprioli, Maura. 1994. *La carità come metodo di governo. Istituzioni caritative a Roma dal pontificato di Innocenzo XII a quello di Benedetto XIV*, Turin: G. Giappichelli editore.

Pollard, Sydney. 1989. *La conquista pacifica. L'industrializzazione in Europa dal 1760 al 1970*, Bologna: Il Mulino.

Polsi, Alessandro. 1993. *Alle origini del capitalismo italiano. Stato, banche e banchieri dopo l'Unità*, Turin: Piccola biblioteca Einaudi.

Porisini, Giorgio. 1969. *Condizioni monetarie e investimenti nel bolognese. La Banca delle Quattro Legazioni*, Bologna: Zanichelli Editore.

Procaccia, C. 1994–1997. *I banchieri ebrei a Roma nella seconda metà del XVII secolo tesi di dottorato di ricerca in storia economica*, Università degli studi di Bari, Facoltà d economia, X ciclo.

Rossi, Gabriello. 1848. *Sulla condizione economica e sociale dello Stato Pontificio, confrontata specialmente con quelle della Francia e dell'Inghilterra*, Bologna: Società tipografica bolognese, vol. II.

Rossi, Vincenzo. 1861. *Delle condizioni dell'Italia nell'agricoltura, nelle manifatture e nel commercio in confronto dell'Inghilterra e della Francia e della libertà di commercio*, Milan: Giuseppe Civelli.

Sereni, Emilio. 1966. *Capitalismo e mercato nazionale*, Rome: Editori Riuniti.

Sereni, Emilio. 1971. *Il capitalismo nelle campagne1860–1900*, Turin: Einaudi.

Tamilia, Donato. 1900. *Il Sacro Monte di Pietà di Roma. Ricerche storiche e documenti inediti, contributo alla storia della beneficenza e della storia economica*, Rome: Tip. Forzani e C.

Toniolo, Gianni. 1988. *Storia dell'Italia liberale*, Bologna: Il Mulino.

Toniolo, Gianni. 1995. *Sull'arte del banchiere centrale in Italia: fatti stilizzati e congetture (1861–1947)*. Temi di discussione del servizio studi di Banca d'Italia, 255: 1–65.

Torri, A. P. 1954. Indagine sulle finanze del Comune di Roma nella prima metà del secolo XIX. *Studi Romani*, II(6): 683–696.

Tosi, Mario. 1937. *Il Sacro Monte di Pietà e le sue amministrazioni. I Banco dei depositi, la depositeria generale della R. Camera Apostolica, la Zecca, la Depositeria Urbana (1539–1874)*, Rome: Libreria dello Stato.

Travaglini, Carlo Maria. 1988. Il Monte di Pietà di Roma in periodo francese, in Atti dl I Convegno nazionale su *Credito e sviluppo economico in Italia dal Medio Evo all'età contemporanea*, Verona 4–6 giugno 1987, Verona: Società italiana degli Storici dell'economia, 463–482.

Travaglini, Carlo Maria. 1991. *Il ruolo del Banco di Spirito e del Monte di Pietà sul mercato finanziario romano del Settecento, in Atti del Convegno internazionale su Banchi pubblici, banchi privati e monti di pietà dell'Europa preindustriale*, Genova 1–6 ottobre 1990, Genoa: Società ligure di Storia Patria, 619–639.

Travaglini, Carlo Maria. 2001. *Monte di Pietà di Roma (1539–1937) Introduzione storico-economica*, Rome: Banca di Roma Archivio storico.

Vaquero Piñeiro, Manuel. 2010. *Il baco da seta in Umbria. XVIII–XX secolo*, Naples: Editoriale Scientifica.

Villani, Pasquale. 1964. *La vendita dei beni nello Stato del Regno di Napoli (1806–1815)*, Milan: Banca Commerciale Italiana.

Villani, Pasquale. 1966. Il capitalismo agrario in Italia. *Studi Storici*, 7(3): 471–514.

Zamagni, Vera. 1990. (1993 II ed.). *Dalla periferia al centro. La seconda rinascita economica dell'Italia (1861–1990)*, Bologna: Il Mulino.

Sources

State Archive of Rome (SAR)

Ministero delle finanze, b. 671.

Archivio Antonelli, b. 31.

Camera di Commercio, b. 28.

Ministero delle Finanze, b. 605.

Ministero delle Finanze, b. 607.

Ministero del commercio, belle arti, industria, agricoltura e lavori pubblici, b. 573.

Edited Sources

Atti Parlamentari, Camera dei Deputati, Legislazione X, sess. 1867–1868, vol III.

Atti Parlamentari, Camera dei Deputati, Legislazione XIV, sessione 1880.

Civiltà Cattolica (roman newspaper) 6 january 1872.

Frusta (roman periodical) 3 january 1871, n. 1

Garrigos, Vincenzo. 1881. *Industria e Commercio, in Monografia della Città di Roma e della Campagna Romana*, Rome: Tipografia Elzeviriana, vol. II.

Giordano, Felice. 1871. *Cenni sulle condizioni fisico-economiche di Roma e del suo territorio*, Florence: G. Civelli.

Jacini, Stefano. 1867. *L'amministrazione dei lavori pubblici in Italia dal 1860 al 1867*, Florence: Edredi Botta.

Maestri, Pietro. 1869. *L'Italia economica nel 1868*, Florence: Stabilimento di G. Civelli.

Maestri, Pietro. 1870. *L'Italia economica nel 1869*, Florence: Stabilimento di G. Civelli.

Raccolta delle leggi e disposizioni di pubblica amministrazione dello Stato Pontificio, n. 42, 1860.

Raccolta delle leggi e disposizioni di pubblica amministrazione dello Stato Pontificio, n. 47, 1865.

CHAPTER 3

Structural Elements of the Rome Stock Exchange: Regulations, Price Lists and Intermediaries

With the industrial revolution, the need emerged to have bodies capable of collecting from savers the large financial resources necessary for the long-term investments of public and private companies, which multiplied in that period. However, already in the Middle Age, merchants would gather in the squares or under the loggias of the civic palace, where they installed a counter on which they placed the bag containing the coin, the exchange letters and the register on which they recorded the operations they performed. The genesis of trading exchanges can be identified in the fairs of the twelfth and thirteenth centuries, which represented the first important organization of trade in goods displayed and handled by merchants. In Italy, stock exchanges were established and began to operate on a large scale starting in the early nineteenth century, when slow economic development made private jobs relatively less important than public ones. The first stock exchange was in Milan, inaugurated on February 15, 1808; in the following years, stock exchanges were also opened in Naples, Rome, Florence, Genoa, Turin, Bologna, and elsewhere in Italy. Prior to the stockbroker, another category of intermediary operated in Rome, the broker. The most substantial information we have regarding the group of brokers in Rome is related to the pontificate of Sixtus V (1585–1590), although as early as 1546, the Consuls of the art of merchants of Rome issued a ban containing rules of conduct. At

D. Strangio, *The Roman Stock Exchange between the 19th and 20th Centuries*, Palgrave Studies in the History of Finance,
https://doi.org/10.1007/978-3-031-00359-2_3

the beginning of the nineteenth century, with the Napoleonic occupation of Rome, a decisive change occurred. In 1809, the French Commercial Code came into force, which led, within the general redefinition of the productive and credit structure of the State of the Church. The Provisional Trade Regulations of June 1, 1821, subsumed the Napoleonic Code and sanctioned the birth of the Rome Stock Exchange.

3.1 Origin and Development of the Stock Exchange

In the Middle Ages, merchants would gather in the squares or under the loggias of the civic palace, where they installed a counter on which they placed the bag containing the coin, the exchange letters and the register on which they recorded the operations they performed. The proper name used for the stock exchange, as Kulisher writes, "first took hold in Bruges. [...] The word Borsa derives from the square in Bruges, on which stood the large old house, which belonged to the patrician family van de Burse, which carried in its coat of arms, carved in stone on the main door, three bags (ter buerse). The 'ter buerse' house became the consular house (loggia) of the Venetians, and immediately, the Genoese and Florentines erected their lodges, which were called the 'Bolsa'. This square served the Italians as a place for their daily business meetings. Although originally the name of these meetings, 'Borsa', was only in a casual connection with the name of the square on which they took place, it spread and became common in linguistic usage due to the circumstance that corresponded to the meaning of the word: stock exchange 'Bursa' (in the Netherlands 'beurs' or 'börs') meant leather purse; in a figurative sense this was already understood in the Middle Ages to refer to the sums of money, later the common coffers, of the mercantile associations".[1] At the end of 1500, the authorities intervened with ordinances and statutes issued above all to regulate the hours and days of these meetings and the customs that were gradually forming. Thus, we know of a Statute for Bologna approved in 1569 by Pope Pius V to regulate the meetings at the Forum of the merchants.

This chapter is divided into two sections. The first concerns the commodity exchange (derived from the ancient markets from which

[1] Kulischer, 1955, II, pp. 461–462.

it differs because of the absence of commodities themselves), where, during special meetings, exchanges were agreed and merchandise sales concluded. Regarding execution, transfer operations could be cash or forward. The latter could give rise to further assignments of the contract before the expiry of its term. A commodity futures market enables one to transfer most of the risk of price changes over time to a particular class of operators suited because of their market knowledge to assume such risks. It is precisely for this reason that the futures market for goods is widely recognized for its important hedging or insurance function in favour of traders and industrialists who deal in the goods (i.e., raw materials or products) traded there.

The second section addresses stock exchanges, which are markets in which, through the activity of specialized intermediaries, the balance between the supply of and demand for debt securities, shares and currencies is established. Starting from this definition, stock exchange activity is divided into three main functions, which, as Baia Curioni notes, consist of the "allocation of financial resources, optimized through extended control, exercised by numerous operators informed in a coherent and uniform manner, and the offer of securities; the liquidity function, which makes it possible to transform long-term investments into short-term investments by reducing the level of risk borne by the individual investor; the information function, which essentially consists in the 'certain' fixing of the prices of the securities traded, in order to obtain a basis for the knowledge of the value of the underlying initiatives and for the definition of portfolio policies by investors".[2] Furthermore, "the stock exchange plays an active role, indispensable for the very survival of companies that are always looking for financial means to support their productivity and management functionality".[3]

The genesis of trading exchanges can be identified in the fairs of the twelfth and thirteenth centuries, which represented "the first important organization of trade in goods displayed and handled by merchants. It was precisely the cities that favoured the exchange of goods between the producers of the countryside who presented their own foodstuffs and the citizens themselves with their handicraft products in the various

[2] Baia Curioni, Bologna, 1995, pp. 17–18; Da Pozzo, Felloni, 1964, part II, chapter I; Cesarini, Gualtieri, 2001, chapters I and II.

[3] Pegorer, 1998, p. 74. Bianchi, 1983; Garbade, 1989.

markets. However, the same cities were the negotiating centres of the local merchant class which soon gave consistency to a market in which goods not produced by local artisans were traded".[4] It is clear, as Bruschini Vincenzini writes, that: "historically, however, it remains established that between the fair and the modern stock exchange there is a very long interval, perhaps no less than three centuries, during which the ancient trade fair institute lost many of its primitive functions and it was transformed to eventually lead to a new form of organized market. In medieval fairs, meeting places for trade currents from different regions and countries, debt and credit relations arising from import and export trade were essentially regulated, while in modern stock exchanges, the income prospects arose from capital investments. Therefore, in medieval fairs, the fundamental instrument was the credit note (the bill of exchange), which originated at that time and place; in the financial field, the development of methodologies suitable for defining the relationship between the purchasing power of individual currencies (the 'exchange' understood as the price of bills of exchange) was of particular importance. In modern stock exchanges, on the contrary, the instrument is the share, a representative security of a real asset, and the obligation, a credit security, whose financial expression is the quotation defined as the capitalization of future income".[5]

As already highlighted, the first official exchanges of the sixteenth century were established in Bruges. Additional exchanges were established in Antwerp, Amsterdam, Lyon and the other main European trading centres. The Antwerp Stock Exchange became the largest, most complex centre of monetary and financial exchange in the sixteenth century. There the development of operating techniques multiplied, and the exchange became the seat of highly speculative exchange rate interventions. It was precisely with the Antwerp Stock Exchange that "the first transactions fixed on 'future' events were established: buyers of goods reserved payment at a future date and, in the event of a price increase before the deadline, they sold them by collecting the difference. Similarly, those who played the seller trusted in the decrease in the prices of goods over time.

[4] Pegorer, 1998, p. 29. Regarding the role and activity of fairs, see in particular Grohmann, 2011; Lanaro, 2003.

[5] Bruschini Vincenzini, 1998, p. 15. Fornasari, 2006, pp. 37–41.

Antwerp, therefore, represented a true centre for the diffusion of innovative financial techniques, and with the success of its stock exchange, it prepared the way for further progress over the years. Antwerp also knew how to open trade to foreign merchants by practising a liberal policy that was unusual for those times".[6]

With the industrial revolution, the need emerged to have bodies capable of collecting from savers the large financial resources necessary for the long-term investments of public and private companies, which multiplied in that period. This period was in fact a phase of diffusion of capital companies and in particular of joint-stock company, which issued their own securities representing share capital.[7] Fornasari observes how the stock market game also made use of the development of probabilistic calculation which, starting in the seventeenth century, made it possible to determine complex probability values and the greater or lesser frequency of the occurrence of uncertain events.[8] Furthermore, as Bruschini Vincenzini said, the capital was divided into transferable shares which were called aktien, shares. Since they gave strong dividends, the shares were easily placed at an ever-increasing price, which rapidly increased tenfold. The joint-stock company therefore developed, for the needs of the distant trade, the trade between distant areas, which froze substantial capital for long periods of time, also considering that, with the increase in the tonnage of the ships and the extended travel, more complex administrative structures became necessary. Their diffusion was linked to the need to transform companies, from personal and family, into social.[9] These securities (i.e., shares) had the characteristic of mobility, enabling their holders to disinvest at any time to easily repossess the invested funds. "It was the daily multiplication of the financial needs of both States and overseas commercial and investment companies, with the creation of the large monopolistic commercial companies and the first joint stock companies, which caused an ever more pressing need to dispose over a single place and an occasion where it was possible to procure from time to time financial means, goods or services, but also

[6] Pegorer, 1998, p. 29.

[7] The origin of joint-stock company dates to the seventeenth century with the formation of the large Dutch, French and English companies and their overseas businesses; see Barron Baskin, Miranti, 2000, pp. 60–64 and chapter III.

[8] Fornasari, 2006, p. 36.

[9] Bruschini Vincenzini, 1998, pp. 16–17.

over a 'space', governed by official rules and able to offer guarantees, where recourse to such supply could be immediate, depending on the needs".[10] Stock exchanges thus spread as a "meeting place for demand and supply of securities with the aim of facilitating their transfer from one subject to another, in order to give them a satisfactory degree of liquidity".[11]

The history of these institutions as public (i.e., publicly regulated) and permanent markets evolves with the formation of nation states and with the emergence of public debt management needs. In particular, in Anglo-Saxon countries, i.e., Britain and America, where open and competitive markets were consolidated, the stock exchange was born "as a private organization that is based on agreements between the operators concerned and elaborates the rules of the exchange".[12] Given the public relevance of this activity, the operational practices privately established by the operators were supplemented and partly replaced by regulatory interventions to make them more suitable to the general interest and to protect investors. The main example is that of the US stock exchanges that "are born and develop as a club of self-regulated intermediaries and receive general discipline with the laws enacted following the great crisis of 1929".[13] As part of the New Deal launched by American President Roosevelt, the main initiative to regulate and protect investors in the securities market was the Securities Act, enacted between 1933 and 1934, whose objective was to tackle information problems and risk and to redefine the legal responsibilities of operators in three different areas: (1) relations between companies and their shareholders; (2) extension of civil and criminal liability to all professionals on whom the efficiency of the operation of the market depended; (3) establishment of the Securities Exchange Commission (SEC), with the task of monitoring the stock market.[14] The London Stock Exchange can be considered the only market comparable with the US market in terms of trading size and number of instruments traded. Important turning points were the series of corrective measures introduced after the collapse of the mid-1840s

[10] Bruschini Vincenzini, 1998, p. 17.

[11] Cesarini, Gualtieri, 2001, p. 14.

[12] Cesarini, Gualtieri, 2001, p. 15.

[13] Cesarini, Gualtieri, 2001, pp. 15–16; Fornasari, 2006, pp. 73–87.

[14] Fornasari, 2006, p. 86; Barron Baskin, Miranti jr, 2000, pp. 196–197.

due to a series of speculative actions, which should have reduced the asymmetries that emerged during the crisis itself, and the mid-1980s, when important reforms were promoted in trading methods, which allowed "growing competition between intermediaries and the lowering of negotiation costs", in particular the Financial Service Act of 1986, i.e., public control over the activities of stock exchanges according to a scheme similar to the US scheme, approved by Margaret Thatcher's government.[15]

In continental Europe, especially in the countries in which Napoleonic codification has had the greatest influence, the evolution of the stock exchanges displays a somewhat different profile; "however, in the last decade they have found solutions substantially similar to those of the Anglo-Saxon countries".[16]

In Italy, stock exchanges were established and began to operate on a large scale starting in the early nineteenth century, when slow economic development made private jobs relatively less important than public ones.[17] As previously mentioned, the Italian stock exchanges were modelled on the French exchange and regulated through application of the Napoleonic code of commerce, while in other European countries, "the stock exchange now had a leading role in economic life. The absorption of capital through the issue of securities reached very considerable dimensions and intensified more and more. It was widely used by public bodies and private companies".[18]

The development of stock exchanges is also linked to several other factors, such as the growth of large industrial and commercial enterprises, the availability and concentration of abundant financial resources and the developments of state loans and private company bonds.[19]

The organization of the stock exchange in Italy, designed as a centre for collecting savings for industrial and commercial activity, was not a response to real economic needs; it was not based "on a free association of operators as in the Anglo-Saxon model, but was in fact 'lowered from above' as in the statist model of the French 'Borsa du Roi', [thus] it is

[15] Fornasari, 2006, p. 59; Cesarini, Gualtieri, 2001, p. 16.

[16] Cesarini, Gualtieri, 2001, p. 16.

[17] Da Pozzo, Felloni, 1964, p. 56.

[18] Da Pozzo, Felloni, 1964, p. 56.

[19] Pivato, 1965, p. 296.

possible to argue that the introduction of the institution of the Stock Exchange in Italy represents more the result of the grandiose Napoleonic political design than a response to the immediate needs of the commercial and industrial classes. Consequently, the failure of the stock exchanges is attributable, at least until 1887, to the inadequacy of the real conditions of the economic and social life of our country and, in this case, to the lack of a significant national industry".[20]

The first stock exchange was in Milan, inaugurated on February 15, 1808[21]; in the following years, stock exchanges were also opened in Naples,[22] Rome,[23] Florence,[24] Genoa,[25] Turin,[26] Bologna,[27] and elsewhere in Italy.[28]

Throughout the nineteenth century, an Italian peculiarity was the presence of independent stock exchanges, which maintained themselves as essentially autonomous organizations and followed independent strategies; until the 1870s, Italy was represented by a set of very different squares in terms of rules, "operating modes and titles dealt with, poorly

[20] Aleotti, 1990, p. 35.

[21] Regarding the importance and evolution of the Milan Stock Exchange in terms of historical profiles and listed shares, see: De Luca, 2002; Baia Curioni, 1991; 1995; 2000; Boccia, 2000; Cafaro, 1993, pp. 107–134; Pivato, Scognamiglio, 1972. For a comparison in the Giolitti era (during the Italian *big spurt*) of the main Italian stock exchanges in Genoa and Milan, see Riva, 2005.

[22] De Rosa, 1962, pp. 1–6; Boccia, 2000; Schisani, 2001; Balletta, 2007.

[23] Strangio, 2007, pp. 251–270; Strangio, 2006, pp. 387–402.

[24] Originally established with a decree of 23 December 1808, the Florence exchange was the subject of a decree of the Grand Ducal government of 1859.

[25] Da Pozzo, Felloni, 1964.

[26] The Turin exchange was founded in 1850 by Vittorio Emanuele II.

[27] The Bologna exchange was established in 1861; it suspended activity in 1909 and resumed operations on September 1, 1926.

[28] The Palermo Stock Exchange was established by the law of 6 July 1862 n. 680 but began to function regularly in 1852. The Venice Stock Exchange was reorganized in 1875 and closed for several years prior to and following the First World War; it reopened in 1927. The Trieste Stock Exchange was established under Austrian rule in 1775, functioning as a mixed stock exchange until, with the annexation of Trieste to Italy, it was split into the Stock Exchange and the Goods Exchange and subjected in 1926 to the law and legislation issued in 1913. In the wake of the international cycle, driven by favourable monetary dynamics, the squares of the Peninsula were particularly active, also giving rise to new official exchanges, such as those of Cuneo (1871), Chieti (1872), Messina (1873).

Table 3.1 Number of companies listed on the major Italian stock exchanges

Years	*N°. firms and listed Companies in Rome*	*N°. firms and listed Companies in Milan*	*N°. firms and listed Companies in Genoa*
1861	6	2	11
1862	6	2	11
1863	6	8	10
1864	6	8	10
1865	6	8	10
1866	6	8	9
1867	6	8	9
1868	5	8	9
1869	4	7	10
1870	4	7	10

Source "Giornale di Roma" from 1861 to 1870

integrated with each other, whose functioning is strongly constrained by the balance between local potentates".[29] Until the end of the nineteenth century, the Genoa Stock Exchange found itself in a position of clear hegemony vis-à-vis its Italian sister exchanges: "the mercantile tradition and the importance of Genoese finance were the factors that determined the centrality of the stock exchange. Genoa is the Italian financial landscape".[30]

Estimates by Da Pozzo and Felloni indicate that for a good part of the nineteenth century, public income played a leading role in the stock exchange, and the distribution of shares was limited to professional speculators, thus not reaching bourgeois and small owners who, instead, subscribed significant amounts of public debt. In particular, "joint stock companies found a place for financial growth on the stock exchange, but the first stock market initiatives had a particular affinity for public debt, and the trading of government bonds has always offered better guarantees by attracting savings".[31]

It was a stock market still in its infancy and therefore rather limited (see Table 3.1 regarding listed companies of the 1860s), which operated

[29] Baia Curioni, 1995, p. 369.

[30] Aleotti, 1990, p. 30.

[31] De Antonellis, 1988, p. 80.

on the sidelines of state investments and whose rises were caused by the favourable opportunities created by a decline of the public title.

It is clear that equities were driven by the rate of public rent. As noted, "share values, not yet forming a market driven by intrinsic fluctuations, are residually driven by the rate of the Annuity (*Rendita*). In fact, it is noted that, for short periods of time, share prices move in the opposite way to those of annuities, demonstrating that in the short term, investments or divestments of capital in shares arose from the opportunities created by the movement of the share price Annuity (*Rendita*). However, in the long run, the underlying trend sees the share prices and those of the Annuity (*Rendita*) move in the same direction, demonstrating how the stock market was undergoing a considerable driving effect by the title of the public debt".[32]

Baia Curioni identified three phases of activity in the period 1800–1915: the first commences approximately 1894; in turn, Baia Curioni identifies other sub-periods, one lasting until 1861 characterized as "like a real genetic moment", the other until 1894, "from an activation of the original organizational model and its progressive crisis, accompanied by a modification of the relations between central and local powers that leads to a weakening of the latter".[33] In particular, with the Royal Decree of December 27, 1882, a unitary regulation was provided for. Despite organizational and decision-making inadequacies, the second phase (1894–1900) was characterized by the telegraphic integration of the various stock exchanges. Here, we observe a desire to create an internal market even if the integration of the price lists would only occur in a slow and progressive way, which coincides with the opening of the Giolitti expansive cycle.[34] The third phase comprised the fifteen years preceding the First World War, when "the evolutionary process built over the previous century comes to fruition, finds a solution that will exert a decisive influence on the future structure of the market".[35]

[32] Aleotti, 1990, pp. 32–33.

[33] Baia Curioni, 1995, pp. 368–369.

[34] Baia Curioni, 1995, p. 370.

[35] Baia Curioni, 1995, p. 370. Angelo Riva (2007, pp. 565–595) studies the liquidity of the Italian rent traded on the Milan and Genoa stock exchanges between 1890 and 1913 using market models, radically different from these structures, as an explanatory variable.

Detailed organization of the stock exchanges and the admission of securities to listing was envisaged in the 1913 regulations, which although modified over time remained in force for approximately sixty years until they were replaced by the law of 7 June 1974 n. 216, which established, among other things, the National Commission for Companies and the Stock Exchange. The establishment of the National Commission for Companies and the Stock Exchange, a public body responsible for monitoring stock exchanges and the transparency of corporate information, favoured the dimensional development of the stock market and helped define its characteristics and the regulatory framework necessary to protect investors. Subsequently, with globalization in the 1990s and the integration of the European Union countries, there was strong growth in the size of the market in terms of number of listed companies, trading volume and overall capitalization. Additionally, the era witnessed rapid progress in modernizing technical and legal structures. In 1997, a transformation from public to private occurred with the establishment of a market company, the Italian Stock Exchange, and the sale of its shares to a group of banks and investment companies that "thus became owners of and responsible for the organization and functioning of the markets".[36]

3.2 The Figure of Brokers and Stockbrokers in the Roman Market

The stockbroker is an intermediary specialized in financial mediation activities without taking direct positions in proprietary securities. The stockbroker is the figure on whom most stock market operations converge and whose origins date to the birth of the stock exchange.

Prior to the stockbroker, another category of intermediary operated in Rome, the broker.[37] Brokers (also referred to as peasants or middlemen) were of particular importance in the Roman market in modern times

[36] Cesarini, Gualtieri, 2001, p. 18.

[37] In the two Roman river ports of Ripa and Ripetta, a particular group of mediators was active: the so-called ripali brokers. Their business was part of a complex network of commercial relations that unfolded around the ports. Their specific task was to put the captains of the boats in contact with city merchants. However, perhaps owing to the restricted economic space provided by the ports, the activity of the middlemen was characterized by rivalries and clashes with other operators in the sector, which the public bodies were unable to repress even through strict rules. The number of ripali brokers varied over time in direct correlation with the economic circumstances, increasing in

because they facilitated a connection between the supply and demand for goods. Towards the middle of the nineteenth century, Moroni defined the matchmaker as the one who "[...] intervenes between contractors for the conclusion of the shop".[38]

Middlemen played a primary role in strengthening commercial and financial relationships. They put their mercantile professionalism at the service of the market with a view to increasing the allocation efficiency of goods and reducing transition costs.

Regarding the activity of the brokers, it is possible to identify two phases during the early nineteenth century that in combination with certain historical events represent an important watershed. The first phase occurred between the sixteenth and eighteenth centuries, when the mediation sector was characterized by the absence of institutions and rules that would have organically governed the various groups of brokers. The regulatory gaps produced uncertainty in the operators and created opportunities for conflicts and illicit activity.

The functions of the brokers involved not only share transactions[39] but also the evaluation of product quality and the establishment of prices. Furthermore, in a period such as this one, when the effects of jurisprudence were ambiguous and proof of the existence of a relationship and a guarantee of compliance with the contract were essential factors, the mediators also acted as solemn witnesses to negotiations.

The most substantial information we have regarding the group of brokers in Rome is related to the pontificate of Sixtus V (1585–1590), although as early as 1546, the Consuls of the art of merchants of Rome issued a ban containing rules of conduct. The brokers were authorized to exercise mediation by a licence issued by the Consuls themselves and had to pay a "[...] safety precaution".[40] Their compensation, the senseria, amounted to one per cent of the value of the negotiated products, paid for half-and-half by the two contracting parties.

phases of expansion and decreasing in recessive periods; see Colzi, 1998, pp. 406–407; Strangio, 1997, pp. 427–450; 2006.

[38] Moroni, 1869, p. 159.

[39] SAR, Camerale II, Arti e mestieri b. 35, "Memoriale di Michelangelo Dorsi et altri possessori dè Sensalati di Ripa contro la Camera Apostolica" del 1715.

[40] Colzi, 1998, p. 402, Bando dei Consoli dei mercanti di Roma "sopra il procedere de tutti i Mercanti, et Sensali, nel loro esercitio".

During the second half of the sixteenth century, the financial assets sector "[...] developed rapidly [...] for a number of reasons, including the growth in working capital and the expansion of public debt, and led to a profound restructuring of the mediation sector".[41] The absence of an organized stock exchange made the work of the brokers decisive, and the brokers became a hub for collecting and disseminating information relating to offers and market demand. To ensure a more coordinated economic system, in 1588, the Apostolic Chamber, the governing body of the Papal State, instituted the first of a series of changes that occurred over the course of several years: the *Deputation of the Forty Sensals* was created.[42]

In 1590, Sixtus V abolished the Deputation, established only two years earlier, and set up the College of the Thirty *Sensali* in order to prevent fraud. In this period of rapid changes, the College of the Thirty *Sensali* was abolished by an edict of the General Treasurer on April 18, 1592, with the generic motivation of the "benefitio publico".[43]

The activity of the brokers did not, however, diminish. In fact, during the seventeenth and eighteenth centuries, exclusivity was increasingly guaranteed in the mediation of merchandise and financial assets. Until the end of the eighteenth century, state authority was directed towards a deregulation of intermediation activities, albeit in compliance with certain basic provisions, such as maximum remuneration and the prohibition of agreements with the secretaries of the pawnbrokers, since the brokers were serving their own interests.[44]

At the beginning of the nineteenth century, with the Napoleonic occupation of Rome, a decisive change occurred. In 1809, the French Commercial Code came into force, which led, within the general redefinition of the productive and credit structure of the State of the Church, to the adoption of new legislation in the mercantile field and therefore also in that of mediation.[45]

[41] Colzi, 1998, p. 402.

[42] Colzi, 1998, p. 403.

[43] SAR, Bandi, vol. 386. Cfr. Colzi, 1998, p. 405.

[44] Edict Camerlengo Aldobrandini 21 may 1624 cfr. Colzi, 1998, p. 405.

[45] "Codice di commercio preceduto dai motivi presentati al corpo legislativo dal Sig. Regnaud di Saint – Jean D'Angely", Roma, s.e., 1809, tit. V, sez. II.

The intermediaries were divided into stockbrokers, operating in the sector of public debt and foreign exchange securities, and brokers (divided into groups dealing in goods, insurance and freight transport by sea and by land).[46]

The functions of the mediators were reduced, and from promoters and guarantors of transactions, they became simple regulators of exchanges. A system was formed in which each group of middlemen tried to increase its privileges, while the state authorities tried to reconcile certain essential needs, such as guaranteeing market functionality, the control of professional orders, the preservation of social consensus and the growth of tax revenues. The new code stipulated that brokers would operate in stock exchanges that would be founded in the main cities of the state. In truth, in Rome, in the eighteenth century, there already existed a prototype of the stock exchange; lacking state sanction, it was simply the meeting place of the main Roman bankers and brokers.[47] The Code therefore brought about the institutionalization of the stock exchange, which from a private meeting of a few operators became a "meeting of traders, ship captains, stockbrokers and brokers that takes place under the authority of the government".[48]

The legislation adopted in the years of French domination, suppressed with the edict of Cardinal Rivarola on May 13, 1814, was reintroduced with slight changes in the years following the second Restoration.[49]

The Provisional Trade Regulations[50] of June 1, 1821, which subsumed the Napoleonic Code and sanctioned the birth of the Rome Stock Exchange, introduced a general regulatory framework that was only partially implemented.[51] In the 1830s, two important innovations

[46] SAR, Congregazione economica (1815–1835) b. 135, *Progetto e motivi della legge*, 1825, p. 467. Colzi, 1998, pp. 414–415.

[47] SAR, Camera di Commercio, b. 44.

[48] Codice di Commercio, cit., tit. V, sez. I, art. 71.

[49] Strangio, 2001.

[50] "Regolamento provvisorio di commercio finora vigente nelle province di seconda recupera e modificato secondo le prescrizioni dell'editto del primo giugno 1821 dall'E.mo e R.mo signore Card. Segretario di Stato da osservarsi in tutto lo Stato Pontificio fino alla pubblicazione ed attivazione del nuovo Codice di Commercio", Tipografia della R.C.A., Rome 1821.

[51] Regolamento di Commercio del 1 giugno 1821, Avviso dell'Editore, Tipografia delle Scienze di Giuseppe Vitali, Bologna 1864, p. I.

occurred: the first was the effective activation of the Roman stock exchange, which in the 1820s was still an "appearance, and a shadow, not a gathering, but only some bankers almost privately", which operated "without regulations, without superiors, without form in sum of legal assembly"[52]; the second was the 1831 establishment of the Rome Chamber of Commerce,[53] "the body that acquired control of the brokers and stockbrokers and that, assumed a basic consultative role for the regulation of the market".[54]

During the nineteenth century, despite regulatory changes made by authorities to better manage the market, the brokers became increasingly concerned regarding ineffective government action to repress illegal activity and safeguard the margins of monopolistic action.[55]

The question of unauthorized use was rather convoluted. That the rules became increasingly detailed and severe represented an incentive for the transgression on the part of the mediators. It should be noted that the grievances and protests voiced in the stock exchange were not only typical of the Roman square but also other stock exchanges, such as that of Milan.[56]

Another issue debated by the brokers was that of defending their business monopoly.[57]

As a demonstration of the conflicting relationships between the intermediary class and public authority, the archive sources offer numerous testimonies, but the one that best summarizes all the various debated

[52] SAR. Congregazioni economiche, b.135, "*Sulla Borsa commerciale di Roma e sulla facoltà di esservi ammesso*" discussa dalla Congregazione economica 22 june 1824.

[53] Edict 8 july 1831 di Papa Gregorio XVI, Titolo I, art. 1, in "Raccolta delle leggi e disposizioni di pubblica amministrazione nello Stato Pontificio", vol. I, 1834, pp. 109–114.

[54] Colzi, 1998, p. 417.

[55] Raccolta delle leggi e disposizioni di pubblica amministrazione dello Stato Pontificio, Rome 1852, n. 34.

[56] Pegorer, 1998, pp. 58–59. For other Italian institutions, see Farolfi, 1999, pp. 444–459; Schisani, 1999, pp. 491–503; De Matteo, 1999, pp. 460–490.

[57] SAR. Camerale II, Arti e mestieri, b. 35, "*Memoriale del sindaco e sensali di commercio*", 11 april 1825.

aspects is from 1842, in which the Chamber of Commerce meticulously replies to the various complaints from matchmakers.[58]

In 1843, the trade union organization of matchmakers was formally recognized by the Chamber of Commerce; the report consisted of thirteen articles that set out how this office should consist of eight individuals.[59] Monthly fees were paid by each matchmaker to a cashier, who at the end of each month deposited them with the Savings Bank; this deposit was used to support the matchmakers if they had health problems or other financial difficulties as a form of welfare.[60] Thus, the brokers were obliged to pay a monthly fee, the nonpayment of which resulted in suspension from the performance of duties and annotation on the register of brokers until the broker returned to good standing.[61]

The activity of pontifical intermediaries continued until 1870 without regulatory change except for the solemn recognition of the order of moneychangers in 1866,[62] whose work partially overlapped with that of stockbrokers, presenting a new source of conflict, as evidenced by a report of the Chamber of Commerce addressed to the Minister of Commerce.[63]

In the long run, the number of stockbrokers operating on the exchange varied with the volume of transactions. Undoubtedly, numerous obstacles hampered access to the profession or its abandonment, but over the years, the group of financial intermediaries adapted to the fickle earning opportunities offered by the stock market.[64]

[58] SAR. Camera di Commercio, b. 14, Avviso della Camera di Commercio del 23 marzo 1839; SAR. Camerlengato, b. 88, "Parere intorno ad alcuni reclami fatti dal Ceto de' Sensali di Roma", 20 july 1842.

[59] SAR. Camera di Commercio, b. 14.

[60] Ibidem.

[61] Ibidem.

[62] SAR. Ministero del Commercio, Belle Arti, Industria, Agricoltura e Lavori Pubblici b.17, Notificazione del ministro Baldini del 20 luglio 1866.

[63] SAR. Camera di Commercio, b. 17, atto della "Camera Primaria di Commercio", con oggetto: "*Dal ricorso degli Agenti di Cambio contro i Cambiavalute ed altri che usurpano le loro funzioni*", 15 febbraio 1868.

[64] Weber, 1924 (edited. it. Tommasi, 1985, p. 81).

3.3 "For the Good Performance and Prosperity of Trade": The Rome Chamber of Commerce

In the first decades of the life of the Roman stock exchange, the Chamber of Commerce represented the main body for regulating and organizing stock exchange activity.

Chambers of Commerce were introduced in Italy when the French Commercial Code came into force on September 1, 1808. Naturally, the existing Chambers of Commerce ceased operation with the founding of the new ones. The objectives that the legislators sought to achieve with the Chambers of Commerce in Italy were the same as in France: to propose projects to encourage trade, to undertake economic analyses to identify inefficiencies that slowed progress and to support the execution of public works, which always concerned the sphere of commerce, such as maintaining the ports in a good state, enforcing compliance with laws and combating smuggling.

Following the 1797 Treaty of Tolentino, the pope was deprived of the Legations of Bologna, Ferrara and Romagna and temporarily of Ancona and its territory. After the French conquest and Napoleonic domination, the territory of the state underwent further reduction and new internal subdivisions. On June 10, 1809, the Papal State was constituted as follows: the city of Rome, the Campagna of Rome and Lazio, the Sabina, the Patrimony of St. Peter and Umbria. The subdivision of the state decreed by the Council in the session of 21 June 1809 consisted of the two Departments of the Tiber and Trasimeno, with the city of Rome independent of these entities. The first of these departments comprised the four "arrondissements" of Velletri-Frosinone-Rieti-Viterbo, with a total of 46 cantons, 372 municipalities and a population of 434,222 inhabitants. The second included the "arrondissements" of Spoleto-Perugia-Todi-Foligno, with 25 cantons, 436 municipalities and 273,685 inhabitants. The two departments were therefore divided into 8 "arrondissements", 71 "cantons" and 808 "communes" and had a total of 707,907 inhabitants, a total that does not include the city of Rome—whose territorial assignment had not yet been defined—and other border cities united to the Kingdom of Italy.[65]

[65] Spizzichino, 1930, pp. 438 e 440; Volpi, 1983, pp. 265–266; Nardi, 1990; 1989; Raponi, 1996.

In the Roman State, the first regulations on the matter of the Chambers of Commerce were issued by the Extraordinary Council with the order of June 17, 1809 relating to the "organization of the legal system of the Roman States".[66] A court was established in Rome and another in Civitavecchia, and after a few months, in the Council's session of 26 December 1809, two Chambers of Commerce were established, one in Rome (with 15 members) and one in Civitavecchia (with 7).[67] After Napoleon's fall, the Roman Chambers of Commerce were overwhelmed by the demands of the Restoration, a fate that did not affect the Chambers on the Adriatic coast. In Rome, there was a strong desire to erase all traces of domination, but despite this desire, it was impossible to stop the modernization triggered by the French[68]: "An example is the Stock Exchange which, albeit in a private capacity, continued to be the point of concentration of the interests of a group, interests that could thus be better managed. As often happens, over time, the reference to the general interest that had undoubtedly animated French institutions disappeared, to give way to particular interest, a degenerative dynamic to which institutions are often not alien".[69] It is precisely in connection with the Roman stock exchange that all the events occur that result in the birth of the Rome Chamber of Commerce in 1831.

The Rome Stock Exchange was established on July 8, 1831, by the edict of the pro-secretary of state Bernetti, with the main tasks of acquiring control over the brokers and stockbrokers and of assuming an advisory role in regulating the market.[70] On July 27 of the same year, the Rome Chamber of Commerce was officially established. Regarding its components, "the prospect of massive State interference in the management of Roman financial affairs"[71]—envisaged in the discussions between the main departments in the early 1820s and of which the edict represented only the final act of this bureaucratic process (thus showing,

[66] Strangio, 2001, pp. 131–132.

[67] Bidischini, 1997; Lodolini, 1962. Martinelli, 2007, pp. 16–22; 133–140. Astraldi, 1956, p. 19.

[68] Formica, 1989; 1994; 2010; Caffiero, 2005.

[69] Martinelli, 2007, p. 20.

[70] Astraldi, 1956, p. 7.

[71] Martinelli, 2007, p. 139.

among other things, strong characteristics of continuity with French legislation)[72]—even if it remained at the level of hypothesis "was perhaps not acceptable to those who had up to then controlled the financial market in perfect autonomy", and it is probable that for this reason the two best-known personalities, Torlonia and Lavaggi, did not want to step aside in favour of other names in Roman finance.[73]

The creation of this body was part of a moderate reorganization of public affairs initiated by Gregory XVI, who also turned his attention to the stock market by ordering, as underlined by the 1836 notification, that more detailed rules be dictated on stock exchanges, agents of exchange and matchmakers.[74]

Having created the Chamber of Rome and subsidiary chambers to several already existing chambers, Pope Gregory XVI subsequently turned his attention to the stock exchanges and with notification from Cardinal Galleffi on 30 August 1836 ordered that rules be dictated on commercial stock exchanges, stockbrokers and brokers.[75]

The activity of the Chamber of Commerce in Papal Rome can be divided into two periods: one preceding and one following the liberal uprisings of 1848–1849, which were accompanied by the pope's exile in Gaeta and his return to Rome after the events of the Roman Republic in April 1850 and which contributed to a phase of limited activity by the pope.[76]

At the time of the dissolution of the Chamber of Papal Rome, the Chambers of Commerce of the Kingdom of Italy were governed by law no. 680 (only replaced with the law of 20 March 1910 n. 121) and

[72] Santoro, 1989; Simonelli, 2000; SAR, Camerale II, Accademie, b. 1, fasc. 15.

[73] They were replaced by Alberto Gnocco and the Marquis Francesco Brancadoro; Nicola Bolasco was replaced by his son Giuseppe, and Giuseppe Truzzi took over from Merolli; the banker Vincenzo Valentini became chairman of the assembly in which the seat of the meetings was temporarily established; the vice president was Giuseppe Antonio Celani, and the secretariat was entrusted to Angelo Carnevalini (Martinelli, 2007, pp. 139–140).

[74] *Raccolta delle leggi e disposizioni di pubblica amministrazione nello Stato pontificio*, I, Roma, Stamperia della R.C.A., 1834, pp. 23–24. Astraldi, 1956, p. 29. Cfr. anche Ascarelli, 1911; Santoro, 1989, pp. 81–95; Bidischini, 1997, pp. 104–114. Farolfi, 1999, p. 459.

[75] Raccolta, 1834, pp. 23–24.

[76] Astraldi, 1956, p. 21. Caracciolo, Caravale, 1978, pp. 659–698; Caffiero, 2001.

charged with satisfying the demands and benefiting the changes occurring in the country and guaranteeing effective industrial development.[77]

3.4 Historical Evolution of the Rome Stock Exchange: From Its Origin to the 1860s

The "Provisional Trade Regulations" of 1 June 1821 established the Rome trading exchange, defining it as "the union that takes place under the authority of the government, merchants, ship captains, stockbrokers, and brokers".[78] Furthermore, article 67 stipulated that the sales and operations carried out on the stock exchange would determine the exchange rate of merchandise, insurance, boat rentals, the price of transport by land and water, public and other effects, the course of which is likely to be indicated in the market tables in the square.[79]

The Economic Congregation[80] established that it was necessary to eliminate any privilege and dominance of a single group within it to maintain the Rome Stock Exchange on the same level as the exchanges of other European capitals.[81]

The Rome Stock Exchange was not governed by a real statute at least until the time of the French invasion. However, the Papal State's code of commerce had already adopted most of the provisions that had been dictated during the French domination. The Roman stock exchange had begun to operate with the decree issued by the French authorities on the "snowy 3rd of the year XI" (24 December 1802). The same decree also established the Chamber of Commerce, which had supervisory duties with respect to the stock exchange and the activity of stockbrokers.

[77] Astraldi, 1956, p. 96.

[78] SAR, Primaria Camera di commercio, b. 2.

[79] SAR, Camerale II, Commercio e Industria, b. 4; SAR, Primaria Camera di commercio, b. 2.

[80] SAR, Congregazione economica (1815–1830), b. 134 *Fogli anonimi presentati alla Segreteria di Stato sulla sistemazione della borsa*, p. 761. The Congregation was the instrument through which the necessary measures were decided and adopted to overcome the purely contingent conditions in which the state found itself (Dal Pane, 1959, pp. 99–102).

[81] SAR, Congregazione economica (1815–1830), b. 134, Sulla borsa commerciale di Roma e sulle facoltà di essere ammesso, pp. 730–738 and p. 763. Da Pozzo, Felloni, 1964; Baia Curioni, 1995; Siciliano, 2001; Boccia, 2000; De Luca, 2002. For an bibliographic review of the nineteenth and twentieth centuries, see Balletta, 2004, pp. 237–311.

Following the entry into force of the new commercial code, in September 1809, the Chamber and the Stock Exchange were reconstituted according to the new system. At the end of the French period, the Chamber of Commerce ceased to exist although the "meetings" of brokers, bankers and moneychangers continued to be held.[82]

New admissions to "meetings" were authorized by the bankers themselves[83]; it was a privilege to be included in the list of "primary bank families", and every year the list was published in the "Cracas" (Diary of Rome), which, as Torlonia affirmed, represented an important form of advertising that went beyond "national" borders and placed the member families in a position "to contribute to the good of the country because the government, protecting and having the utmost trust in the banking body, always directed itself to the needs of the state".[84]

Previously, the "bankers" had always constituted a closed caste such that only seven or eight private bankers were recognized in Rome[85]; these individuals gathered once a week (usually on Friday) in a room of the "Archiginnasio della Sapienza" in the company of only two "mezzani" (stockbrokers) and fixed the "exchange".[86] At the end of the eighteenth century, the negotiations were held in the *Sapienza palace*. Later, during the 1820s, bargaining meetings were held at the *Valentini palace*. It appears that in the beginning the Chamber, which also arranged the Stock Exchange and probably also the Court, rented rooms in the *Sciarpa palace* in *Corso place* and that at the end of 1842 it moved to the *Viscardi palace in Gesù place*, renting a large set of chambers there for twenty years at 450 scudi per year.[87] According to a letter from the vice president of the primary Chamber of Commerce of Rome, Giuseppe Guerini, to the Councillor of the Lieutenancy for Finance Affairs on November 15,

[82] On the financial problems inherent in the French period, see among others: Strangio, 1997; 2001.

[83] SAR, Congregazione economica (1815–1835), b. 134, *Sulla borsa commerciale*, p. 771.

[84] SAR, Congregazione economica (1815–1835), b. 134, *Sulla borsa commerciale*, p. 795.

[85] In 1818, they were the bankers Torlonia, De Rossi, Valentini, Isola, Ardenti Loprano and Brancadoro.

[86] SAR, Congregazione economica (1815–1835), b. 134, *Fogli*, p. 815.

[87] Astraldi, 1956, p. 27.

Table 3.2 First stock market listing

Public effects	*Quotes scudi romani*
Roman Consolidated at 5 per 100	69
Folders from the *Monte di Milano* in favour of the pontifical subjects with the commencement of the interests from 1814 to all of 1817	74
Debt in favour of foreign subjects from 1814 to 1819	81
Non-interest-bearing restrictions, including Boni Stefanini	33.50
Debt for the purchase of Chamber of Commerce fees	–
Community credits for the purchase of funds	34
Interest-bearing debts	–
Bills payable in cash in instalments	84

Source "Diario di Roma" 7 September 1821

1870, it was proposed to provide a more suitable and respectable location for the meetings, as in other Italian cities. Thus, the Rome Stock Exchange was located in a building that would become the property of the Chamber (Convention of 18 June 1873 and its approval with law no. 1804 of 8 February 1874). The building was inside the temple of Hadrian on the piazza di Sciarra at no. 234 A. The temple, built in 145 AD by Antonino Pio in honour of his predecessor, Adriano, became a land customs office under Pope Innocent XII. The building was transformed in the years 1879–1884 as part of a project by Virginio Vespignani to house the Chamber of Commerce and the stock exchange. It was subsequently restructured in 1925 by Tullio Passatelli, who "managed to evoke, through the complete and severe quality of the Doric columns and frieze, Romanity of the Adrianeo, and to clearly celebrate the international nature of the myth of capitalism". This architectural clarity was immortalized in several dramatic sequences of the film Eclisse (1962) by Michelangelo Antonioni.[88]

The first stock market listing that appeared in the "Diary of Rome" was that of September 7, 1821 (Table 3.2).

A peculiarity of this list is the absence of securities of private companies. This "snapshot" reflects the economic situation of the papal State,

[88] Ciranna, 2005, pp. 233–269, pp. 233, 243, 245, where the phases of the definitive acquisition of the building are well described, and pp. 257–259; Galletti, 2005, p. 13; SAR, Intendenza di Finanza-Demanio, b. 459, fasc. 412.

which was traditionally lacking in private initiatives by certain entities; public debt securities, which have long been the main form of guaranteed investment, were the main protagonists.[89] It is true that "stock exchange listing in itself offers the possibility of easier access to the raising of risk capital (understood as the sum of self-financing and capital increases), to the extent that the constraints in terms of recourse to self-financing, linked to the need to maintain a certain dividend policy, are less stringent than the opportunities for raising fresh assets".[90] However, this way of directing capital into interest-bearing investments through trading on the stock exchange presupposes the existence of a mature "capital market", i.e.:

(a) the presence of companies and companies in an adequate number and representative of the economic activity in the territory;
(b) adequate public knowledge of the reliability of the securities representing the assets (i.e., shares or quotas) of companies and companies that aspire to admission to trading (i.e., quotations) on the stock exchange; such public knowledge was obviously linked to information on the economic potential of these aspirants (information which equally evidently must be furnished by qualified "controllers").

Such assumptions that qualify a capital market as "mature" were not present in the Papal State or in truth in the other Italian states at the time.

With the regulation of 1822, it was established that to ensure the legality of any bargain the signature of two stockbrokers was necessary.[91]

More than ten years passed until subsequent regulation (February 16, 1833), which introduced further provisions. The most important of the new provisions provided that the stockbroker had to transcribe the trades made on a certified note and that, in turn, an employee of the Chamber

[89] Stumpo, 1985; Piola Caselli, 1988, pp. 191–216; 1991; 1993, pp. 21–55; Strangio, 2001, 2005, pp. 7–42; Sabatini, 2004, pp. 89–145; 2003, pp. 79–128; Della Torre, 2008, pp. 401–420; Postigliola, Strangio, 2017, pp. 313–330. See also Conte, 2021; Tedoldi, Volpi, 2021.

[90] Siciliano, 2001, p. 128.

[91] SAR, Collezione bandi, b. 401, "Regolamento di Monsig. Tesoriere Generale" del 19 agosto 1822.

of Commerce should record on a list all the transactions carried out. This list had to be posted on the premises of the stock exchange and remain there for the entire week to make public the increase or decrease in the value of public effects. The price list had to indicate the maximum and minimum price of the trades and their opening and closing prices on the stock exchange. Article 8 and the final part of the previously mentioned notification of 1833[92] confirmed a trend, as noted, in these early years of the new stock market, that of the particular attention paid by the papal government to public debt securities and papal finances in general.[93]

3.4.1 The Notification of 1836

The subsequent notification of 1836 (referring to all commercial exchanges of the Papal State) established more detailed rules and introduced a new figure, that of the stock exchange deputy. This individual was chosen annually, subject to approval by the members of the Chamber of Commerce, from among the members belonging to the class of merchants and was deputed to settle any disputes that could arise between parties during negotiations.[94]

The operating days and hours of the stock exchanges were fixed, and the activity of the brokers, with which much of the notification was concerned, was regulated in a stricter manner.[95]

Regarding the subject of "privacy", art. 32 stated that stockbrokers and brokers had to maintain secret the name of those who intervened in the negotiations unless "the nature of the business requires it... under penalty of reimbursement of the damages, which they might have caused thereby, to be liquidated civilly".[96]

Furthermore, in the cities of the state in which there was greater trade in securities, it was necessary to appoint so-called "secondary" brokers,

[92] SAR, Primaria Camera di commercio b. 2, Notificazione della Segreteria di Stato del 16 febbraio 1833; SAR, Primaria Camera di commercio, b. 15.

[93] Felisini, 1993.

[94] SAR, Primaria Camera di commercio b. 14, Avviso della Camera Primaria di Commercio di Roma del 29 settembre 1836.

[95] Ibidem.

[96] SAR, Primaria Camera di commercio, b. 2, "Notificazione: borse commerciali, agenti di cambi e sensali dell'Emo. e Rmo. Pier Francesco Card. Galleffi Camerlengo di S.R. Chiesa", pubblicata il 30 agosto 1836.

trusted agents of the government, who had the task of facilitating the conclusion of negotiations.[97]

Perhaps because for the first time it set precise precepts that strictly and scrupulously defined the field of action of stockbrokers, the notification of 1836 gave rise to numerous grievances, as documented by a reply from the Roman Chamber of Commerce.

Among these precepts, as stated in Articles 3 and 6, was one establishing that agents, like brokers, must be subordinate to the members of the Chamber, uphold the good order of the stock exchange and report the negotiations they concluded.

One provision that provoked the protest of the agents concerned the need to make a deposit as a guarantee of their probity (art. 25); in this regard, the agents stated that by having practised their profession for a long time they had provided sufficient proof of honesty thus were not required to provide a further pledge or other guarantees, underlining that the practice of foreign nations was contrary to this ordinance.[98]

In the face of these criticisms, however, the legislator noted that it was not sufficient protection against all fraud to have exercised an office for a short time or for a long time, adding that this provision was necessary not so much to prevent fraud but, rather, the errors that anyone could make without detriment to their own estimation. In this regard, it was observed that the law had already provided to reduce the required deposit by two-thirds for currently active agents and brokers.

The third provision concerned the right "of one per thousand, payable half by the seller half by the buyer, which is fixed to them for exchange transactions in any square [...] Bankers, Freight Forwarders and Dealers, who bring in support of their claim". It was emphasized that it was improper to cite the example of "neighbouring" stock exchanges, "where they say that for bills of exchange you pay two per thousand".[99] In Livorno, for example, one per thousand was paid according to the requirements of a notification, just as in Genoa. If there were bankers and shopkeepers who wanted to pay the stockbrokers two per thousand for "their particular purposes", they could do so privately without the practice being adopted as a general rule. The fourth provision concerned the right

[97] SAR, Camerale II, Commercio e Industria, b. 4.

[98] SAR, Primaria Camera di commercio, b. 2, "Notificazione: borse commerciali".

[99] SAR, Camerale II, Camerlengato, b. 88, Rome 24 september 1836.

of "Sensaria for interest-bearing reinvestments", which was reduced to a quarter per cent of the sums contained in the contract, as for consolidated annuities.[100]

3.4.2 The Regulations of 1848 and 1854

The subsequent legislation on the subject was a "Disciplinary Regulation" concerning the stockbrokers of the Papal State stock exchanges on 13 September 1848. This legislation made changes especially at the accounting level, establishing that each stockbroker was obliged to maintain four accounting books: "to register in one the mediations of the purchases and sales of public effects; in the other, the brokerage of bills and other effects likely to be noted in the merchant tables; in the third, the return accounts; in the fourth, the certificates issued for the interrogation of the Castrensi requirements".[101]

The books were written on stamped paper, signed by a judge of the commercial court, updated chronologically and compiled according to ordinary accounting rules. It was forbidden for stockbrokers to create any company among themselves, whether for transactions or profit.[102]

The presence of intermediaries within the official securities market was therefore fundamental because "The Stock Exchange tends to be a 'reserved', closed, oligopolistic market, in which technical information, such as credit access capacity differentials (also obtained through networks of consolidated social relations), determines the creation of tendentially unequal exchange relationships".[103] As Baia Curioni writes, "The history of the Stock Exchange markets and their effective functioning thus largely coincides with that of the intermediaries who, in various capacities and with different objectives, find themselves orchestrating the market"; therefore, "The story of the Stock Exchange summarizes [...] the history of intermediaries' activities, their relations with the public authorities, the

[100] Ibidem.

[101] SAR, Primaria Camera di commercio b. 14, "Regolamento disciplinare per gli agenti di cambio nelle piazze dello Stato Pontificio" del 13 settembre 1848.

[102] Ibidem.

[103] Baia Curioni, 1995, p. 23.

economic culture of those who, as regulators, investors or intermediaries, decide on its functioning".[104]

In the regulation of 1854, the stock exchange was characterized in a more nuanced manner than in the definition provided in the deed of its foundation in 1821: "the place where, on established days and with the established rules, the trading of foreign exchange, public effects, of the goods, and anything else that can be negotiated, and the Price Lists are compiled to make the prices of the same negotiations known to the public".[105]

The difference between the two definitions was that in addition to greater specificity, after more than thirty years of history and experience, it was preferred to refer to the objects of trade "and anything else that can be negotiated" and not to the individuals interested in stock exchange transactions ("[...] under the authority of the Government, traders, ship captains, stockbrokers, and brokers").[106]

This difference is significant because by now, at least from a theoretical perspective, there were no longer many restrictions on admission to the stock exchange. Anyone who had money to invest could do so, perhaps with the help of an intermediary.

The role of bankers was formally recognized: "The Stock Exchange is open to bankers recognized as such in the square of Rome by the Chamber of Commerce".[107] In fact, the main phase of stock exchange activity, that of bargaining, termed enchantment, was regulated through the presence of "three bankers, who are currently banking in the capital, or first-rate merchants, and two stockbrokers, the number of attendees is legal, and the spell begins. After half an hour, and since there are not even many, the exchange rate that is in the previous stock exchange price list is confirmed, and the auction is closed".[108]

Art. 7 established that "The agent who enchants, before fixing the exchange rate, must consult all those present, and among these also the

[104] Baia Curioni, 1995, pp. 24 e 31.

[105] See paragraph 3.1.

[106] SAR, Primaria Camera di commercio b. 14, "Regolamento per la Borsa di Roma approvato dalla Santità di Nostro Signore Papa Pio IX, li 4 gennaio 1854".

[107] Ibidem.

[108] SAR, Primaria Camera di commercio b. 14, "Regolamento per la Borsa di Roma approvato dalla Santità di Nostro Signore Papa Pio IX, li 4 gennaio 1854".

agents, who were instructed by the bankers and shopkeepers to sell or buy. The same must be done at each change in the price of the so-called currency that enchants, and the reservations made by the customers must be respected, as well as the injunction to be understood again before fixing".[109]

Based on art. 8, at the time of negotiation, it was forbidden for other agents to interrupt the course of the auction until it ended except if they represented other subjects.[110]

According to art. 12, notice of successful negotiation had to be provided to both contractors.[111]

An important novelty concerned the agents, who in each negotiation could only be linked to one other agent and therefore did not have the right double mediation.[112]

The special regulation for the Rome Stock Exchange of January 1854 defined more precisely the pre-eminent functions of the stock exchange deputy[113]; under his direction, the list containing the quotations of the securities was compiled. He also acted as arbiter; i.e., the deputy resolved all issues that might arise on the stock exchange, including disciplinary matters, with full authority and definitively, and legal matters as conciliator if the contracting parties reported to him.[114]

Once the auction was over, the securities traded on the stock exchange had to be delivered to the agents and the stock exchange deputy according to specific procedures.[115]

Moreover, with this regulation, reference was made for the first time to the term "shares": The trading, both on the stock market and off, of consolidated annuities, and of industrial shares, was regulated in the same way as the exchange rates.[116]

[109] Ibidem.

[110] Ibidem.

[111] SAR, Primaria Camera di commercio b. 14, "Regolamento per la Borsa di Roma approvato dalla Santità di Nostro Signore Papa Pio IX, li 4 gennaio 1854".

[112] Ibidem.

[113] Astraldi, 1956, p. 36.

[114] SAR, Primaria Camera di commercio b. 14, "Regolamento per la Borsa di Roma".

[115] SAR, Primaria Camera di commercio b. 14, "Istruzioni per il Deputato di Borsa, su la concorrenza tra la carta e la moneta" 4 january 1854.

[116] SAR, Primaria Camera di commercio b. 14, "Regolamento per la Borsa di Roma".

With the set of rules of 1854, the Roman stock exchange now had more defined and nuanced regulation; the subsequent legislation of 1862 made only small additions to the regulation of Roman stock exchange activity.[117] On April 27, 1872, a new internal regulation was issued for the Chamber of Commerce; it included administrative provisions for the stock exchange, which adopted the name of Deputation of the Stock Exchange and which, pending completion of the remodelling of the Hadrianeum, had a temporary seat in the premises of the Banca Romana.[118] The subsequent regulation of 1884, which had the approval of the Ministry of Agriculture, Industry and Commerce, had wider application; it assigned tasks to a deputation consisting of seven members of the chamber, who alternated in turn but deliberated collectively, determined the functioning of cash and term and their modalities and established criteria for the assessment of courses.[119]

References

Aleotti, Alessandro. 1990. *Borsa e industria. 1861–1989: cento anni di rapporti difficili*, Milan: Edizioni di Comunità.

Ascarelli, Pellegrino. 1911. *La Camera di Commercio di Roma dal 1831 al 1911*, Rome: Tipografia I. Artero.

Astraldi, Romolo. 1956. *La Camera di Commercio di Roma nei centoventicinque anni di vita. (1831–1956)*, Rome: Fratelli Palombi Editori.

Baia Curioni, Stefano. 1991. Sull'evoluzione istituzionale della Borsa Valori di Milano (1898–1914). *Rivista di Storia economica*, 8: 41–80.

Baia Curioni, Stefano. 1995. *Regolazione e competizione. Storia del mercato azionario in Italia (1808–1938)*, Bologna: Il Mulino.

Baia Curioni, Stefano. 2000. *Modernizzazione e mercato. La Borsa di Milano nella "nuova economia" dell'età giolittiana (1888–1914)*, Milan: Egea.

Balletta, Francesco. 2004. Borsa, assicurazioni e finanza pubblica in età contemporanea, in Angelo Moioli and Fausto Piola Caselli (ed.) *La storiografia finanziaria italiana. Un bilancio degli studi più recenti sull'età moderna e contemporanea*, Cassino: Edizioni dell'Università degli Studi di Cassino, 237–311.

Balletta, Francesco. 2007. *Borsa di Napoli: protagonisti, etica, finanza e politica economica (1946–1953)*, Naples: Arte Tipografica Editrice.

[117] Astraldi, 1956, p. 37.

[118] Astraldi, 1956, p. 57.

[119] Astraldi, 1956, p. 57.

Barron Baskin, Jonathan and Paul J. Miranti jr. 2000. *Storia della finanza d'impresa*, Rome-Bari, Editori Laterza.

Bianchi, Tancredi. 1983. *La Borsa Valori e il mercato finanziario*, Turin: Utet.

Bidischini, Elisabetta. 1997. La Camera di commercio di Roma. Breve storia istituzionale e notizie sulle fonti, in *Gli Archivi Economici a Roma. Fonti e Ricerche, Atti della giornata di studio* (Roma, 14 dicembre 1993), Rome: Ministero per i beni culturali. Ufficio Centrale per i Beni Archivistici, 104–114.

Boccia, Elisa. 2000. *La Borsa di Milano tra miracolo e crisi, 1958–1978*, Naples: Edizioni Scientifiche Italiane.

Bruschini Vincenzini, Loretta. 1998. *Storia della Borsa*, Rome: Editoria Newton.

Cafaro, Pietro. 1993. La Borsa di Milano: origini vicende e sviluppi, in Ezio Antonini (ed.) *La Borsa di Milano. Dalle origini a Palazzo Mezzanotte*, Milan: 24Ore Cultura, 107–134.

Caffiero, Marina. 2001. Roma Repubblicana 1798–99, 1849. *Roma moderna e contemporanea*, IX(1–3): 9–28.

Caffiero, Marina. 2005. *La repubblica nella città del papa. Roma 1798*, Rome: Donzelli editore.

Caracciolo, Alberto and Mario Caravale. 1978. Lo Stato Pontificio da Martino V a Pio IX, in Collana Giuseppe Galasso (ed.) *Storia d'Italia*, Turin: Utet.

Cesarini, Francesco and Paolo Gualtieri. 2001. *La Borsa*, Bologna: Il Mulino.

Ciranna, Simonetta. 2005. *The Stock Exchange of Roma capital. The "difficult and rare invention in joining the modern with the ancient"* [La Borsa di Roma capitale. La «difficile e rara invenzione di raccordare il moderno con l'antico»], Roberto Novelli (ed.), Hadrianeum, Rome: Camera di Commercio Industria Artigianato e Agricoltura.

Colzi, Francesco. 1998. "Per maggiore facilità nel commercio". I sensali e la mediazione mercantile e finanziaria a Roma nei secoli XVI–XIX. *Roma moderna e contemporanea*, IV(3): 397–425.

Conte, Giampaolo. 2021. *Il credito di una nazione. Politica, Diplomazia e Società di fronte al problema del debito pubblico italiano, 1861–1876*, Rome: Edizioni Storia e Letteratura.

Da Pozzo, Mario and Giuseppe Felloni. 1964. *La borsa valori di Genova nel secolo XIX*, Archivio Economico dell'Unificazione Italiana, s II, vol. X, Genoa.

De Antonellis, Giacomo. 1988. *La storia della Borsa*, Milan: Vallardi.

De Luca, Giuseppe. 2002. *Le società quotate alla borsa valori di Milano dal 1861 al 2000. Profili storici e titoli azionari*, Milan: Libri Scheiwiller.

Della Torre, Giuseppe. 2008. Collocamento del debito pubblico e assetto normativo del sistema creditizio in Italia (1861–1914), in Alberto Cova, Salvatore La Francesca, Angelo Moioli and Claudio Bermond (eds.) *La banca, Storia d'Italia*. Annali 23, Torino, Einaudi, 401–420.

De Matteo, Luigi. 1999. «La tolleranza della violazione». Agenti di cambio e mediatori di borsa a Napoli tra età Borbonica e anni postunitari, in Guenzi Alberto, Paola Massa and Angelo Moioli (eds.) *Corporazioni e gruppi professionali nell'Italia moderna*, Milan: FrancoAngeli, 460–490.

De Rosa, Luigi. 1962. Le origini della Borsa di Napoli. *Orizzonti economici*, 43, Pozzuoli: 1–6.

Farolfi, Bernardino. 1999. Sensali e mediazione commerciale a Bologna dal XVI al XIX secolo, in Alberto, Guenzi, Paola. Massa and Angelo Moioli (eds.) *Corporazioni e gruppi professionali nell'Italia moderna*, Milan: FrancoAngeli, 444–459.

Felisini, Daniela. 1993. Le finanze pontificie nell'ottocento tra inquietudine politico-sociale e crisi economica, in Antonio Di Vittorio (ed.) *La finanza in età di crisi*, Bari: Cacucci, 181–211.

Formica, Marina. 1989. Potere e popolo. Alcuni interrogative sulla Repubblica Romana giacobina, *Studi Romani*, XXXVII(3–4): 235–257.

Formica, Marina. 1994. *La città e la rivoluzione. Roma 1798–1799*, Rome: Istituto per la Storia del Risorgimento Italiano.

Formica, Marina. 2010. Alla ricerca di nuove identità: Roma e la rivoluzione del 1798–1799, in *Mémoires d'Italie. Identités, représentations, enjeux (Antiquité et Classicisme). A l'occasion du 150° anniversaire de l'Unité italienne (1861–2011)*, sous la direction de Angelo. Colombo - Sylvie. Pittia - Maria.Teresa. Schettino, Como, New Presse Edizioni: 201–212.

Fornasari, Massimo. 2006. *Finanza d'impresa e sistemi finanziari. Un profilo storico*, Turin: G. Giappichelli Editore.

Galletti, M. 2005. *L'intervento di valorizzazione dell'ex Borsa Valori di Roma a Piazza di Pietra. Problemi di restauro del restauro*, Roberto Novelli (ed.), Hadrianeum, Rome, Camera di Commercio Industria Artigianato e Agricoltura.

Garbade, Kenneth. 1989. *Teoria dei mercati finanziari*, Bologna: Il Mulino.

Grohmann, Alberto. 2011. *Fiere e mercati nell'Europa occidentale*, Milan: Mondadori Bruno.

Kulischer, Joseph M. 1955. *Storia economica del Medio Evo e dell'epoca moderna*, Florence: Sansoni vol. II.

Lanaro, Paola (ed.). 2003. *La pratica dello scambio. Sistemi di fiere, mercanti e città in Europa. (1400–1700)*, Venice: Marsilio.

Lodolini, Elio. 1962. Camere e tribunali di commercio nello Stato romano (sec. XIX), in *Studi in onore di Amintore Fanfani*, vol. I, Milan: Antonino Giuffrè.

Martinelli, Manuela. 2007. *Le origini della Camera di Commercio di Roma*, Rome: Camera di Commercio Industria Artigianato e Agricoltura.

Nardi, Carla. 1989. *Napoleone a Roma. La politica della Consulta romana*, Rome: Ecole francaise de Rome.

Nardi, Carla. 1990. *Consulta straordinaria per gli Stati romani (1809–1810). Inventario*, Rome: Archivio di Stato, Scuola di archivistica paleografia diplomatica.

Pegorer, Paolo. 1998. *Il ruolo della borsa nella integrazione dei mercati*, Padova: Cedam.

Piola Caselli, Fausto. 1988. La diffusione dei luoghi di monte della Camera Apostolica alla fine del XVI secolo. Capitali investiti e rendimenti, in *Credito e sviluppo economico in Italia dal Medio Evo all'Età Contemporanea*, Atti del primo convegno nazionale della SISE (4–6 june 1987), Verona, 191–216.

Piola Caselli, Fausto. 1991. Banchi privati e debito pubblico pontificio a Roma tra Cinquecento e Seicento, in *Banchi pubblici, Banchi privati e monti di Pietà nell'Europa preindustriale. Amministrazione tecniche operative e ruoli economici*, Atti del Convegno, Genoa 1–6 october 1990, Genoa.

Piola Caselli, Fausto. 1993. Una montagna di debiti. I monti baronali dell'aristocrazia romana del Seicento. *Roma moderna e contemporanea*, I: 21–55.

Pivato, Giorgio. 1965. *Il mercato mobiliare*, Milan: Giuffrè Editore.

Pivato, Giorgio and C. Scognamiglio. 1972. Scorcio storico della Borsa Valori di Milano (1808–1970), in *Aa.Vv. La Borsa Valori dal 1808 ad oggi*, Milan: Camera di Commercio.

Postigliola, Michele and Donatella Strangio. 2017. Il debito pubblico italiano. Una serie storica dal 1861 al 2012. *Storia economica*, XX(1): 313–330.

Raponi, Nicola. 1996. Il trattato di Tolentino, in *Lo Stato della Chiesa in epoca napoleonica, Atti del XIX convegno del centro di studi Avellaniti* (Fonte Avellana, 24–26 agosto 1995), Fonte Avellana: Arti grafiche stibu di Urbannia (Pesaro), 9–22.

Riva, Angelo. 2005. *Competition entre places financieres: les bourses de Milan et de Genes a l'epoque giolittienne, 1894–1913.* sous la direction de P.-C. HAUTCOEUR, soutenue le 12 december 2005, University of Genoa.

Riva, Angelo. 2007. La negoziazione della Rendita nelle borse italiane, in Giuseppe De Luca and Angelo Moioli (eds.) *Debito pubblico e mercati finanziari in Italia. Secoli XIII–XX, Storia della Società, dell'economia e delle istituzioni. Collana promossa dal Dipartimento di storia della società e delle istituzioni dell'Università degli Studi di Milano*, Milan: FrancoAngeli: 565–595.

Sabatini, Gaetano. 2003. La storiografia più recente sulla finanza italiana dell'età moderna: gli studi sul debito pubblico. *Rivista di storia finanziaria*, 10: 79–128.

Sabatini, Gaetano. 2004. Il debito pubblico in età moderna, in Angelo Moioli and Fausto Piola Caselli (eds.) *La storiografia finanziaria italiana. Un bilancio degli studi più recenti sull'età moderna e contemporanea*, Cassino: Edizioni dell'Università degli Studi di Cassino, 89–145.

Santoro, Raffaele. 1989. La Camera di Commercio in epoca pontificia e la documentazione della Camera di commercio sussidiaria di Foligno, in Giampaolo Gallo (ed.) *Gli archivi delle Camere di Commercio. Atti del II Seminario Nazionale sugli archivi d'impresa* (Perugia, 17–19 novembre 1988), Foligno: Editoriale umbra.

Schisani, Maria Carmela. 1999. Gli agenti di cambio a Napoli dal decennio francese all'Unità. I caratteri regolativi e socio economici di una professione tra esigenze di tutela e finalità di indirizzo del mercato finanziario, in Alberto, Guenzi, Paola Massa and Angelo Moioli (eds.) *Corporazioni e gruppi professionali nell'Italia moderna*, Milan: FrancoAngeli, 491–503.

Schisani, Maria Carmela. 2001. *La Borsa di Napoli (1778–1860). Istituzione, Regolazione e attività*, Naples: Edizioni Scientifiche Italiane.

Siciliano, Giovanni. 2001. *Cento anni di borsa in Italia. Mercato, imprese e rendimenti azionari nel ventesimo secolo*, Bologna: Il Mulino.

Simonelli, Fabio. 2000, La Camera di Commercio di Roma: un profilo storico-istituzionale, in Bruna Colarossi (ed.) *Economia e cultura, l'archivio e la collezione d'arte della Camera di Commercio di Roma*, Rome: Gangemi editore.

Spizzichino, Jader. 1930. *Magistrature dello stato pontificio (470–1870)*, Lanciano: Editore Carrabba.

Strangio, Donatella. 1997. Il mercato primario del debito pubblico (1814–1846), in Anna Lia Bonella, Augusto Pompeo and Manola Ida Venzo (eds.) *Roma fra la Restaurazione e l'elezione di Pio IX. Amministrazione, Economia, Società, Cultura*, Rome: Herder, 427–450.

Strangio, Donatella. 2001. *Il debito pubblico pontificio. Cambiamento e continuità nella finanza pontificia dal periodo francese alla restaurazione romana. 1798–1820*, Padova: Cedam.

Strangio, Donatella. 2005. Il sistema finanziario del debito pubblico pontificio tra età moderna e contemporanea. *Rivista di Storia Finanziaria*, 14: 7–42.

Strangio, Donatella. 2006. "Facilitare al governo il mezzo di conoscere e di soddisfare i veri bisogni del commercio e delle arti". La disciplina della Borsa di Roma nella prima metà del XIX secolo. *Studi storici Luigi Simeoni*, l(LVI): 387–402.

Strangio, Donatella. 2007. Debito pubblico e mercato finanziario a Roma e nello stato pontificio tra XVIII e XIX secolo: l'istituzione della Borsa di Roma, in Giuseppe De Luca and Angelo Moioli (ed.) *Debito pubblico e mercati finanziari in Italia. Secoli XIII–XX, Storia della Società, dell'economia e delle istituzioni. Collana promossa dal Dipartimento di storia della società e delle istituzioni dell'Università degli Studi di Milano*, Milan: FrancoAngeli: 251–270.

Stumpo, Enrico. 1985. *Il capitale finanziario a Roma fra Cinque e Seicento. Contributo alla storia della fiscalità pontificia in età moderna (1570–1660)*, Milan: Giuffrè.

Tedoldi, Leonida and Alessandro Volpi. 2021. *Storia del debito pubblico in Italia. Dall'Unità a oggi*, Rome-Bari: Editori Laterza.

Tronci, Anotonio. 1891. *Le operazioni in materia di Borsa*, Turin-Rome: L. Roux e C. Editori.

Volpi, Roberto. 1983. *Le regioni introvabili. Centralizzazione e regionalizzazione dello Stato Pontificio*, Bologna: Il Mulino.

Weber, Max. 1924. Die Borse, in *Gesammelte Aufsätze zur Soziologie und Sozialpolitik*, Tübingen, Mohr, trad. it. Claudio, Tommasi. 1985. *La borsa*, Milan: Unicopli.

Sources

State Archive of Rome (SAR)

Bandi, vol. 386.

Collezione bandi, b. 401.

Camerale II, Accademie, b. 1.

Camerale II, Arti e mestieri, b. 35.

Camerale II, Commercio e Industria, b. 4.

Camerale II, Camerlengato, b. 88,

(Primaria) Camera di Commercio, bb. 2,14,15, 17, 44.

Congregazioni economiche, bb. 134,135.

Ministero del Commercio, Belle Arti, Industria, Agricoltura e Lavori Pubblici, b. 17.

Intendenza di Finanza-Demanio, b. 459, fasc. 412.

Edited Sources

Diario di Roma (roman newspaper) 7 september 1821

Codice di commercio preceduto dai motivi presentati al corpo legislativo dal Sig. Regnaud di Saint – Jean D'Angely, Roma, s.e., 1809, tit. V, sez. II.

Moroni, Gaetano. 1869. *Dizionario d'erudizione storico–ecclesiastica*, Venice: Tipografia Emiliana, voll. LXXXIV.

Raccolta delle leggi e disposizioni di pubblica amministrazione dello Stato Pontificio, Rome 1852, n. 34.

Raccolta delle leggi e disposizioni di pubblica amministrazione nello Stato pontificio, I, Roma, Stamperia della R.C.A., 1834.

Regolamento di Commercio del 1 giugno 1821, Avviso dell'Editore, Tipografia delle Scienze di Giuseppe Vitali, Bologna 1864.

Regolamento provvisorio di commercio finora vigente nelle province di seconda recupera e modificato secondo le prescrizioni dell'editto del primo giugno 1821 dall'E.mo e R.mo signore Card. Segretario di Stato da osservarsi in tutto lo Stato Pontificio fino alla pubblicazione ed attivazione del nuovo Codice di Commercio, Tipografia della R.C.A., Rome 1821.

CHAPTER 4

The Rome Stock Exchange and the Evolution of the Roman Financial Market (1821–1870)

How was the Rome Stock Exchange organized and developed "in the long nineteenth century"?

Who were the underwriters? What were the interests and the real value of the securities? What weight did the "currency crisis" have and what was the size of the Rome stock exchange compared to other Italian stock exchanges?

Rome and its state, of which it had been the point of reference ever since, with the return of the popes, which began with Martin V, after the so-called period of the "avignant captivity", a policy of unification of the ecclesiastical territories was carried out (Caravale, Caracciolo, 1978, pp. 26–42). But the changes that occurred from the end of the eighteenth century and the early nineteenth century during the Napoleonic occupation, and in the course of the nineteenth century, as received by the Rome Stock Exchange, in particular by the transition from the capital of Papal State to the capital of the Kingdom of Italy?

D. Strangio, *The Roman Stock Exchange between the 19th and 20th Centuries*, Palgrave Studies in the History of Finance,
https://doi.org/10.1007/978-3-031-00359-2_4

4.1 The Period 1821–1847

Although the governing bodies were aware that new issues would cause further financial turmoil, it was necessary to resort to redeemable debt, which was placed partly within the state and partly, through loans granted by major banking houses, on the European markets.[1]

> Among the loans contracted internally, that from 8 July 1832 (one hundred thousand scudi) between the Reverend Apostolic Chamber and Luigi Boncompagni, Prince of Piombino, deserves attention. The loan was amortized over 12 years (in gold and silver) according to the capability of the Holy See at a rate of 5% tax-free through income from the Campanoli estate pertaining to the Chapter of St. Peter.[2]

The state also resorted to various international loans, in particular by entering into agreements with the Rothschilds; by 1846, there were seven loans, of which six were provided by the Rothschild house; the loans were contracted to obtain loans abroad.[3] The Rothschilds performed 3 functions during the first decades of the nineteenth century: (1) the oldest, the commercial one, on which the house originally based its fortune; (2) banking in the traditional sense, that is, the movement of bills and gold; and (3) the financial function, whereby the house was primarily interested in investments in securities issued by governments and companies.[4] In November 1831, in response to Austrian pressure, the Rothschild house in the person of James Rothschild, who signed the bond, granted a loan of 3 million Roman scudi to the Papal State.[5] However, unlike other European states, which could resort to debt as a development tool, the Papal State was virtually strangled by its need to finance increasingly significant current and unproductive expenses, which reduced the funds that could be allocated to investment in infrastructure and other areas.

In particular, with the *Motu Proprio* of 11 June 1831, a new internal annuity was established for internal debt that could be extinguished in

[1] Felisini, 1990, pp. 73–74.

[2] SAR, Camerale II, Debito pubblico, b. 14, fasc.4.

[3] Morandi, 1933, pp. 502–503.

[4] Felisini, 1990; Corti, 1950, pp. 239–241.

[5] Fatica, 1973, p. 7.

10 years at a nominal interest of 5%[6]; 1000 bonds equal to 500 thousand scudi were issued at 500 scudi each; they were easily negotiable and further subdivided, like the old *Luoghi*.[7]

On July 8, 1831, a regulation was promulgated regarding the issue and extinction of the certificates of the new annuity. The consolidated annuity certificates were referred to as folders and divided into ten classes, each comprising a capital of 50,000 scudi, with an income of 2,500 scudi. These classes were further divided into twelve additional classes. The amortization of the securities occurred, as in former times, through extraction. To avoid or at least limit fraud and make the marketability of the securities safer, a coupon was added to each certificate, which recorded for a period of five years the interest instalments to be collected (each quarter postponed). On expiry of the five years, if the bond had not yet been extracted, the Directorate General for Public Debt issued a new coupon, which reported the serial number of the reference certificate with the new interest instalments to be collected (for the remaining five years). At the time of the drawing, the owner had to return the title to the bodies in charge, at which moment the interest stopped accruing. Subsequently, the coupons were destroyed through incineration.

The Depreciation Fund was officially established with art. 246 of the *Motu Proprio* of 1816 and operated in other regions of Italy, such as the Kingdom of Naples,[8] with the specific purpose of amortizing the obligations of the old and new consolidated debt. Subsequently, the notification of January 24, 1825, issued by Leo XII, endowed the Cassa with funds, intended exclusively to provide for the progressive extinction of the debt.

> The individual assets with which the Cassa was endowed consisted of the estate of Nettuno (later, the estate was alienated in favour of Prince Camillo Borghese for 40 thousand scudi, and the Cecchignola estate was sold to the Torlonia brothers, as established following the issue of the new redeemable of 1831), the Allumiere, the pine forests of Ravenna, the Mesola, S. Felice, Scavolino and the "relapse" of life pensions.[9]

[6] Raccolta di leggi, 1871, pp. 1–16.

[7] Lodolini, 1956, pp. 263–278; Piola Caselli, 1988, pp. 191–216; Masini, 2005; Felloni, 1971; Strangio, 1994, pp. 179–202.

[8] Ostuni, 1992, pp. 48–49.

[9] Raccolta, 1871, pp. 282–283. SAR, Camerale II, Debito pubblico, b. 14. See Capalbo, 1995, pp. 173–199.

In addition, a group of major creditors of the state assumed administration of the assets; above all, this body had to remain independent.[10] The fund was obliged to provide an annual payment to extinguish the "old consolidated debt" through "the net income of the assets" of the allocated funds and of the "new debt" established with the *Motu Proprio* of 1831 using the fifty thousand scudi that by law the "regalia de 'salts and tobaccos" was obliged to pay annually for this purpose.[11]

In reality, the state, having to face pressing financial needs, violated the independence of this body, which was unable to operate according to its original criteria.

4.1.1 The Securities Market

The legislative provisions recognized the full negotiability of the public securities in circulation, as in former times. The individual transfers were recorded in special registers housed at the Public Debt Directorate. The securities were nominative, but it was determined to make them also bearer.[12] The consolidated public was undoubtedly the main title of the Roman financial market even in this phase of the nineteenth century, as it had been in previous centuries with the *monte* system. Public debt securities up to 1833, in addition to the Roman consolidation at 5%, included the listing of the *Monte di Milano* folders, pertaining to the Papal State after the Vienna Convention, both issued in favour of subjects and foreigners residing in the territory of the Church, and until 1834, the non-interest-bearing credit certificates could be extinguished in numerary and for the purchase of "community goods in the provinces of first and

[10] Raccolta, 1871, pp. 6–7; SAR, Tesorierato generale, titolo I, affari generali, b. 279, Sullo stato delle finanze, p.13. Unlike the other amortization funds, that of the Papal State was part of the Ministry of the Treasury (SAR, Camerale II, Debito Pubblico, b. 14, fasc. 3).

[11] SAR, Camerale II, Debito pubblico, b. 14, fasc. 3.

[12] SAR, Direzione generale del debito pubblico, b. 2854; SAR, Tesorierato Generale, b. 277, p. 5 "Rapporto del Tesoriere Generale sullo stato della finanza per la Congregazione Cardinalizia del 16 luglio 1834".

second recovers".[13] In 1838, the first shares of the Pontifical Insurance Society were listed.[14] Subsequently, towards the end of the 1850s, the Stock Exchange experienced a certain liveliness in the negotiations regarding shares of companies that operated in the service, railway and insurance and banking sectors (the only shares were those issued by the bank of the Papal State).[15]

In a dispatch dated 21 December 1821, the Secretariat of State ordered stockbrokers to open a public stock exchange that every merchant was free to access.[16] The economic group reiterated that it was necessary to eliminate any privilege of or dominance by a subgroup within it so as to maintain the Rome Stock Exchange on the same level as those of other European capitals,[17] from Naples, "where the stock exchange is public and bankers and merchants without distinction at the sound of the bell gather in it", to Livorno, from Genoa to Marseille, to Ancona, not to mention London and Paris, where the exchange is open to "shopkeepers of every nation" without any subjection to local bankers and merchants, as previously mentioned.[18] Starting in 1790, newly admitted participants had to deposit 25,000 scudi at the *Sacro Monte di Pietà* or the *Banco di S. Spirito*.[19] Until then, the "bankers" had customarily constituted a closed caste such that only seven or eight private bankers were recognized in Rome,[20] who gathered once weekly (usually Friday) at the *Archiginnasio della Sapienza* with only two "middlemen" (stockbrokers) to fix

[13] SAR, Bandi b. 312, *Motu Proprio* di Papa Pio VII "Sulla dimissione de' debiti delle Comunità" pp. 3–19. The term "first and "second recover" refers to those parts of the territory that were re-annexed to the Papal State on the basis of the European conventions stipulated in the aftermath of French domination (Strangio, 1997, pp. 155–159).

[14] Diario di Roma, a.1838 supplement to n.43 del 28/05/1838.

[15] Giornale di Roma, listini di borsa, aa. 1850–1860.

[16] SAR, Congregazione economica (1815–1830), b. 134 Fogli anonimi presentati alla Segreteria di Stato sulla sistemazione della borsa, p. 761.

[17] SAR, Congregazione economica (1815–1830), b. 134, Sulla borsa commerciale di Roma e sulle facoltà di essere ammesso, pp. 730–738.

[18] SAR, Congregazione economica (1815–1830), b. 134, Fogli, pp. 763 and 771.

[19] At the end of the eighteenth century, the Stock Exchange was located in the Palazzo della Sapienza; it was later transferred to the Palazzo Ruspoli.

[20] In 1818, this closed group included the following bankers: Torlonia, De Rossi, Valentini, Isola, Asdenti Loprano e Brancadoro.

"the exchange".[21] The fixation of the exchange rate between square and square was determined by negotiation and fluctuated relative to the supply and demand of exchange letters while also considering current values at foreign commercial centres.[22]

Because the government linked the nominal value of the bonds of the "old" consolidated public debt to these prices, as was customary in the major European markets, while those relating to the 1831 issue continued to be repaid at par, the lists were of particular importance. The *Motu Proprio* of 11 June 1831 established that even the "old consolidated debt" had to be repaid at par, "that is, at the rate of one hundred scudi in capital over five scudi of annuity, through the extraction to be done annually of as many certificates".[23] Subsequently, the governing bodies agreed to amortize the old consolidated debt by linking the securities "to the commercial price" because "the repayment at par with the annual extraction method has little effect on public effects, which in the current circumstances have a continuous movement, and because the net product of stable assets destined for amortization is not in proportion to the total of the old consolidated debt to be amortized".[24]

4.1.2 The Subscribers

The major capitalists of the state were invited by the government (the securities market had suffered negative repercussions from recent events) to subscribe to the new securities for the "good of public affairs". The recourse to individual private capitalists and "institutional investors" (to use current terminology), whose assets and income could ensure the placement of the securities, was nearly obligatory. The vicissitudes of the old debt, which, as mentioned, had reduced the repayment expectations of the underwriters (the loss percentages were 75 and 76%), did not allow public and indiscriminate underwriting except at high risk.

Figure 4.1 shows that only 18% of the redeemable bonds (1832–1835) were issued to the bearer, while 46% were subscribed by "institutional

[21] SAR, Congregazione economica (1815–1830), b. 134, Fogli, p. 815.

[22] SAR, Congregazione economica (1815–1830), b.134, Fogli, p. 795.

[23] Raccolta, 1834, p. 30, Metodi, coi quali debbono impiegarsi i fondi della cassa di ammortizzazione per le rendite consolidate, 21 novembre 1832.

[24] Raccolta, 1834, p. 31. SAR, Tesorierato Generale, b. 277, p. 18.

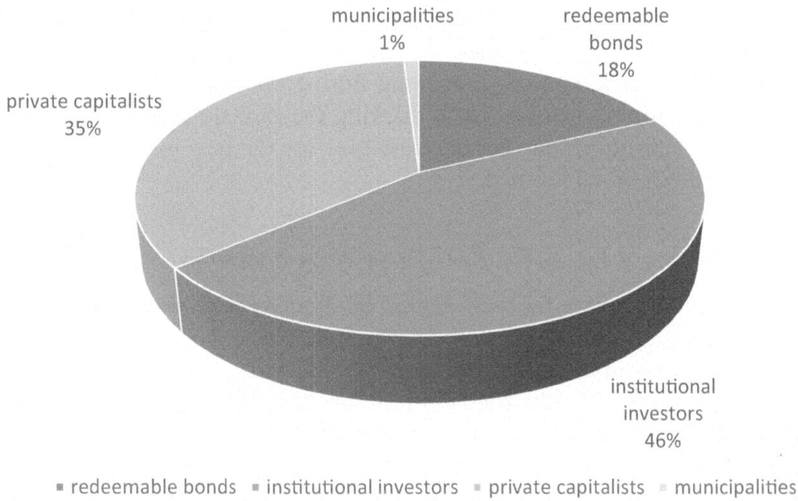

Fig. 4.1 Unit holders of redeemable public debt (1832–1835) (Tot. scudi 196,288) (*Source* SAR, Camerale II, Debito Pubblico b.14)

investors" (e.g., convents, hospitals, chapters) and 35% by private capitalists. Of the latter, more than half (60%) were issued to the private banker Torlonia and the remainder to a small number of individuals belonging to the Roman nobility (Agostino Rampicci, Vincenzo Grazioli, Angelo Galli, Angelo Polucchio, Pietro Forti, Ugo and Pietro Spinola, Galeppi) or high prelates of the Church (Brignole Apostolic Nuncio of Florence, Archbishop of Bologna, Monsignor Benedetto Costantini).

Meanwhile, the members of the Roman nobility noted above and the private capitalists invested in subscriptions as holders of significant liquidity. Then, strengthened by this position, they were able to place the securities held on the secondary market when the opportunities of that market allowed them to sell at the most convenient quotations.

The knight Alessandro Torlonia, for example, reallocated securities acquired in the subscription of the redeemable debt on the secondary market. The reallocation was facilitated by his position as official banker of the State. One should recall that the role of the banker as an intermediary between the Apostolic Chamber (i.e., the issuer) and the securities market was widespread if not essential in the sixteenth and seventeenth centuries. In the eighteenth century, this figure was overshadowed by the increasing role played by the *Monte di Pietà* and the *Banco di S. Spirito.* Under French domination, these two credit institutions were suppressed. However, after a temporary reopening during the first restoration, they became operational again in 1818. Lacking the capital necessary for their effective reactivation, they became easy prey for the new institutions that slowly came to be established.[25]

4.1.3 The Real Value of the Securities

Consolidation displayed a high degree of elasticity with respect to political institutions. Regarding these constraints, Table 4.1 shows how the stock market trend identifies economic periods with completely dissimilar peculiarities, as marked by the fall in the price at the quarterly maturities of interest. Between 1814 and 1848, the break in the historical series of quarterly average courses of consolidation is represented by the minimum of 1831. As was previously pointed out, 1831 stands as a watershed in papal finances, which, due to the state's crises, record greater deficits.[26] The public debt burden underwent a surge starting in 1831, and between 1831 and 1832, it reached a maximum of 34%, settling at approximately 30% with small fluctuations except for a surge in 1838, when it reached nearly 35%.[27]

The inconsistent price trend between 1814 and 1848 is partly explained by the economic and financial policy phases of the restoration period and by the economic and financial emergency measures. The cyclical sweep of the quarterly average prices of the public securities traded on the square in Rome recorded expansionary and recessive phases that coincide precisely with the political, economic and financial events of the State, characterized by medium expansion phases (2–3 years) and short recessive phases (1 year to a maximum of 2 years). From 1821 to 1833, securities relating to the *Monte di Milano* are also listed (for an annual average of 80–90 scudi up to and exceeding par only for the third quarter of 1830, reaching a maximum quota of 103 scudi)[28]; previously, it was determined to combine the public debt with the consolidated debt (in

[25] SAR, Bandi, b. 312, Chirografo di Pio VII, 7/4/1818.

[26] Felisini, 1993.

[27] Felisini, 1990, p. 25 e p. 80.

[28] Diario di Roma, a.1830 n. 61 del 30 luglio.

Table 4.1 Quarterly and annual quotations of the Roman consolidated debt at 5%

Years	*I quarter*	*II quarter*	*III quarter*	*IV quarter*	*Annual*
1822	71	70.16	70.83	74.54	71.63
1823	76.65	74.17	74.9	78.58	76.08
1824	83.79	93.34	94.38	93.25	91.19
1825	92.88	91.87	90.27	91.08	91.53
1826	90.67	89.25	91.06	91.71	90.67
1827	94.77	95.98	96.25	95.25	95.56
1828	95.44	95	95	94.42	94.97
1829	94	94.12	95	95.1	94.56
1830	98.94	100.48	102.21	99.46	100.27
1831	92.29	84	79.77	74.98	82.76
1832	74.66	73.36	71.9	71.47	72.85
1833	72.86	79.62	78.69	78.9	77.52
1834	79.5	83.09	83.35	87.85	83.45
1835	90.33	96.13	92.56	91.6	92.66
1836	94.5	94.56	91.88	90.34	92.82
1837	91.16	91.09	91.52	93.9	91.92
1838	96.25	98.62	99.66	100.77	99
1839	101.29	100.67	100.69	101.25	100.98
1840	101.83	103.73	103.08	97.27	101.48
1841	101.52	103.98	103.21	104.51	103.31
1842	105	103.81	104.74	107.29	105.21
1843	108.31	110.06	110.57	107.83	109.19
1844	106.13	106.48	110.58	110.6	108.45
1845	111.76	109.75	108.27	108	109.44
1846	106.31	104.48	104.4	104	104.8
1847	104.46	104.92	104.46	100.71	103.64

Source Data processing based on Diario di Roma, 1821–1847

1832), non-interest-bearing debts (which fluctuated between 91 and 95 scudi and then fell after 1831) and community debts until the community debt was completely liquidated.[29] Quotes remained fairly stable for the shares of the *Cassa di Risparmio* (equal to 190 scudi), while the anonymous insurance company reached 166.86 in 1847 (with nominal shares of 107.13 scudi; Fig. 4.2).

[29] Lodolini, 1956, pp. CXXII–CXLVI, p. CXLIV.

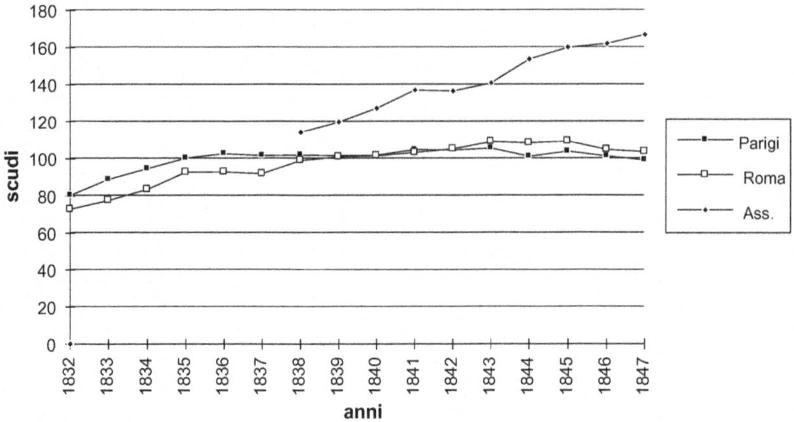

Fig. 4.2 Trends in Roman bond prices on the Paris stock exchange, internal Roman consolidation folders (both at 5%) and the insurance company shares (*Source* Data processing based on Diario di Roma aa.1832–47. For the quotations of Roman bonds on the Paris stock exchange, see Felisini, 1990, p. 107)

The gradual increase in prices from 1831 onwards probably underpinned the constant interest of the state not only to obtain less burdensome credit conditions in contracts with domestic banker merchants but also to maintain and obtain international credit. This type of conditioning damaged the interests of the subjects of the new enlarged circuit (state—private finance—international finance), which required an increase in prices that would move the internal market and lighten the burden of the conditions of the loans taken out at the prices of the Paris market and at the same time create an impression of a certain economic and financial stability of the state on the European market. The consolidation surpassed par after 1838, reaching its maximum price in the first quarter of 1845: 112 scudi. The price of domestic securities closely resembled that of the bonds listed on the Parisian market (Fig. 4.2).[30] This superimposition of the Roman hypercycle on the Parisian hypercycle reflected a certain balance in the internal market and a degree of success in the external market. In 1847, prices underwent a significant decrease from 104 scudi

[30] Felisini, 1990, p. 107.

to 100. The republican phase was approaching, and a new pontiff had been selected. However, the share price no longer went below par.

In conclusion, various parties reiterated the need to intervene with new rigor to improve the financial system, but these investment proposals remained for the most part ineffectual and concerned only single sectors of the financial landscape rather than that landscape as a whole, in the sense in which Benedict XIV had tried to proceed.[31] Among the individual proposals was one to convert the consolidated annuity from 5% to nominal 4% or even less; had it been adopted, it would have represented an important step since it would have allowed the Papal State to adapt to the general trend of other countries while lightening the public burden of interest on public securities.[32] It remained an opportune moment to create greater demand for direct consumer goods and decrease the armed and civilian military forces,[33] and the public treasury would have had to make sacrifices to invest in new sectors, such as rail transport, which was gaining ground in the largest European countries.[34] Therefore, if at first, thanks to the work of Cardinal Consalvi, a policy of modernization was pursued, profound political dissatisfaction, financial difficulties, the chronic use of budget revenues in unproductive expenditure and the recurrent and systematic recourse to debt to finance the deficit made it difficult for the state to manage and forced it to depend on foreign powers for its survival.

4.2 The Period 1847–1860

To avoid insubordination, denounced in 1846 by the provincial magistrates, and to address an agricultural harvest not expected to be particularly positive, the papal government adopted several customs measures that while aiming to favour the supply of goods to the working classes contributed to a slowdown in commercial traffic in 1847.[35]

[31] Strangio, 1997, p. 150.

[32] SAR, Tesorierato generale, titolo I, Affari generali, b. 279, Sullo stato delle finanze pontificie e de' modi di migliorarle—Rapporto di Monsignor Carlo Luigi Morichini Arcivescovo di Nisibi, p. 6.

[33] Pepoli Napoleone, 1858, p.118.

[34] SAR, Camerale II, Debito pubblico, b. 8, fasc. 5, Rapporto cit., p. 6 e p.16.

[35] Raccolta, 1834, vol. 1, pp. 115–116, vol. 2, pp. 109, 126–128; SAR., Consulta di Stato, b. 2.

The value of exports decreased from 5,640,000 to 3,642,000 scudi, while imports increased from 2,176,000 to 3,087,000 scudi.[36]

The greater imports did not translate into profits for the traders, who had responded to speculative pressure by requesting since the summer of 1847 free trade measures[37]; as it turned out, good harvests disappointed the expectations of the traders and the communities of the Papal State, who had taken steps to build up stocks, which were then left unsold "with very serious damage to the owners and contracting communities".[38] The dynamics of the commercial crisis that afflicted the State of the Church were similar to those afflicting other European countries in 1847. The budget deficit caused by increased cereal imports resulted in a drain of cash abroad and a slowdown in monetary circulation.[39] The outflow of capital to service loans contracted in Paris and Genoa increased the negative state trade balance.[40] One immediate consequence was an increase in requests for deposit reimbursements at the *Cassa di Risparmio di Roma*. To meet these requests, the Bank withdrew ever more substantial shares of the funds deposited at the issuing institution, depriving this institution of an important metal reserve needed for the exchange of tickets. The economic situation that emerged in the autumn of 1847 was accentuated in the following year.[41] Due to public debt burdens and lower customs revenue, the 1848 deficit budgeted by the treasurer for financial management was more than double that of previous years.[42]

The budget deficit of November 1847 increased dramatically at the end of March 1848, when preparations to intervene in the war of independence required the public debt burden, the largest component of the papal budget, to be added to the "expenditure for arms", which doubled, as previously noted, from 1,954,000 to 4,000,000 scudi, among other difficulties. Government intervention in support of the banking institutions (ordinance of 11 April 1848) *Banca Romana* and *Cassa di Risparmio* had occurred in the context of financial circumstances such

[36] Bonelli, 1961, p. 74.

[37] SAR, Camerlengato, parte II, Annona e Grascia, b. 766.

[38] SAR, Consulta di Stato, b. 2.

[39] Morichini, 1847.

[40] Farini, 1853, p. 48.

[41] Morichini, 1847, p. 16.

[42] D'Errico, 1990.

that, having set aside extraordinary finance projects, had no other way to ensure the coverage of expenses except by creating liquidity through printing fiat-backed securities to guarantee they would be held by the public. The decree of April 1848, which marked the first issue of government bonds, was only the beginning of a monetary policy in which subsequent issues of bonds and notes caused an increase in paper inflation. In December, it was necessary to print another three titles at a value of 600,000 scudi to be added to the first 800,000.[43] The printing occurred despite the contrary opinion expressed by the representatives of the Chamber of Commerce regarding the danger of the depreciation of paper money and the consequent premium placed on gold.[44] The financial conduct of the provisional government (from 25 November 1848 to 9 February 1849) and of the republican government (from February 1849 to the following 3 July) did not differ from that of the pontifical authorities. During the Republican period, the number of fiat bonds in circulation increased to 6,890,160 scudi.[45] To these were added the tickets printed by the Banca Romana for 1,500,000 scudi on the orders of the republican authorities.[46] The 3.6% yield enjoyed by all government issues up to January, equal to 3,900,000 scudi, was abolished in March 1849, thus assimilating public debt securities to banknotes.[47]

Until 1852–1853, while in the rest of Western Europe and in certain areas of the Italian Peninsula the money supply increased and access to credit was facilitated, in Rome, the continuation of the compulsory course of government notes caused a premium of gold on paper, which reached 17–18%. This phenomenon penalized the profits of the export trade and the resumption of commercial transactions. Shopkeepers complained that "metal species are commonly used today at 5–6%", while in the years preceding the crisis, the cost of money was below 4.5%.[48]

To restore the convertibility regime and ease tensions on the money market, the papal government ordered in April 1853 that the remaining

[43] SAR, Camerale II, Debito Pubblico, b. 14. SAR, Ministero delle finanze, b. 551.

[44] Bollettino delle leggi, proclami, 1849.

[45] Bollettino delle leggi, 211.

[46] Raccolta, 1848, vol. II, pp. 38–39 and 105–108.

[47] Bollettino delle leggi, 1849, decreto del 26 marzo, 1849, pp. 211–213.

[48] SAR, Ministero delle Finanze, b. 635 Memoria del ceto dei negozianti di Roma alla Commissione governativa del 10 august 1849.

amount of paper money be withdrawn from circulation within the year and "gradually replaced with actual money".[49] The new bond loans, obtained abroad between 1853 and 1854, provided the government with the financial means necessary to undertake from the summer of 1853 to April 1855 the issue of metal money for a total amount of 4,538,280 scudi, which was used in the withdrawal of securities.[50]

The operation conducted by the Treasury, however, did not have the desired outcome because of the effects of the new ration crisis that developed in the Papal State and other Italian and European states, precisely in the two-year period 1853–1854.[51] The serious deficit that occurred in foreign trade in those years, caused by the greater imports of cereals, was such that "the metallic currency issued in place of treasury bonds soon disappeared from circulation, mostly drawn abroad by the force of circumstances, in response to the scarcity of representative or circulating values of any kind".[52]

In the autumn of 1854, internal monetary tensions worsened, causing a slowdown in the inflow of deposits from the Savings Bank of Rome. In November 1854, the government authorized the issuing institution to limit the exchange of its notes to 10,000 scudi daily. At the end of the year, a credit balance 30% lower than that of the previous year was recorded. This outcome was attributable to the 59% increase in withdrawals in the second half of the year compared to a 22% decrease in deposits. Reimbursement requests increased sharply, culminating in a rush of depositors for liquidity starting in December 1854 and continuing in 1855. It was necessary to wait until the beginning of 1856 to normalize the situation and to remove all limits on the exchange of tickets.

The development of new forms of collection during this period in competition with the Roman deposit banks helped slow the withdrawal of deposits. This phenomenon explains, for example, the annual balance of the collection of deposits, which remained modest at the *Cassa di Risparmio di Roma* despite the presence of a larger depositor base.

[49] Raccolta, 1954, vol. VII, circular from the Minister of the Interior del 28 April 1853, pp. 47–53.

[50] Felisini, 1990, pp. 151–153.

[51] Romani, 1982, pp. 149–164.

[52] SAR, Camerlengato, Commercio, b. 319, Lettera di tre delegati della Camera di Commercio al Ministro del Commercio del 22 agosto 1854. Bonelli, 1961, pp. 73–74.

The articulation of the financial market due to the increased supply of securities, both public and private, favoured investment opportunities that were more profitable than the 4% that the *Cassa di Risparmio* paid its depositors. The internal placement of several public debt issues facilitated the purchase of 5% annuity bonds, which were also made attractive by stock market prices that remained below par for the entire decade.[53] Other investment opportunities were offered by anonymous companies established in Rome in the 1850s.[54] In this decade, there were 22 anonymous companies, whose total capital amounted to 18,670,000 scudi spread over 218,310 shares. Among such companies, the railway construction sector stood out, which alone accounted for 85% of the total share capital.

The dimensions of the Roman financial market were undoubtedly more modest than those of other Italian cities, such as Genoa, Turin or Milan, where the modernization process in those years was more pronounced.[55]

Due to fragmentary and nonhomogeneous archive sources, it is difficult to assess what effects the new investments had on production levels and on the Roman economy of the 1850s. However, one factor that must be considered is the presence of the names of well-known businessmen and members of the Roman nobility in the founding documents of the companies established in those years. In fact, excluding the railway company and the Anglo-Roman company for gas lighting, which were established primarily with foreign capital, the local financial elite was among the most active promoters of the most important commercial companies in recent years. Its presence was dominant in the insurance sector, where three companies operated, and in the mining sector, where the Roman Society of Iron Mines operated, one of the few companies remaining active in the aftermath of 1870.[56] The subscribers of these

[53] Starting in 1853, in addition to consolidated debt securities, the list of the Rome Stock Exchange reported the prices of redeemable debt certificates issued by the Treasury in the summer of 1850 for the withdrawal of paper money. Between 1855 and 1857, the series of public securities listed in Rome was enhanced by two new issues placed by the treasury on the domestic market (Giornale di Roma, 1850–1860).

[54] SAR, Camera di Commercio, bb. 40–41.

[55] Ministero di Agricoltura Industria e Commercio, (ed.) 1865.

[56] The Roman Society of Maritime and River Insurance began operations in 1851 although its statute was approved in 1847, and the Commercial Company for maritime insurance was founded in 1852 (SAR, Camera di commercio, b. 40; SAR, Camera di commercio b. 29).

companies include the names Rospigliosi, Borghese, Feoli and Costa, among those other prominent figures.

The decade preceding 1860 is important for understanding the evolution of the Roman stock market, which until then had been based on the quotations of Roman consolidated securities and since 1838 on those of the shares of the Pontifical Insurance Company.

4.2.1 The Stock Trend

Securities prices in this period vary from the second semester of 1849 to 1860.

That the primacy of the Roman consolidation and its trend was closely linked to the political and economic situation of the State was immediately evident when in 1848 share prices collapsed.

The decline of the two-year period 1850–1851 was followed by an expansion phase (approximately three years) and a recessive phase (1 year). In fact, the ration crisis of the two-year period 1853–1854 caused a serious shortage of representative or circulating values of any currency.[57] In this period, stock prices reached their minimum in 1855. After the critical period, there was an increase until 1859, the year before Unification, during which political tensions were the fundamental cause of a new fall in stock prices.[58] The considered period witnessed a substantial increase for the Roman market in listed securities due to the investment opportunity they represented for "the aristocracy".[59]

The redeemable debt certificates for the withdrawal of paper money constituted a valid alternative to the consolidation. The first trace was issued in 1850 and listed in 1853; in 1856, two additional traces appeared, the first with a nominal value of 100 scudi and the next at 50 scudi. While the first series was proposed with a nominal interest rate of 5%, the following series were proposed at 3%.[60]

For the first-issued annuity certificates, the year of greatest decline was 1855. Subsequently, until 1857, when this security was delisted from the stock exchange, the trend settled on values close to par.

[57] Caravale, Caracciolo, 1978.

[58] Giornale di Roma, 1858, n. 112, 19, May.

[59] SAR, Ministero delle finanze, b. 607.

[60] Giornale di Roma, Stock Exchange lists 1853–1856.

The second issue of the certificates exhibited a gradually decreasing trend.

In the insurance sector, the first listed title was that of the Privileged Pontifical Insurance Society. Its value was 500 scudi, of which only 100 had to be paid at the time of subscription. The stock maintained a constant trend until 1854, when its price decreased by 30%. It decreased by half the following year. The course of the quotations subsequently increased again, settling at approximately 80 scudi in 1859, the year the title was delisted. The other two listed insurance companies were the Roman Society of Maritime and River Insurance and the Rome Commercial Company for Maritime Insurance. The first, whose shares had a nominal value of 300 scudi and an effective value of 30 scudi, exhibited strong growth from 1851, the year of the listing, until 1854, the year of the crisis. Its values subsequently decreased, and the stock was delisted in 1857.

The second company, whose capital consisted of shares with a nominal value of 500 scudi and an effective value of 50 scudi, displayed a similar trend. Its value increased starting in 1852, the year of listing, until 1854, when it reached its maximum, whereupon it decreased in subsequent years. In September 1855, its effective value was 2/10 of its face value. The stock remained listed until May 1859.

The Bank of the Papal State, established in 1850, was listed on June 17, 1853. Its shares had a par value of 200 scudi, and the quotation series displays rapid growth in the price of the stock until the first half of 1854. Beginning in the second half of that year, the stock began to decline, reaching its nominal value at the beginning of 1855 and remaining there until the middle of the following year. The monetary tensions that had intensified at the end of 1854 and the consequent decrease in deposits were the fundamental reasons for the fall in price. The expansion phase of the title recommenced in 1856 and lasted until 1859. It was then slowed by the shock of political events, including the loss of legations by the State of the Church and its relative weakening on the international scene. The Roman Society of Iron Mine (Società Romana delle Mine di Ferro), whose shares had a nominal value of 100 scudi, similar to that of other listed securities, reached its lowest listed value in 1855; during the remainder of the period considered, after increasing to approximately 80 scudi, it remained stable; this trend is probably attributable to support measures by the Treasury, which held a good number of shares in this company.[61]

The *Regia Pontificia dei Sali e Tabacchi*, which beginning 1 January 1856 was administered autonomously by the government and no longer subject to a joint administration contract, was constituted with a fund of one million scudi divided into shares of 200 scudi each. Its price trend shows strong growth from March 1856 until the end of 1858, after which it reached its maximum. The following two-year period witnessed a sharp decline in the stock, the explanation for which could be linked to a contraction in the consumption of the goods the firm produced, as indicated by the decrease in indirect tax income from these goods during that period.[62]

The Anglo-Roman Society for Gas Lighting, established in 1852, was listed in 1857. Its shares, issued at 50 scudi, increased steadily in value for the entire decade under consideration. As noted in other parts of this work, this increase was due to the great importance the service sector was assuming in Rome, whose population was increasing annually.[63]

This company, created thanks to the contribution of foreign capital, is undoubtedly representative of the increasing significance of the Roman securities market, which nevertheless remained at an embryonic level compared to that of other Italian and European stock exchanges.

In the railway sector, the first company to list shares was the *Società delle Strade Ferrate Romane*, known as the *Pio Centrale Line*; its shares were valued at 500 francs, each equivalent to 92.94 scudi (at the usual exchange rate of 5.40 francs per scudo), but the shares were actually issued at only 150 francs.[64] The shares displayed a constant trend for the entire decade considered and then were delisted. The delisting was inevitable given the financial difficulties of the company, which was damaged by the loss of the Legations of the Roman State and by a decree of the government of Paris that prohibited the listing of securities not fully released on the Paris Stock Exchange.

[61] SAR, Camera di Commercio, b. 29.

[62] SAR, Computisteria della Reverenda Camera Apostolica, b. 237.

[63] SAR, Camera di Commercio, b. 40.

[64] Given the participation of French capital for the construction of the works, the documents relating to the establishment of this company were drawn up in both Italian and French; the establishment of the Anglo-Roman Society for Gas Lighting was similarly bilingual.

The so-called liberated shares were those of the same Pio Central Society, which issued securities in a ratio of one new share to two old shares on payment of 100 francs. The newly issued shares valued at 400 francs actually cost 250 francs each. These stocks also exhibited a constant trend throughout the period. Bonds valued at 500 francs but issued at 252.50 francs behaved similarly.

During this time span, another listed company was Pio Ostiense for the Saline d'Ostia. This company's presence in the listing testifies to the shareholding role played in it by the pontifical government. The company was noted for a moderate increase in the value of its listing.

The price data for Pio-Latina stock were too scarce for a significant trend to be identified; the company experienced ups and downs.

4.3 The Period 1860–1870

For the Italian stock exchanges, the 1860s were a period of profound uncertainty. A certain instability reigned throughout the Italian Peninsula for various reasons. On the one hand, as a corollary of the taxing political and economic fusion of the former autonomous Italian regions, the new Kingdom of Italy had to face difficulties with no immediate solution. On the other, to the Papal State, the approaching opening to the new territory, with a consequent lack of tranquillity and certainty (indispensable conditions for balanced financial and economic development) was increasingly evident. These factors could not fail to be reflected in "the mirror" of a country's economy: "On the other hand, the stock exchange is a device that measures and regulates the economic forces of a country and there is no fact or event that, directly or indirectly, is connected with the production, exchange or consumption of goods, or that directly or indirectly affects the conditions of private or public credit, which does not have an impact on the stock exchange".[65]

In the decade under consideration, the Rome Stock Exchange had a single main set of regulations, which replaced the previous one of 1854: the Regulation issued by Pope Pius IX on 23 July 1862.[66]

[65] Camaiti, 1996, p. 2.

[66] SAR. Camera di Commercio, b. 14.

It should be noted that as in all other stock exchange regulations forward contracts were not considered[67]; it is possible, however, that even if not legally recognized such contracts had their own illicit market.[68] As previously mentioned, in 1866, the figure of the moneychanger was formally introduced although initially moneychanging was not directly connected to stock exchange activity.[69]

The work of the moneychangers, however, also extended to other environments, as the interested parties themselves did not respect their limitations, invading both the sphere of stock exchange and banking activities, as evidenced by a currency exchange established by the Chamber of Commerce.[70]

Following the monetary reform of 1866 and the consequent replacement of the Roman scudo by the Italian lira, the stock exchange deputy, at the end of the same year, announced it was obligatory to operate using the new currency.[71]

The stock exchange listing represented an indispensable tool for the official securities market. It was the only secure source of information available regarding quotes, that is, the prices fixed by the confluence of demand (for money) and supply (of securities credit, shares and currency). "The point at which the buyer and seller meet forms the level of the exchange rate. Therefore, the price list does not fix but indicates this meeting point between the seller and the buyer, as the stone indicates the more or less high level of the course of the waters".[72] In this regard, Da Pozzo and Felloni write, "as is well known, stock market fluctuations are attributable to extremely numerous and variable factors, which can be roughly classified into two large groups: 1. intrinsic or particular factors, which concern exclusively the issuing company of the security and which directly affect its economic solidity, its income capacity and the volume of the free float; for government bonds (and those of public bodies in general), the situation of public finances, the prospects for

[67] Villani, 1964, pp. 25, 91.

[68] SAR, Camera di Commercio, b. 14 and 22.

[69] SAR, Camera di Commercio, b. 17, Notificazione del Ministero del Commercio e dei Lavori Pubblici, 20 July 1866.

[70] SAR, Camera di Commercio, b. 17.

[71] SAR, Camera di Commercio, b. 14.

[72] SAR, Congregazione economica (1815–1830), b. 134.

repayment of capital and for the payment of interest, etc. can be considered as such. Extrinsic or general factors affect the entire stock market and are connected with investment opportunities, with the availability and orientation of capital, with the monetary situation, etc. In reality, the intrinsic factors indirectly affect the entire stock market; any alteration in the profitability of a security modifies the pre-existing equilibrium, tending towards the equality of the average incomes envisaged for the various securities investments, and through speculation sets in motion a phenomenon of revision to restore the equilibrium, of course at different levels of profitability and therefore of quotations".[73]

As in much of past stock exchange history, the 1860s were accompanied by repeated rebellions and conflicts, which mainly occurred between two opponents; on the one hand, there were the brokers and stockbrokers, who demanded from the public authorities a more energetic fight against illegal activity within the profession[74]; on the other hand, there was the Chamber of Commerce, which blamed the middle class for the continuing shortcomings in transaction declarations and therefore the consequent lack of full validity of the stock exchange lists. After numerous appeals, the speaker of the chamber turned to the minister of the interior, asking for greater speed and incisiveness in punitive procedures.[75] A letter from the Minister of Commerce, dated 1869, announced the name and number of the brokers operating in the Roman square, trying in this way to neutralize interlopers and protect those who used the brokers.[76] In July 1869, in Rome, there were forty-eight "primary" and twenty-nine "secondary" brokers (at least officially; that is, in possession of the necessary operating licence), of which eleven were involved in wine and oil goods.

In 1870, the life of the Rome Stock Exchange did not conclude with the same epilogue as the Papal State. After that famous 20 September the trading of goods and securities continued under the authority of the new Italian government. The description of the Rome Stock Exchange that

[73] Da Pozzo and Felloni, 1964, p. 89.

[74] SAR, Camera di Commercio b. 17.

[75] SAR, Camera di Commercio, b. 17.

[76] Ibidem.

appeared on 29 January, 1871, in "L'Italia Economica", the Italian business newspaper, is highly instructive[77]; in it, one peculiarity of the Rome Stock Exchange emerges. In terms of importance, the Roman square, while ranking among the top Italian stock exchanges, never represented the top of the stock market pyramid. If in the nineteenth century it had to "submit" to the superiority and greater fame of the Genoa stock exchange, in the twentieth century, it will be dominated by that of Milan.

As they do today, stock market prices reacted negatively to political and military events that create instability and uncertainty. It is precisely these two elements, instability and uncertainty, that repeatedly hindered Roman investors during the transition from the Papal State to the Kingdom of Italy. How could one expect that after the reduction of the Papal State to Lazio alone or after major military battles or after the financial crisis of 1866 investors could be found willing to forgo safer uses of their money, such as investing it in land, to try a stock market adventure? With the end of the Papal State imminent, how could one hope to find holders of capital willing to purchase share packages in companies with little idea of what was in store for them in the new Italian context? To all this, we must also add the strong aversion to risk-taking of the few Roman capitalists. Often, the largest financial transactions of the decade were made by foreign investors who managed to find opportunities for profit in the Roman environment. An example was the Belgian De Merode, who was able to foster a wave of entrepreneurial and business ideas that encouraged the entry of economic and financial forces. These forces began to change certain features of the economic and urban face of Papal Rome as it neared its end.

It should also be remembered that the only company listed on the Rome Stock Exchange whose shares rose at the end of the decade was the Anglo-Roman Company (Table 4.6), which was funded primarily by English capital.

Already in this nineteenth-century stock exchange we can note a peculiarity that has persisted to the present: the formal freedom of access to stock market trading was only apparent. In essence, the stock exchange became an oligopolistic, closed and reserved market, as Weber states:

77 L'Italia Economica, n. 4, Rome-Naple, 29 January 1871.

> On a formal level, stock exchange trading can also be accessible to anyone, without any distinction, but the fact is that the private sector is excluded from it by a natural barrier, which prevents it from operating independently and successfully. What he [the investor] lacks, in fact, is a knowledge of the market that is acquired only with the profession, and which, in any case, for those who possess it, is in fact also the basis of their position of privilege. On the other hand, this means that only those who possess (or of whom it is known, in some way) a sufficient amount of credit can participate in the trade. Those who do not know the market or are not known to it (due to the fact of not operating permanently) must instead turn to professional merchants with strong capital and become their customers. A formal freedom of access does not serve to modify, but only to hide, this situation which is both real and necessary at the same time.[78]

Therefore, at this juncture, the Rome Stock Exchange, perhaps because it still belonged to a state other than the Italian one, presented rather rare characteristics. It could be said that it enjoyed a unique character compared to the other stock exchanges of the peninsula. The low number of economic subjects present, the simple and formal rules due to good faith in bargaining, and the absence of public security officials can be highlighted. The Roman business centre was comparable to "... a family reunion to sincerely conclude a deal".[79]

However, the already porous borders of the late 1860s were demolished on that famous 20 September, starting a process of homogenization and "globalization" of the Rome Stock Exchange and of the other Italian stock exchanges.

4.3.1 Stock Exchange Lists: 1860–1870

The following tables present the stock exchange lists from 1860 to 1870; they are adopted from the main daily newspaper of the time, the "Giornale di Roma",[80] which recounted the main events in politics, economics and other areas that occurred in the Papal State.

[78] Weber, 1924 (edited Tommasi 1995).

[79] SAR, Primaria Camera di Commercio b. 14.

[80] From the time of their introduction, the quotations of the Rome Stock Exchange were always published in the same newspaper, which, however, had different names over the years: until January 15, 1848, the quotations appeared in the «Diario di Roma»; from 17 January 1848 to 30 January 1849 in the «Gazzetta di Roma»; from 31 January

Table 4.2 Consolidato Romano: 5% interest

Year	*1° Sem*	*2° Sem*	*Annual*	*Variation (%)*
1860	78.045	75.192	**76.619**	
1861	63.748	69.928	**66.838**	**−12.766**
1862	66.910	66.815	**66.860**	**+0.033**
1863	66.860	66.256	**66.558**	**−0.452**
1864	66.490	70.480	**68.480**	**+2.289**
1865	71.508	71.088	**71.298**	**+4.115**
1866	65.733	59.300	**62.516**	**−12.317**
1867	56.782	57.351	**57.066**	**−8.718**
1868	57.639	59.105	**58.372**	**+2.289**
1869	62.621	66.357	**64.489**	**+10.479**
1870	67.951	59.021*	**63.486**	**−1.555**

*Until 17 September
Note The quotations of 1868–69–70 were originally in Italian lire; to facilitate temporal comparison, they have been converted into Roman scudi

Securities quotations[81] were published weekly, but for a better summary analysis, in this study, it was preferred to summarize them through half-yearly arithmetical averages to better reveal their trend.

The lists with the prices of securities, exchanges and currencies had a rather simple and essential form: they were limited to indicating the name of each item and the corresponding price.

During the considered decade, the number of listed securities did not vary much. The public securities quotations also included the prices of the Roman Consolidation and Treasury Certificates (Tables 4.2 and 4.3). In fact, six private companies were listed, one for each of the following economic components: salt and tobacco (Table 4.4), the bank of the pontifical state (Table 4.5), ironworking (Table 4.6), lighting (Table 4.7), railways (Table 4.8) and land reclamation (Table 4.9).

1849 to 6 July 1849 in the ‹‹Monitore Romano››; from 7 July 1849 to 17 September 1870 in the ‹‹Giornale di Roma››.

[81] Regarding the denominations of the securities, the original denominations that appeared on the price lists have been maintained.

Table 4.3 Treasury certificates: scudi 100 al 3%

Year	*1° Sem*	*2° Sem*	*Annual*	*Variation (%)*
1860	72.747	65.850	**69.298**	
1861	63.748	69.928	**66.838**	**−3.550**
1862	75.138	88.680	**81.910**	**+22.550**
1863	90.880	92.416	**91.648**	**+11.889**
1864	93.490	95.990	**94.740**	**+3.374**
1865	87.400	85.882	**86.641**	**−8.549**
1866	82.877	83.840	**83.358**	**−3.789**
1867	85.180	86.483	**85.831**	**+2.967**
1868	84.105	85.918	**85.011**	**−0.955**
1869	91.971	93.108	**92.540**	**+8.857**
1870	92.638	88.527*	**90.583**	**−2.115**

*Until 17 September
Note The quotations of 1868–69–70 were originally in Italian lire; to facilitate temporal comparison, they have been converted into Roman scudi

Table 4.4 Pontifical direction of salts and tobacco: shares: 200 scudi, 5% interest

Year	*1° Sem*	*2° Sem*	*Annual*	*Variation (%)*
1860	214.609	195.450	**205.029**	
1861	190.933	193.314	**192.124**	**−6.294**
1862	196.100	192.470	**194.290**	**+1.127**
1863	191.950	194.800	**193.375**	**−0.471**
1864	191.020	195.310	**193.160**	**−0.111**
1865	193.921	195.960	**194.940**	**+0.922**
1866	195.381	194.710	**195.045**	**+0.054**
1867	193.020	195.833	**194.426**	**−0.317**
1868	–	–	–	–
1869	–	–	–	–
1870	–	–	–	–

It should be noted that throughout the decade certain companies did not submit quotations but nevertheless continued to maintain their names on the stock exchange (e.g., the Privileged Pio latin Company that owned the railway line from Rome to Frascati; the Debt line from Rome to the Neapolitan border; the Maritime and fluviali commercial company of Rome).

Table 4.5 Bank of the pontifical state: shares: 200 scudi

Year	*1° Sem*	*2° Sem*	*Annual*	*Variation (%)*
1860	225.620	214.910	**220.266**	
1861	214.222	224.333	**219.277**	**−0.449**
1862	228.300	244.010	**236.150**	**+7.695**
1863	250.350	253.175	**251.762**	**+6.611**
1864	242.950	252.590	**247.770**	**−1.586**
1865	248.840	252.870	**250.850**	**+1.243**
1866	227.050	180.504	**203.780**	**−18.764**
1867	139.544	164.068	**151.806**	**−25.505**
1868	157.673	153.862	**155.767**	**+2.609**
1869	167.111	175.860	**171.486**	**+10.091**
1870	187.227	181.705*	**184.466**	**+7.569**

*Until 17 September

Note The quotations of 1868–69–70 were originally in Italian lire; to facilitate temporal comparison, they have been converted into Roman scudi

Table 4.6 Roman iron mining company: shares: 100 scudi, 5% interest

Year	*1° Sem*	*2° Sem*	*Annual*	*Variation (%)*
1860	81.800	81.115	**81.459**	
1861	80.468	79.910	**80.189**	**−1.559**
1862	79.680	79.480	**79.580**	**−0.759**
1863	82.400	77.337	**79.868**	**+0.362**
1864	64.910	65.100	**65.010**	**−18.603**
1865	51.155	44.165	**47.660**	**−26.688**
1866	47.150	44.198	**45.674**	**−4.167**
1867	38.219	31.096	**34.657**	**−24.121**
1868	21.339	24.558	**22.949**	**−33.782**
1869	23.256	23.617	**23.437**	**+2.126**
1870	24.457	–	**24.457**	**+4.352**

It should also be noted that after the introduction of the Italian lira in 1866, the values were no longer expressed in Roman scudi. However, to facilitate comparison over the years, it was determined to convert the securities prices into the old accounting unit: the Roman scudo (Table 4.10).

Table 4.7 Anglo-Roman company for gas lighting: shares: 50 scudi

Year	*1° Sem*	*2° Sem*	*Annual*	*Variation (%)*
1860	55.730	55.047	**55.388**	
1861	54.965	57.387	**56.176**	**+1.423**
1862	61.890	59.590	**60.740**	**+8.124**
1863	63.390	63.162	**63.276**	**+4.175**
1864	62.760	55.240	**58.990**	**−6.774**
1865	64.015	62.960	**63.490**	**+7.628**
1866	63.173	66.394	**64.783**	**+2.037**
1867	63.217	57.283	**60.250**	**−6.997**
1868	87.225	102.363	**94.794**	**+57.334**
1869	104.811	104.654	**104.732**	**+10.484**
1870	94.054	93.271*	**93.663**	**−10.569**

*Until 17 September

Note The quotations of 1868–69–70 were originally in Italian lire; to facilitate temporal comparison, they have been converted into Roman scudi

Table 4.8 Roman railway roads Pio Centrale Line: shares scudi 92.94 as franchi 500, interest fr. 25 all'anno

Year	*1° Sem*	*2° Sem*	*Annual*	*Variation*
1860	70.035	68.940	**69.488**	
1861	54.404	40.954	**47.679**	**−31.385**
1862	42.470	62.720	**52.600**	**+10.321**
1863	73.980	80.019	**76.999**	**+46.386**
1864	68.340	61.160	**64.750**	**−15.908**
1865	52.640	41.450	**47.050**	**−27.336**
1866	29.041	16.278	**22.659**	**−51.841**
1867	15.458	10.296	**12.877**	**−43.170**
1868	9.302	–	**9.302**	**−27.763**
1869	–	–	–	–
1870	–	–	–	–

Note The quotation of 1868 was originally in Italian lire; to facilitate temporal comparison, it has been converted into Roman scudi

Table 4.9 Pio Ostiense Company for the salt pans and remediation of the Ostia pond: shares franchi 500, sc. 92, 59

Year	*1° Sem*	*2° Sem*	*Annual*	*Variation (%)*
1860	59.314	50.838	**55.430**	
1861	38.854	41.758	**40.306**	**−27.285**
1862	49.220	45.270	**47.250**	**+17.228**
1863	46.740	47.335	**47.038**	**−0.449**
1864	44.760	48.720	**46.740**	**−0.634**
1865	44.060	51.610	**47.840**	**+2.353**
1866	52.770	46.016	**49.393**	**+3.246**
1867	34.932	34.772	**34.852**	**−29.439**
1868	36.041	40.206	**38.124**	**+9.388**
1869	33.915	31.150	**32.532**	**−14.668**
1870	24.444	20.093*	**22.258**	**−31.581**

*Until 17 September

Note The quotations of 1868–69–70 were originally in Italian lire; to facilitate temporal comparison, they have been converted into Roman scudi

Table 4.10 Fluctuation in securities prices over the decade 1860–1870

Securities listed on the stock exchange	*1860*	*1870**	*Variation over the decade (%)*
Roman consolidated	76.619	63.486	−17.141
Treasury Certificates of sc. 200	69.298	90.583	+30.715
Pontifical Direction De 'Sali e Tabacchi; shares of sc. 200	205.029	194.29[a]	−5.171
Bank of the Pontifical State; shares of sc. 200	220.266	184.466	−16.253
Roman Society of Iron Mines; shares of sc. 100	81.459	24.46[b]	−69.976
Anglo-Roman Society for Gas Lighting; shares of sc. 50	55.388	93.663	+69.103
Via Ferrate Company, Pio Centrale Line; shares of sc. 92, 94	69.488	9.30[c]	−86.613
Pio Ostiense Society for the Salt Pans of Ostia and reclamation of the Stagno di Ostia; shares of 500 French francs	55.430	22.258	−59.845

*Until 20 September

[a]The quotation refers to 1867 (last available)

[b]The price refers to the 1st half of 1870 (last available)

[c]The price refers to the 1st half of 1868 (last available)

References

Bonelli, Franco. 1961. *Il commercio estero dello Stato Pontificio nel secolo XIX*, Rome: Archivio Economico dell'Unificazione Italiana", S.I., vol. XI.

Camaiti, Romolo. 1996. *Borse valori in Italia e in Europa*, Padoa: Cedam.

Capalbo, Cinzia. 1995. Dal proibizionismo al monopolio. L'istituzione della privativa del tabacco nello Stato pontificio in età moderna. *Roma moderna e contemporanea*, III (1): 173–199.

Caravale, Mario, and Alberto Caracciolo. 1978. *Lo Stato pontificio. Da Martino V a Pio IX*, Torino: Utet.

Corti, Egon. 1950. *La casa Rothschild*, Milan: Mondatori.

Da Pozzo, Mario, and Giuseppe Felloni. 1964. *La borsa valori di Genova nel secolo XIX*, Archivio Economico dell'Unificazione Italiana, s II, vol. X, Genoa.

Fatica, Michele. 1973. Nicolas Micard nel quadro delle operazioni economiche e politiche francesi nello Stato Pontificio nell'età di Gregorio XVI e di Pio IX, *Annuario dell'Istituto Storico Italiano per l'età moderna e contemporanea*, Rome: Tip. Castaldi, 1969–1970, vols. 21–22.

Felisini, Daniela. 1990. *Le finanze pontificie e i Rothschild (1830–1870)*, Naples: Edizioni Scientifiche Italiane.

Felisini, Daniela. 1993. Le finanze pontificie nell'ottocento tra inquietudine politico-sociale e crisi economica, in Antonio Di Vittorio (ed.) *La finanza in età di crisi*, Bari: Cacucci, 181–211.

Felloni, Giuseppe. 1971. *Gli investimenti finanziari genovesi in Europa tra il Settecento e la Restaurazione*, Milan: Giuffrè.

Lodolini, Armando. 1956. *I «Monti» camerali nel sistema della finanza pontificia*, «Archvi storici delle aziende di credito», vol. I Associazione bancaria italina (ed.): 263–278.

Masini, Roberta. 2005. *Il debito pubblico pontificio a fine Seicento. I monti camerali*, Rome: Edimond.

Morandi, Mario. 1933. Le condizioni economiche dello Stato pontificio al tempo della Repubblica Romana (1848–1849), *Rivista italiana di statistica, economia e finanza*, V(3), XI: 490–545.

Kindleberger Charles P. 1987. *Le crisi finanziarie*, in Charles P. Kindleberger (ed.), *Storia della finanza nell'Europa occidentale*, Milano, Cariplo Laterza, 367–389.

Ostuni, Nicola. 1992. *Finanze ed economia nel Regno delle due Sicilie*, Nales: Liguori Editore.

Pepoli Napoleone, Gioacchino. 1858. Il debito pubblico pontificio. Lettera al Conte Costa della Torre, *Rivista contemporanea*, XIV(6): 120–125.

Piola Caselli, Fausto. 1988. *La diffusione dei luoghi di monte della Camera Apostolica alla fine del XVI secolo. Capitali investiti e rendimenti*, in *Credito e sviluppo economico in Italia dal medio evo all'età contemporanea*, Atti del

primo convegno nazionale della SISE (Verona 4–6 giugno 1987), Verona, 191–216.
Romani, Marzio. 1982. *Storia economica d'Italia nel secolo XIX*, Bologna: Il Mulino.
Strangio, Donatella. 1994. Debito pubblico e riorganizzazione del mercato finanziario nello Stato ecclesiastico del '700, *Roma moderna e contemporanea* II(1): 179–202.
Strangio, Donatella. 1997. *L'economia dello Stato pontificio tra il 1860–1870*, in Fiorella Bartoccini and Donatella Strangio (eds.) *Lo Stato del Lazio. 1860–1870*, Rome: Istituto Nazionale di Studi Romani, 147–187.
Villani, Pasquale. 1964. *La vendita dei beni nello Stato del Regno di Napoli (1806–1815)*, Milan: Banca Commerciale Italiana.
Weber, Max. 1924. Die Borse, in *Gesammelte Aufsätze zur Soziologie und Sozialpolitik*, Tübingen, Mohr, trad. it. Claudio, Tommasi. 1985. *La borsa*, Milan: Unicopli.

Sources

State Archive of Rome (SAR):
Bandi b.312.
Camerale II, Debito pubblico, b. 8, fasc. 5; b. 14, fasc. 3 and 4.
Congregazione economica (1815–1830), b.134.
Camerlengato, Commercio, b. 319.
Camerlengato, parte II, Annona e Grascia b. 766.
Camera di Commercio, bb. 14, 17, 22, 29, 40, 41.
Computisteria della Reverenda Camera Apostolica, b. 237.
Consulta di stato, b. 2.
Direzione generale del debito pubblico, b. 2854.
Ministero delle Finanze, bb. 551, 607, 635.
Tesorierato generale, titolo I, affari generali, bb. 277, 279.

Edited Sources

Diario di Roma, a.1830 n.61, 30 July.
Diario di Roma, a.1838 supplement n.43, 28/05/1838.
Stock exchange list (roman newspaper):
1821 to 15 January 1848 in Diario di Roma.
From 17 January 1848 to 30 January 1849 in Gazzetta di Roma.
From 31 January 1849 to 6 July 1849 in Monitore Romano.
From 7 July to 17 September 1870 in Giornale di Roma.
L'Italia Economica, n.4, Rome-Naple, 29 January 1871.
Bollettino delle leggi, 1849, decreto del 26 marzo 1849, pp. 211–213.

Ministero di Agricoltura Industria e Commercio (ed.) 1865. *Bollettino Industriale del Regno d'Italia*, Rome: MAIC.
Raccolta delle leggi e disposizioni di pubblica amministrazione nello Stato pontificio, I, Roma, Stamperia della R.C.A., 1834.
Raccolta delle leggi e disposizioni di pubblica amministrazione nello Stato pontificio, II, Roma, Stamperia della R.C.A., 1848.
Bollettino delle leggi, proclami, regolamenti e altre disposizioni della Repubblica Romana, Rome, 1849.
Raccolta delle leggi e disposizioni di pubblica amministrazione nello Stato pontificio, VIII, Roma, Stamperia della R.C.A., 1854.
Raccolta delle leggi e disposizioni di pubblica amministrazione nello stato pontificio emanate nel pontificato della Santità di nostro signore papa Pio IX°. Volume XXIII° dal 1 gennaio 1869 al 20 settembre 1870, 1871.

CHAPTER 5

The Stock Exchange and the Roman Financial Market from the Annexation of Italy to the Great War (1870–1914)

The globalization of the world economy did not necessarily go hand in hand with the abolition of trade barriers: the historical period 1870–1914 was characterized by the opening of the world following the revolution that occurred in transport and communications, by migratory waves, by the free movement of capital that accompanied the birth of the colonial empires and by the ability of the great powers of the time to extend their direct and indirect dominion over a large part of the world (Cassis 2008). Rome and the "State" must be viewed in this context. In the decade following the annexation of part of the papal territory to Italy, with respect to the Papal State's trading exchange, prices were low and discontinuous except for banking sector securities. In Italy, from 1871 to 1873, a lively increase in industrial activity, especially in the northern regions, prompted conspicuous construction and urban growth by attracting labour from the countryside, accompanied by steadily increasing financial and banking activity. This growth was interrupted by an international crisis that reinforced the idea of greater state intervention, especially in the area of customs. Following this crisis, changes occurred in government economic policy and in the financial structures of various countries, including Italy. As said by Jeremy Atack, some institutional designs have worked better than others. As financial innovations work their way through the exiting financial institutions and

D. Strangio, *The Roman Stock Exchange between the 19th and 20th Centuries*, Palgrave Studies in the History of Finance,
https://doi.org/10.1007/978-3-031-00359-2_5

structures, crises have occurred (Atack 2009). Each Time, critics have railed against the innovations that appear to have played a role in the crisis, arguing that the unseemly profits for the early innovators could not be justified by the real contribution to the economy (Atack 2009, p. 5). But it is important to look to the past to understand what lessons to draw for the present and the future in the financial and stock market fields (Neal 2009).

5.1 The Age of the First Globalization

Cassis argues that the historical period 1870–1914 was characterized by the opening of the world following the revolution that occurred in transport and communications, by migratory waves, by the free movement of capital that accompanied the birth of the colonial empires and by the ability of the great powers of the time to extend their direct and indirect dominion over a large part of the world. In particular, the political and economic environment prior to 1914 was especially favourable to the development of international financial centres.[1]

Also Cassis, examining eight global financial crises since the late nineteenth century, offers insights into how the financial landscape—banking, governance, regulation, international cooperation and balance between partners—has or has not been reshaped after a systemic shock (Cassis 2008).[2]

The first wave of globalization following the consolidation and spread of the capitalist economic system was characterized by several important factors: (a) flows of exported capital; (b) closer integration between international financial centres and (c) an increase in the number of international financial centres.[3] In particular, the construction of railway lines, which began in the 1830s, continued on an increasingly large scale, bringing the total kilometres of railway tracks worldwide from 205,000 in 1870 to 925,000 in 1906; maritime transport also made considerable

[1] Cassis, 2008b, p. 89.

[2] At the Italian level see among others: Pecorari, 2006; Conti, Cova and La Francesca, 2017. Cassis and Schenk, 2021, invite us to know and learn from financial crises and how the past is used by financial crises and what impacts they produce, in a series of public and private contexts, in order to intervene and correct distortions.

[3] Cassis, 2008b, p. 90.

progress, thanks to steam navigation, which established itself in the 1890s, when steamship tonnage exceeded that of sailing ships.[4]

The globalization of the world economy did not necessarily go hand in hand with the abolition of trade barriers: between 1880 and 1914, there was an increase in protectionism after a period of free trade that had been initiated by the Cobden Chevalier treaty between France and England in 1860.[5] Paul Bairoch observed that foreign trade increased faster during the protectionist phase than during the free trade phase, a paradox that Bairoch explains by the fact that economic growth was stronger during the protectionist period.[6] The characteristics of this globalized economy had repercussions for the international financial centres. For example, beyond its economic and sociocultural impact, emigration furnished a supply of talented individuals who enriched the financial centres and other areas. Furthermore, the growth of trade resulted in an increase in international trade activity (particularly in the major squares), while the transport revolution not only supported trade growth but also required substantial investments that only the large financial centres were able to undertake.

5.2 The Quotations of 1870–1880

Rome and the "State" must be viewed in this context. In the decade following the annexation of part of the papal territory to Italy, with respect to the Papal State's trading exchange, prices were low and discontinuous except for banking sector securities.

In Italy, from 1871 to 1873, a lively increase in industrial activity, especially in the northern regions, prompted conspicuous construction and urban growth by attracting labour from the countryside, accompanied by steadily increasing financial and banking activity.[7]

This growth was interrupted by an international crisis that reinforced the idea of greater state intervention, especially in the area of customs. Following this crisis, changes occurred in government economic policy, and with the fall from power of the historical Right and the rise of the

[4] Cassis, 2008b, p. 91.

[5] Pollard, 1981.

[6] Bairoch 1976.

[7] Izzo, 1962; Jacini, 1867.

historical Left, there was a shift from a liberal approach to a more protectionist orientation, in line with what was occurring in the rest of Europe and the globalized world of that time.[8]

The "great depression" of 1873 (as defined by Anglo-Saxon economists), lost its momentum as early as 1878, when a recovery began that by 1880 reached higher levels of production in postunification Italian economic development. Rome too began to change: after 20 September 1870, it found itself fulfilling the role of capital of a Kingdom, one much larger than the Papal State, to which until then it had belonged from a temporal perspective; the city, therefore, underwent several profound transformations.[9]

At the time of unification, Rome presented a degraded urban framework, which was unsuitable as a backdrop for the government of a young Kingdom; there was a lack of housing, which became especially insufficient when after the city's selection as capital it attracted numerous new inhabitants.[10]

Thus, a speculative construction fervour was triggered that lasted until 1873, when Rome was afflicted by an economic crisis, which substantially slowed work to enlarge the city.

With the fading of the crisis of 1876 and in particular starting in 1878, the impulse for construction resumed. As Caracciolo wrote, it is unknown who first used the term "building fever" to describe the life of the city of Rome at that particular historical moment, but it is certain that for approximately eight years the city experienced what could be termed a frenzy in the area of business and building speculation.[11] The special laws for Rome (in particular that of 20 May 1881 n.209 and that of 1883)[12] combined with loans and the help of the state fuelled this business euphoria. Undoubtedly, however, the growth had originated in the early 1870s, when the activity in Rome of several financial groups intensified, causing property and building prices to increase in the manner of a race

[8] Toniolo, 1992; see also Cassis, 2008a.

[9] Regarding Cavour's decision to proclaim Rome the national capital, cf. above all Chabod, 1997, pp. 179–209; Galasso, 1970, pp. 71–92; Aquarone, 1972, pp. 215–279; Romeo, 1984, pp. 921–930; Vidotto, 1997, pp. 7–20; Viarengo, 2010, pp. 465–467. Also see Formica 2021.

[10] Insolera, 1995.

[11] Caracciolo 1984, p. 169.

[12] Caracciolo, 1984, pp. 173–176. See also Ciampani, 1998, pp. 483–504.

to the top to avoid dangerous immobilizations.[13] Several companies were involved in designing the new urbanization of Rome, such as Mariotti & Frontini and Moroni. The company Moroni Brothers[14] is an emblematic case from this period. Moroni was one of the major companies engaged in the Roman industry of brick production, which even in the years of the crisis (lasting approximately ten years from 1888 to 1899) played a leading role in national production; established on 17 May 1886, as stated in article 3 of its deed of constitution, the company should have had a life of 3 years.[15] In reality, its activities lasted until 1893 as the serious crisis in the capital's construction industry and the uncertainty of land buyers blocked the mechanism for increasing the prices of building areas and caused such companies to buy and sell land using bank credit, which during the period of the building boom seemed inexhaustible.[16] This phenomenon helps clarify the objectives of this company: to obtain profits in the short term. Although involved in this crisis, thanks to its relations with several large banks and major Piedmontese financial groups, the company was helped by the Bank Nazionale del Regno and managed to obtain the support of the concordat. The complex management circumstances that ensued reflected the need to protect the capital linked to the Piedmontese financial world. The other mentioned company, Mariotti & Frontini, was a construction company that like Moroni engaged in buying and selling land and in building construction in the decades following Rome's proclamation as Italy's capital. However, it did not undertake other activities in the sector, such as the supply of building materials, as Moroni did. Another difference is that Mariotti & Frontini did not extend its business to the east (Prati district) and to the north (Parioli district) but to the south into the areas of Testaccio, San Paolo and Villa Walkonsky, where its interests were concentrated. Like Moroni, this company was financed by capital belonging to banking groups of northern origin. However, Mariotti & Frontini was also supported by Ugo Geisser, a leader of the financial and banking world of the Kingdom of Italy and member of the Board of Governors of the Bank of Italy as well as of

[13] Caracciolo 1984, pp. 169–176.

[14] Alessandro, Scipione and Giuseppe Moroni were born in Cori and lived in Rome (SAR, Tribunale del Commercio di Roma, Atti di società, b. 414).

[15] SAR, Tribunale del Commercio di Roma, Atti di società, b. 414.

[16] Ibidem.

the Compagnia Fondiaria Italiana. Another difference is that Mariotti & Frontini operated nearly exclusively in the field of public construction, while Moroni specialized in private construction.[17]

At the end of the 1870s, Roman trade appeared to be in full recovery and expanding.[18]

The securities that managed to endure within the fragile Roman stock exchange belonged to the banking sector: behind the construction, industrial and commercial activity was a complicated movement of capital, as Rome had attracted considerable liquid assets not only from other regions of Italy (e.g., Piedmont, Lombardy, Liguria, Tuscany, Veneto) but also from abroad, creating a significant turnover.[19]

Until 1870, Rome had never been a major banking centre. With Rome's definitive designation as Italy's capital, the Bank of the Papal State, established in 1851, changed its name to *Banca Romana* and strengthened its activity as a circulation, deposit and discount bank. As of 30 September 1880, it represented only the fifth-largest bank of circulation in the Kingdom of Italy, after the National Bank, the Banks of Naples and Sicily and the *Banca Nazionale Toscana*.

After 1870, the banking structure of the capital was enhanced by the presence of ordinary credit banks, among which the Italo-Germanic Bank and the Italo-Austrian Bank stood out in importance, followed by the General Bank and the General Real Estate Credit Company, a group extended by new institutes in the following years (Fig. 5.1).

Rome in 1870 was the scene of a new system of interests and activities in the area of production and labour that helped break down the customs and political barriers that isolated the city. The doors were opened to goods, men and ideas.

As previously noted, from the north, representatives of the capitalist and industrial world began to arrive, individuals who viewed Rome as an attractive place for investment.

The "Romans" found themselves having to face not only the loss of ancient occupations and forms of assistance following the demise of the "paternalistic" attitude, which had constituted a kind of charity

[17] Historical Archive of the Bank of Italy, Liquidazioni, Pratt., c.13, fasc. 1; Liquidazioni, Ufficio Legale Pratt., c. 209, fasc. 1.

[18] Bonelli, 1961.

[19] Fenoaltea, 2006.

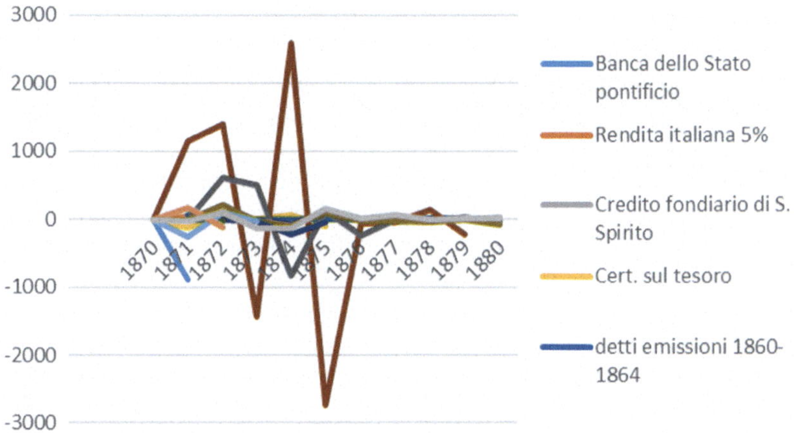

Fig. 5.1 Main listed banks (*Source* "La Tribuna", daily newspaper, Giorn.104, Library of the Senate of the Italian Republic "Giovanni Spadolini"; several years)

on the part of the previous papal government, but also competition from "immigrants" (capitalists and shopkeepers) who did not offer work but, rather, worked themselves or were seeking employment. As of 31 December1871, Rome had 244,484 inhabitants, Turin 212,644, Milan 199,009 and Palermo 219,398, whereas Naples alone, capital of the old Kingdom of Naples, had 448,335 residents. The population in Rome doubled between 1871 and 1901 and tripled by 1921.[20]

Immigrants contributed to the severe and sudden collapse, even in sectors that had been vital under the papal government. A large number of artisans and merchants of consumer goods or artistic objects were supplanted by the arrival of numerous new shopkeepers and merchants, who not only offered the products of "perfected" northern industry but also introduced new needs and sales systems.[21]

Unemployment affected the servant class and, more generally, all those who lived under the protection of a family as the demand for this type of employee decreased due both to a general reduction in overall disposable

[20] Martinelli, 1964; Comune di Roma, 1872, 1960.

[21] Martinelli, 1964, pp. 42–43 and 57–58.

income available to support former standards of living and the closure of large noble palaces.[22]

Only those who possessed property, agricultural and real-estate income and solid assets managed to survive the first crisis, in certain cases; thanks to marriages and other alliances of interest.

For those who lived on income from work alone, the failure was aggravated by the increase in the cost of living. Among the most sought-after professionals were medical doctors in addition to engineers and architects who could contribute to building the new Rome.

The circumstances were aggravated by increased taxes and the introduction of new taxes. In addition to other consumer duties, the ground tax affected everyone. The average tax burden of the Roman population increased from approximately 16 lire per person under the popes to 40 (in Milan, approximately 30; in Turin, just over 20; in Naples, 25). In the early phase of this period of increased tax burden, the Romans failed to understand the meaning of taxation, the main features of the new government, and the citizen-state relationship, particularly because they saw little return for their contributions, certainly less than those formerly guaranteed by the pontiff. The tax burden was a cause of protest and rebellion, as was pro-papal propaganda. Petitions were circulated calling for the abolition of certain taxes.

As previously argued, another problem, already difficult at the time of Pius IX, was that of housing. The city continued to become increasingly crowded. People lived where there was any free space, even if small and uncomfortable. The doubling and tripling of rents were inevitable. Most of the population, having lost nearly all forms of public assistance, was in painful circumstances. The number of Romans reduced to begging, that is, accustomed to daily aid, increased considerably. Under the popes, this segment of the population had never fallen to this degree of misery because the cost of food and housing was kept low and the papal welfare system of charity alleviated the most urgent needs. To the poor of the city were now added the peasants of the surrounding countryside, directly or indirectly overwhelmed by the agrarian crisis as well as by the confusion generated by the advent of private property.[23]

[22] Friz, 1980, 1972; Bocci, 1999, pp. 125–146.

[23] Giordano, 1871; Piccialuti, 1991, pp. 367–380; Strangio 1997, pp. 149–187.

After the transition, the Romans encountered a new range of occupations required by the changed economic and productive system. The influx of tourists inspired by the appeal of the city, Italy's capital, a metropolis, was enhanced by a significant improvement in the railway network, which favoured both individual and group transportation.

The non-native population increased from 10.7% in 1870 to 13% in 1881.

One began to speak of a mixed generation and above all one free from ancient structural and behavioural bonds.

The population increase gave rise to a new spirit of commerce and consumption, such that Gabriele D'Annunzio could write, "the shop window invades the city".[24]

Rome became a suitable place for encounters between different forces and interests, and it opened up other spaces of contact and understanding between financial groups in close connection with the government and central administrative circles. Various credit, social security and insurance institutions were established with headquarters and branches and with representatives from strong European institutions (such as the Italo-Germanic Bank and the Italo-Austrian Bank).[25]

Additionally, in Rome, as was occurring in the rest of the peninsula, the demand for housing was increasing, which attracted investment in the form of both large capital and small savings. In Rome, the economy of those years was characterized by the strong link between building investments and the credit sector. Private bankers and joint-stock companies operated by making loans to builders but also intervened in various ways in the sale of land and by founding real-estate companies.

As for the industrial sector of the 18 wool factories still existing in 1870 eight years later only 8 remained and of the 1,240 workers only 21.

Tobacco manufacturing ranked first, a state-owned industry like the mint, followed by paper and printing, which supplied not only the church but also the new government.[26] The railways were the exception in the metalworking field. At the end of the decade, 4,000 workers were employed in the industry.[27] In the agricultural sector, there were changes

[24] Castelli, 1913, p. 57 and pp. 48–52.

[25] D'Errico, 1999.

[26] Capalbo, 1995, p. 185; Capalbo, 1999.

[27] Martinelli, 1964, p. 57.

in ownership, reductions in the number of underemployed and a dispersion of collective goods. The legislation of the Kingdom was extended to the city of Rome. Thus, the rule of conservative senators was replaced by that of an elected mayor and municipal council. For a long time, interest and discussion focussed on the problems of the city of the new regime, whereby the government's relations with the Holy See, i.e., of liberals with Catholics, remained a constant theme.

5.3 The Quotations of 1880–1890

In the following decade (1880–1890), there was an increase in the number of listed companies and their prices, especially in the middle years of the decade, when national and special laws as well as innovations encouraged the speculative and operational activity of the previously noted firms.

After 1880, there were 21 newly listed companies, representing exponential growth for the nineteenth-century market. By 1883, there were 30 companies, which became 43 by 1890.[28] In a decade, the number of listed companies doubled, with growth of over 100%. The interests of credit institutions in fact coincided with those of public service companies. However, the companies that actually moved the market were the construction companies expanding Rome's urban structure, which in this way gave impetus to service companies, such as those providing water, gas, lighting and credit.

Urban expansion, free and feverish, benefited both the construction and the services sectors while encouraging activity in other sectors, as the price values indicate. All sectors that were not involved in construction, credit and urban services created a real market for small companies. Their prices have much lower values, and when the Vatican markets and the national income are compared with respect to the prices of Roman services, such as water and lighting, Roman prices are approximately 10 times lower. The "Vatican" titles survived more for their historicity and as representatives of a sort of religious ethic than for their actual commercial value. The same argument could be valid for the national income, while for the other securities, given their poor listing and marketing record, it is difficult to outline a trend.

[28] "La Tribuna", daily newspaper, Giorn.104, Library of the Senate of the Italian Republic "Giovanni Spadolini"; several years.

Another peculiarity of the Roman market was the monopoly in the expanding sectors: the Banco di Roma controlled local capital, while Vatican finance controlled services; here certainly the political power of the Vatican and the Roman bourgeoisie managed to defend themselves at least in part from the sectors that could potentially mount real competition and/or from the total hegemony of foreign capital; it must, however, be remembered how advanced the convergence of these two groups was by now.[29]

The issuing banks represented the creditors and moderators of the economic forces operating in Rome. There were 10 Italian and foreign banks and 5 land companies. Companies that supplied gas, water and lighting included *Acqua Marcia* for water distribution and Omnibus for public transport.

Between 1881 and 1883, there was an increase in the number of credit institutions and an increase in their prices until 1887; for example, in 1880, the Tiberina Bank possessed real-estate assets of 2 million lire, which increased within a few years to five and a half million lire.[30]

From 1887 onwards, there was a slight but constant decline, which was a clear prelude to crisis. Small and large savers suddenly found themselves holding securities that formerly had a high value and that now suddenly collapsed. For example, real-estate securities listed at 1,260 lire per share in 1887 decreased in 1892 to 114 lire (see Fig. 5.2). The maximum point of movable development was reached in 1886–1887; constant growth characterized the first five years, whereas a slight and constant loss of value characterized the last 2 or 3 years.

The decade can be divided into 3 phases. The first, from 1880 to 1883, was characterized by growth in the number of companies. In 1880, there were 21 companies. At the end of 1883, there were 36. As noted in a previous chapter, this period was marked by the establishment of the new Chamber of Commerce, and special laws were enacted. The market was opened to new capital, and there was strong growth in the number of new investors.[31] The stock market was heavily influenced by the policies of the new government. The government evaluated the potential of the Roman market and issued laws aimed at creating new regulations in the movable

[29] Pollard, 2005, pp. 65–67.

[30] Palermo, 2006.

[31] Astraldi, 1956.

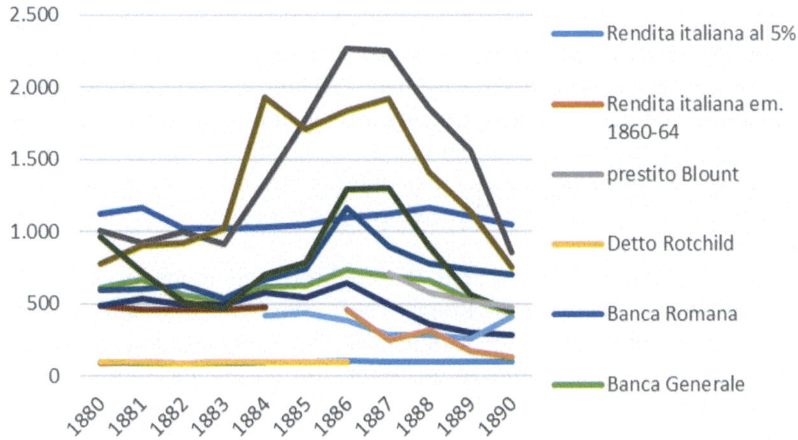

Fig. 5.2 Trend of the main securities of listed banks (*Source* "La Tribuna", giornale quotidiano, Giorn.104, Biblioteca del Senato della Repubblica "Giovanni Spadolini"; several years)

sector and special laws designed to support Rome's urban development (such as, for example, the law of 14 May 1881 n. 209).

The second phase, 1884–1888, was characterized by strong monopolies on the part of the companies in their respective sectors. Only in the banking field was there any competition. At this juncture, the market consisted of 42 companies, of which only 12 drove the Roman market and were marketed. The highest quotations were achieved by service companies supplying primary goods, such as water, gas and lighting. Several service companies even achieved quotations four times higher than those of banks.

From 1888 to 1890, there was a generalized decrease in securities prices. After 1887, the prices of securities began to decline slowly, then more suddenly. The market also started to list shares that a few years earlier had not received interest from investors because they belonged to sectors other than construction, services and credit.

At the end of the considered decade, it was evident that the most prudent investors of the time understood how, even in the face of a crisis, the most expansive companies, e.g., *AngloRomana a gas* and *Antica Acqua Marcia*, still guaranteed gains higher than any losses.

This mechanism went hand in hand with the construction fever, which lasted as long as the bills could be discounted abroad. However, when this chain was interrupted, Capitoline economic growth suddenly stopped. One by one, the builders were called on to pay their bills in cash: all went bankrupt and consequently dragged the banks down with them; the first bank to fail was *Banca Tiberina* in 1890, which had been one of the major promoters of Rome's urban and economic growth; the bank that experienced the greatest repercussions was *Banca Romana*, which also had to cope with the excessive inflation, given its function as regulator of paper money.[32]

5.4 The Quotations of 1890–1900

In the following decade (1890–1900), the number of listed securities consolidated at approximately fifteen. An interesting fact is that nearly all the companies on the lists were from the local Roman market, with the exception of certain banking securities, as previously noted, such as the General Bank and, starting in 1891, the Mediterranean Railways and the Southern Railways.[33]

The securities as well as the Roman economic and financial system of the late 1890s were influenced by a financial crisis that involved all of Italy and by a construction crisis that resulted in the collapse of several banking institutions.

For the Roman stock market, these events translated into a stasis if not a reduction in the volume of trading and listed securities, as also underlined in the financial reports of the newspaper "La Tribuna".[34]

The number of listed companies reached eighteen in 1891 and then decreased until 1897, the year growth resumed. Two periods can be identified: the first starts at the end of the 1880s and lasts until 1896 and

[32] Graziani, 1995.

[33] Confalonieri, 1982, vol. II, pp. 268; La Francesca, 1965. About Mediterranea see Deslex, 1914; http://www.lombardiabeniculturali.it/archivi/soggetti-produttori/ente/MIDB000D10/.

[34] The data were collected by the newspaper "La Tribuna" at the library of the Senate in Rome. They are weekly quotations (every Friday) published on the Rome Stock Exchange. The same newspaper points out that since 1913 the quotations of the securities were suspended due to the outbreak of the First World War. These will resume starting from December 1918.

during which the effects of the economic-financial crisis are evident; the other starts in 1897 with a resumption of trading and listed securities with the presence of new companies of national importance, which also registered their prices on other stock exchanges of the peninsula, such as Genoa and Milan.[35]

Between the beginning and the end of the decade, the number and type of listed companies varied. In 1899, there were thirty companies that had at least one listing during the year (compared to eighteen in 1891), sixteen of which concerned the local market, while fourteen were of national relevance. There were ten companies that displayed a certain continuity throughout the decade: *Rendita Italiana, Banca Generale, Banco di Roma, Ferrovie Mediterranee, Ferrovie Meridinali, Società dell'Acqua Marcia, Società Angloromana Gas, Società Condotte Acqua, Società Rinascimento Napoli* and *Società Omnibus tramway*.

Regarding banking and real-estate companies (e.g., *Banco di Roma, Banca Tiberina, Banca Romana, Banca Generale, Banca Industria e Commercio* and *Società Generale Immobiliare*), from 1890 to 1895, these firms exhibited a downward trend, which then led to the financial crisis of 1897. In accordance with the law of 1874, Bank Romana held the privilege of issuing paper money together with other banking institutions. As a consequence of the serious scandals of 1893, which highlighted a heavy debt situation, the bank was liquidated. The liquidation contributed to a reorganization of the issuing system, which in 1894 resulted in the creation of the Bank of Italy; in the following years, this bank would also see its securities listed on the Roman square.[36]

5.5 Prices and the Period 1900–1910

In the early years of the twentieth century, united Italy began to reduce its economic gap with the most industrially advanced countries; thanks to a significant increase in industrial production.[37] In certain large industrial sectors, Taylorist systems of work organization were introduced. In this initiative, the state played a fundamental role: customs protectionism and tariff policies together with active participation through orders and

[35] Da Pozzo, Felloni, 1964; De Luca, 2002.

[36] Negri, 1989; Cardarelli, 1990; Bonelli, 1991.

[37] Gehering and Fohlin, 2006; Fohlin, 2008; Fohlin and Reinhold, 2010.

support to private industry in the form of requests for public works and for military supplies.[38] In this way, the state sought to redistribute wealth while guaranteeing Italy's political and social stability. The circumstances in the countryside were different: here, backwardness contributed to creating a large reservoir of low-cost labour that could be poured into industry and the tertiary sector; the only alternative was emigration, which in those years was high.[39]

This development was characterized from the outset by heavy imbalances, the most serious of which was the territorial imbalance, i.e., the north–south economic dualism, accentuated by protectionism.[40] The industrial fabric formed in a nonhomogeneous way, concentrating in the "industrial triangle" (Milan, Turin, Genoa). Thus, the southern question emerged as one of the great problems of Italian society.[41]

As even this brief examination reveals, the Italian economy, after overcoming the Great Depression and the increase in prices, thanks to the policy of an increasingly active state presence, was the protagonist of an increase in investments necessary to attract foreign capital.[42] There was a climate of optimism and trust that spanned all of Europe in this period referred to as the Belle Époque, which lasted until the beginning of the First World War.[43] Furthermore, labour productivity in the Giolitti era[44] increased 2.5% annually in the industrial sector and 2.2% in the services sector.[45]

This optimism also had repercussions for the stock exchanges; a transition towards a "modern" stock market, not only in terms of the number

[38] Toniolo, 1990; Zamagni, 1990.

[39] Sori, 1979 and 1984; Fauri, 2015.

[40] Daniele and Malanima, 2011; Cafagna, 1989; D'Antone, 1996; Felice, 2007.

[41] Fortunato, 1911; Nitti, 1900; Cafagna, 1989.

[42] Fenoaltea, 2011.

[43] The expression "Belle Époque" originated in France in the late nineteenth century. In that period, inventions and advances in technology and science occurred that were unparalleled in previous eras. Electric lighting, radio, automobile, cinema, pasteurization, and other novelties all contributed to an improvement in living conditions and the spread of optimism.

[44] This phrase refers to that period of Italian history that extends from 1903 to 1914, a decade that took its name from the governments of the liberal Giovanni Giolitti, who views characterized Italian political life until the eve of the First World War.

[45] Toniolo, 2013, p. 23.

and quantity of securities traded but also with respect to greater information efficiency (which mainly involved several Italian squares, such as that of Milan) occurred in 1894 when the market was connected by telegraph to the main Italian stock exchanges and those of Paris and Berlin.[46] At the same time, as mentioned, Italy was undergoing intense industrialization, which involved the concentrated investment of new capital in certain sectors, increasing production needs but at the same time increasing the availability of capital; thanks to the containment of state debt; the latter was partly due to the slowdown in railway investments (a sector that increasingly turned to the financial market for support) in view of the expiry dates of the concessions (1905) combined with the growth of internal savings; thanks to remittances from emigrants.[47] This dynamic is significantly reflected in the number of companies listed on the Roman stock market, which between 1900 and 1910 made an unparalleled leap in size for the Roman market (that of Milan reached 127 stocks),[48] doubling its number of listed stocks to a peak in 1908 with 55 stocks. These stocks included qualitatively important companies destined to play an important role, e.g., Terni, Edison, Banca Commerciale Italiana, Credito Italiano and Metallurgia Italiana. The mixed banks favoured the transformation of entrepreneurial activity into anonymous companies and accompanied their entry: for example, Comit participated in the placement, underwriting and support of Molini Alta Italia, Carburo Calcio and Export of Water in addition to Edison and Richard Ginori, while Credit intervened in favour of Italian Metallurgy, Italiana Gas and Montecatini.[49] These years saw the Milan Stock Exchange pursue recognition as the "Great International Stock Exchange for Central Europe".[50] Nevertheless, the Roman stock exchange was also representative, although not on the scale of Milan, of the development of industrial capital together with banking and financial capital, which until then had characterized its

[46] Baia Curioni, 1995, pp. 13 e ss. Baia Curioni and Fantacci (2004) assess the contribution of telegraphy to Italy's financial-market integration between 1890 and 1910. They find Italian bond markets converging with each other and with the Paris exchange over time, suggesting a role for improved communications, but conclude that integration between stock markets depended primarily upon the changing volatility of securities.

[47] Bonelli, 1968, pp. 261–263.

[48] De Luca, 2002 p. 52.

[49] Confalonieri, 1994.

[50] Cafaro, 1993, p. 125.

list. In addition to the transport sector, whereby, however, the Southern and Mediterranean transport firms were transformed into financial ones after the nationalization of 1905, the most innovative and dynamic sectors appeared to be electricity, iron mining and steel production, while emerging sectors included the chemical, machinery and food industries. The crisis of 1907 saw a reduction in the number of securities listed on the Roman stock exchange and in general a financial centralization increasingly on the Milanese square; the Genoese square, which together with the Milanese and Roman ones, had experienced an increase and played a central role in the Italian financial market, was where in November 1906 the fall in prices began, triggered by the impossibility of refinancing carryover operations, and where the flight of private savings, due to the negative effects of speculative excesses, had the most profound consequences.[51]

In response to these events, the Italian government issued two decrees, of which the first prohibited the listing of companies that had not published at least two financial statements and the second instituted the discount right, considered an instrument that prevented downward speculation although the overall index of the Italian stock exchanges did not reflect major benefits.[52] Starting at the end of the 1800s, Italy's accession to the gold standard and the increase in foreign funding resulting from the now increased confidence in Italian economic development resulted in the growth of the securities market.[53] Two economic and financial crises characterized the end of the nineteenth century and the beginning of the new century: that of 1893 and that of 1907.

Whereas the 1893 crisis led to a net decline in capital inflows because of the shock received by the financial and banking system, the 1907 crisis worsened the situation.[54] Despite the financial crisis affecting bank loans, which suffered a sharp decline, and consequently afflicted the industrial system, the exchange rate remained relatively stable.[55] In 1906, therefore,

[51] Siciliano, 2001, pp. 19–20. About the events of the 1907 crisis see Bonelli, 1971, 1982; La Francesca, 2006, 2009; Riva, 2018. About the crisis after and before the great war I see Conti, Cova and La Francesca 2014 and 2017. For more information on financial crises, see Kindleberger, 1987, pp. 367–389.

[52] Siciliano, 2001, pp. 21–24.

[53] James and O'Rourke, 2013, cap. II, cit., p. 73.

[54] *Ibidem*, pp. 75–76.

[55] Cesarano et al., 2012, pp. 253–275.

a year before the second crisis, the Bank of Italy attempted to promote the sale of government bonds through expansionary monetary policies[56]: the gap with French government bonds still existed and decreased, albeit not by much, reaching approximately two-tenths of a percentage point around 1910.[57] In 1907, however, both Credit and Comit, as mixed banks, were forced to suddenly scale back their investments.[58]

5.6 The Period 1911–1920

The second decade of the twentieth century was a period of particular importance. Most significantly, it witnessed, following Giolitti's development, a rebirth of the Italian country from an economic perspective.

From an economic viewpoint, one can note that Italy's per capita GDP had varied since the end of the 1800s.[59] The GDP was 38% of that of Great Britain at the end of the 1890s, and only in 1913 did it rise to 54% of the British GDP's value.[60] This performance was due not only to Italy's economic development but also to a general change in historical reference trends.[61]

However, the regional gap within the Italian Peninsula, which presents different data according to the regions considered, became increasingly important.[62] In fact, 55% of Italian added value was produced in 1911 in the northwest, more precisely, in the territories of Milan, Genoa and Turin.[63]

Italy, in general, as has been mentioned several times, was experiencing a favourable period, which had spread to nearly all the country's regions and increased the demand for both Italian and foreign investment, such that the country could afford to convert the Italian Rendita

[56] Confalonieri, 1974, p. 137; Forsyth, 1993, p. 43.

[57] James and O'Rourke, 2013, p. 76.

[58] Forsyth, 1993, pp. 35–36.

[59] Baffigi 2015, pp. 195–196.

[60] Toniolo, 2013, p. 23.

[61] Ciocca, 2007, cit., pp. 142–143. Toniolo, 1990; Zamagni, 1993.

[62] Felice, 2007.

[63] *Ibidem*, p. 24; Fenoaltea, 1987; Ciccarelli and Fenoaltea, 2009.

from 5 3.75%[64]; nevertheless, nearly all the owners of these bonds determined to continue to subscribe to them, although the title yielded less. The trade balance of payments, however, did not show positive signs, as imports of raw materials and cereals as well as machinery with new technology contributed to increasing deficits due to the high costs of trading with foreign countries.[65]

According to a 1985 study by Sanna Randaccio, it is possible to trace the share of investments made by Italian companies starting from the last years of the nineteenth century.[66] Latin America, in particular Argentina, was one of the first regions to host direct investments abroad by Italian companies in the early 1900s; the flow of investments, complementary to that of migration, reveals Italy as a country entering the process of globalization[67]: Dunning's research is useful for tracing Italy's first investments and international involvements, which commenced in approximately 1880.[68] In this regard, a scheme drawn up by Acocella in 1985 relating to the period 1911–1920 shows that the international activity of Italian companies involved six key firms, among which Pirelli stands out.[69] Pirelli initially established itself in Spain, but with the subsequent increase in customs duties, the company determined to circumvent the increased import tariffs by opening a factory in Villanueva y Geltrù.[70] After 1907, rubber production began to become increasingly important; in particular, in tyre production, by 1912, Pirelli's share in overall turnover increased from nearly 8 and a half percentage points to 23.7%.[71]

As mentioned, the crisis of 1907 affected both the credit system and the Italian government. The problem originated in the downward speculations that consequently had to be combated or at least limited by a specific government measure: the right to discount. The provision remained in force until 1936 and enabled all purchasers of shares to postpone delivery of the same (securities) to a predefined deadline,

[64] Toniolo, 2013, p. 24.

[65] Warglien, 1985, 1987.

[66] Sanna Randaccio, 1985, pp. 25–50.

[67] Barbero, 1991.

[68] Dunning, 1983.

[69] Acocella, 1985.

[70] Bezza, 1987, p. 411.

[71] Bigazzi, 1981.

thus penalizing those who engaged in short sales.[72] In addition, in 1913, legislative measures were issued to regulate real-estate brokerage activity.[73] These were among the first measures to increasingly limit the influence of banks and "access to the cries of the latter", unlike stockbrokers, for whom most of the trading activity on the stock exchange was reserved.[74]

At the dawn of the First World War, liquidity became a fundamental resource, so much so that it was necessary to convert bank deposits into currency.[75] Thus, the nonstate sector witnessed a reduction in the use of the financial market to sell shares, from 30 to 20% over the following ten years, in favour of bank financing.[76]

The war period was particularly stimulating for the Italian economy and financial market (although, as Baia Curioni writes, "it seemed as if over-the-counter exchanges during the war were more active than when the stock market was open"[77]; in fact, during the First World War, the stock exchanges were affected by war events and were closed on 1 August 1914, only to be reopened in 1917, suspended in the same year and reopened again in 1918); on the other hand, the war facilitated the development of certain sectors, such as steel and machinery, increasing the growth rate to 15%.[78] This growth was experienced in particular at companies that significantly contributed to war production, such as Fiat, Ansaldo and Ilva.

The increasingly close ties between the Italian discount bank, Ansaldo and the Comit are important for the history of the Italy's stock exchanges.[79] The shareholders of Ansaldo, the main customer of the Italian discount bank, at the same time held an important controlling stake in the same.

The Italian discount bank was therefore an important financier for the production of the famous company and one on which the Perrone

[72] Aleotti, 1990.

[73] Siciliano, 2001.

[74] Baia Curioni, 1995.

[75] Toniolo, 1989; Cotula and Raganelli, 1996.

[76] Cotula and Garofalo, 1996.

[77] Baia Curioni, 1995.

[78] Castronovo, 1995.

[79] Toniolo, 1993.

brothers relied for many years.[80] The circumstances of the postwar period, however, forced the company to search for new loans at other banks and ultimately to resort to history's first hostile attempt to take over the Comit.[81]

5.6.1 *Financing the First World War*

The economic aspect of the First World War and the war's economic consequences assume a special significance in the period under consideration. Vera Zamagni calculated the resource allocation choices made to finance the war (the author finds total expenses of approximately 1/3 the nation's income) and during the following years.[82]

Despite its entry into the war, Italy, in 1915, recorded a decrease in state resources, caused decreased tax revenues; unlike Great Britain, which had multiplied its tax burden 5 times, and France, which like Germany, albeit to a lesser extent, had also increased its tax burden, Italy was the only country that (at constant prices) left the tax burden unchanged.[83] Thus, according to the calculations and elaborations of Vera Zamagni, the exploitation and contraction of public debts became the chief instrument adopted by the Italian State.[84] The state issued five national loans in 1914; with the ever-increasing inflation resulting from the increase in the free float, it became more difficult to resort to long-term debt, consequently increasing the share of short-term debt, which reached and exceeded at the end of the conflict 1/3 of the total debt.[85] The weight of the public debt was also a relevant issue for other European countries, such as France, an issue highlighted in the research of Confalonieri and Gatti.[86]

The public debt after Unification (thanks to the law of 10 July 1861, the Great Book of Public Debt of the Kingdom of Italy was established,

[80] Castronovo, 1990; Falchero, 1990.

[81] Cotula and Spaventa, 1993.

[82] Zamagni, 1990, pp. 266–267.

[83] Frascani, 1975, p. 254; Zamagni, 1990, p. 268.

[84] Zamagni, 1990, p. 269.

[85] Zamagni, 1990, p. 270.

[86] Confalonieri and Gatti, 1986.

which recorded all the debts of the pre-unification states)[87] continued to play a prominent role within the list of the Roman stock exchange, and in this case, it is interesting to analyse the relationship between this debt and the nominal and real GDP of the examined period (1911–1920).[88] Starting from the Unification of Italy, the debt, despite a certain physiological decline, exhibits important growth, registering a share of 126% in 1894.[89] In the following years until 1911, thanks to Italy's economic boom at the end of the century, the value of the ratio undergoes a decline, reaching a share of less than 80%.[90] From 1911 to 1920, this ratio was the driver of an important increase, equal to approximately 160%.[91] This last reconstruction is especially important because it followed the economic and financial consequences of the First World War; at the beginning of the conflict, in fact, the issuance of public debt securities, accompanied by a strong investment by companies in the industrial sector, resulted in a significant increase in not only internal but also external debt, while also registering an important increase in the foreign component of debt; subsequently, therefore, from the end of the conflict and in subsequent years, the debt increase was accompanied by a decrease in GDP, which negatively affected the country.[92] The economics literature has often addressed the dynamics of these events; for example, the discussion on the nascent relationship between government debt growth and economic growth has been highlighted: many economists question the sudden economic recovery of a country when it is difficult to reduce public debt since it is easy to envisage a policy aimed at increasing taxation,[93] but such a policy also has devastating macroeconomic effects, including the discouragement of investment,[94] which makes a country financially fragile.[95]

[87] De' Gennaro, 1934.

[88] Baffigi, 2011.

[89] Francese and Pace, 2008.

[90] Reconstruction presented in Francese and Pace, 2008.

[91] *Ibidem*.

[92] Balassone et al., 2013.

[93] Elmendorf and Mankiw, 1999.

[94] Servén, 1997.

[95] Bernanke and Gertler, 1990.

5.6.2 *The Italian Annuity on the Main Foreign Stock Exchanges*

The Italian State instilled security in savers regarding its ability to repay the debts incurred to consolidate the relationship: the State had also gained financial credibility in foreign markets, where the main and potential investors resided, for instance, in the Parisian market.[96] In fact, the yield of the Italian public debt bond was primarily influenced and largely established, together with its price, by the Paris Stock Exchange.[97]

Nevertheless, foreign investors appropriated a large part of Italian public debt securities through Italian private banking circuits.[98] To ensure that the political instability and turbulence of the financial markets did not negatively affect the prices of Italian public debt securities and the quantity of quotas requested both inside and outside the country, a fundamental role was assigned to the Bank of Italy, which, after the reform of 1893, distributed public securities not only through its branches but also through its savings banks and its main banks and was thus able to divert a prevalent share of the money destined for savings.[99]

This period of dependence on the foreign market and the will of the main Paris financiers regarding the trend in prices and quantity of stock traded witnessed important growth until 1890 and a sharp decline dictated by the need to invigorate the Italian stock market; the share of debt placed abroad only increased until 1889, when growth within the Italian stock market began to become more prevalent (from a peak of 40%, the percentage of such debt decreased to between 13.5 and 20.2% between 1906 and 1913).[100]

The reason for the fall in the share of public debt abroad and the consequent increase in the same on the Italian stock exchanges lies hidden in the conversion of the rent, which occurred at the behest of the government in July 1906, to 3.75%, as previously mentioned; the rent subsequently underwent a further conversion to 3.5% and a further decline in July 1912.[101] Artoni and Biancini (2003) underline that this

[96] Berta, 1990; Zamagni, 1998, pp. 207–242; Volpi, 2002.

[97] Aleotti, 1990; Conte et al., 2003, pp. 443–461.

[98] De Cecco, 1990; Fenoaltea, 2006.

[99] Baia Curioni, 1995; Volpi 2002.

[100] Consob, 2011, Chapter IV, p. 115.

[101] Zamagni, 1998.

conversion of rent was clearly possible not only because of the general economic recovery of the Giolitti era but also because of the consequences of the latter, which led, among other things, to a reduction in the ratio of the public debt to the GDP (Fig. 5.3).[102] As noted, with the entry of Italy into the First World War, this ratio underwent a new rise.[103] At the beginning of the 1900s, the Bank of Italy also began to contribute to the development of the Italian annuity, which while maintaining a stable relationship between reserves and circulation was able, thanks to the contribution of certain local and savings banks, to place public debt securities and allow them to circulate as efficiently as possible, giving strength and continuity to Italy's monetary policy.[104]

Unlike the Bank of Italy, mixed banks preferred not only the stock exchanges but also the private circuit, giving more consistency to their investments destined for the private enterprise market; these two models, in contrast and despite this approach, in the first few years did not negatively affect the Italian Stock Exchange or the liquidity of savers.[105]

Conversely, compared with the prewar period, the substantial decline that occurred from the end of the First World War to 1920 was due not only to the increase in the ratio of public debt to GDP but also to a further scenario: the effect of general price inflation as a consequence of the worldwide conflict. All this affected the value of the stocks listed on the stock exchanges, including the Roman exchange.[106]

5.6.3 *A Technical Analysis of the Variations in the Title of the Italian Annuity*

According to Siciliano, there was a negative correlation between the inflation rate and real yields; from 1911 to 1920, the real rate of short-term government bonds and therefore the difference between the nominal rates and the changes in the annual price indices was negative in the period of the First World War.[107]

[102] Artoni and Biancini, 2003; Fratianni and Spinelli, 1997; Postigliola, Strangio 2017.

[103] Artoni and Biancini, 2003.

[104] Conti, 1999.

[105] Nardozzi and Piluso, 2010.

[106] Fratianni and Spinelli, 1997.

[107] Siciliano, 2001, p. 88.

Fig. 5.3 Ratio of public debt to gross domestic product in Italy: 1894–1933 (*Source* Fratianni and Spinelli, 1997)

Siciliano defines this period at the beginning of the twentieth century as "disappointing" for government bonds compared to the returns that companies in the private sector achieved, especially in the areas of metallurgy and steel, where production increased; thanks to the Great War.[108] Starting in 1915, the latter production increase in fact contributed in real terms to a higher return on the shares of Italian companies compared to long- and short-term government bonds. Beginning in 1915, the return on the entire stock market will always, except for a few years, have a higher yield than government bonds.[109]

5.6.4 *Role of Mixed Banks in the Rome Stock Exchange*

By analysing the structure of banking and industrial securities listed on the Rome Stock Exchange, one can note that banks, especially mixed banks, were the key and perhaps only drivers of development during the Giolitti era of the Italian industrial system, both in terms of risk capital and credit.[110]

In fact, to maintain stock market efficiency, albeit occasionally with a speculative character, the mixed banks supported many of the companies that represented the Italian industrialization of the early twentieth century (even if their capitalization did not have a large impact on national GDP).[111] Many scholars have contrary opinions regarding these dynamics, and among these scholars, the main critic is Bonelli, who describes the stock market as a highly opaque place, where mixed banks together with certain large industrial conglomerates exerted too much influence on banking management, leading it to provide financing to a network potentially unreliable businesses.[112] However, this analysis cannot ignore the consequences of the 1907 crisis, which caused a fall in real share prices of 76 percentage points; the origin of this crisis can in fact be explained from a technical perspective by the increase in short-term interest rates and the international liquidity crisis.[113] Here, the

[108] *Ibidem*, p. 89.

[109] *Ibidem*.

[110] Castronovo, 1995; Confalonieri, 1975, 1976; Gershenkron, 1965.

[111] Consob 2011, p. 15.

[112] Bonelli, 1971.

[113] Consob, 2011, p. 16.

most vital data are reported by Bonelli, who shows the importance of the link between mixed banks and the Italian industrial system: approximately one-third of the loans made by these banks consisted of equity investments in industrial companies.[114]

Therefore, the liquidity crisis, the tangled negotiations of the banks with the industrial world and, in particular, the crisis of 1907, caused a slow detachment of the banking world with regard to carryovers, but the holdings in shares and bonds remained stable and strong; nevertheless, this system was too complex and, due to a lack of solid legislation in this regard, could only lead to serious financial problems, such as those experienced by the Italian Banking Company.[115]

5.6.5 *First Attempts to Regulate Bank–Business Relationships and the Evolution of Securities Listed on the Rome Stock Exchange Based on an Analysis of the War Period*

The power of the mixed banks was based on their relationships with the companies, including the intertwined board memberships of the banks and companies and the favouritism this entailed. More specifically, the banks had holdings in the companies in their portfolios and consequently were forced to speculate on these companies to drive their value upwards and thus generate profits and raise cash in the short term.[116] After the crisis of 1907, there were numerous attempts to curb speculation to avoid running the risk that the value of corporate securities and consequently that of banks, mainly mixed banks, would collapse due to stock market speculation. Precisely for this reason a provision was enacted, the discount right, which despite its initial temporary nature remained in force until 1936. This provision allowed the holders of the share rights not to deliver them on expiry. In this way, those who sold short were constantly afraid of finding themselves in serious difficulties and facing penalizing conditions.[117]

In "The four major Italian credit institutions", Bava analyses the balance sheet assets, in millions of lire, of Italian mixed banks to 1914;

[114] Bonelli, 1971.

[115] Consob, 2011, p. 16.

[116] Bonelli, 1971.

[117] Aleotti, 1990.

Table 5.1 Balance sheet assets of the four main "mixed banks" (millions of current lire): 1895–1914

Bank	*Year*	*Balance sheet assets*
Banca commerciale Italiana	1914	1,101.9
Credito Italiano	1914	633.7
Banco di Roma	1914	413.1
Banca Italiana di sconto	1914	368.2
Share of the 4 institutions on the total assets of the Italian banking system	1914	14.7

Source Bava, 1926

this research reveals the percentage weight of these institutions on the Italian banking system and their financial circumstances at the outbreak of the First World War.[118]

Extrapolating from Bava's data concerning the Rome Stock Exchange, Table 5.1 shows the balance sheet situation and the percentage of stock value owned by mixed banks on the Rome Stock Exchange in 1914, prior to Italy's entry into the war.

In a separate study, Alexander Gerschenkron considers the development of these banks to be fundamental for the economic development of nineteenth-century Germany; compared to others, these banks had the strength to collect savings across a large territory, even through small branches, and thanks to good relationships and personal bonds, the banks succeeded in investing these savings as venture capital in numerous industrial companies.[119]

Analysis of this strategy reveals that it was focussed primarily on the electricity and steel sectors and in a more limited way on the railway and navigation sectors; in any case, it was strategically relevant for the war period.[120] Other scholars, such as Confalonieri, confirm the main role of mixed banks, even if they were unable on their own to satisfy the credit demand of all Italian companies; nevertheless, the growth clearly reflects the long-term credit they provided beginning in the postwar period.[121]

118 Bava, 1926.

119 Gershenkron, 1965.

120 Cohen, 1967.

121 Confalonieri, 1985.

5.6.6 *The Italian Commercial Bank and the Mediterranean Company*

During the First World War, the newspaper La Tribuna did not provide data on the stock exchange because the quotations had been suspended since the end of 1913; according to the Rome commercial stock exchange, off-exchange trading was highly active.[122] Numerous requests were made to banks to reconvert bank deposits into currency, which negatively affected the financial system.[123]

Between 1914 and 1918, the sectors that benefited most from the war period were steel and machinery, which increased their profits. Industrial production accelerated by approximately 15%. The companies mainly involved in this profitable period were Fiat, Ansaldo and Ilva. Each of the 4 mixed banks was engaged in different industrial sectors, which enabled them to increase the value of their shares listed on the Rome Stock Exchange in the period immediately following the end of the First World War. It is appropriate to follow their trends individually to understand their function within the Roman financial and stock exchange system. The sector in which Comit primarily operated was the production and distribution of electricity. The bank supported both Italian and German initiatives, also contributing to the founding of Sade.[124]

Comit stock underwent a significant rise after the end of the First World War. The stock increased from a value of 727 at the beginning of the war to approximately 1000 by war's end, when a number of companies reported substantial gains. Consequently, those who had invested in these companies, such as the mixed banks, whether in the form of venture capital or debt, also reported large profits. This was the case in the electricity sector, which took advantage not only of the capital of the Comit but also of that of the former railway companies following their nationalization in 1905.[125] This circumstance also explains the different performances of the shares of the Comit and the Mediterranean railway company on the Roman commercial exchange. Confalonieri highlights that the Mediterranean Company preferred to continue investing in the railway sector while avoiding investing in the growing electricity sector

122 Baia Curioni, 1995.

123 Cotula and Raganelli, 1996; Toniolo, 1989.

124 Zamagni, 1990, p. 195.

125 Confalonieri, 1982, pp. 235 and 353.

and engaging in new construction projects, a policy that did nothing good for the firm but, rather, brought it to the financial collapse in 1914 (Table 5.2). From a strategic perspective, Credit aimed, like Comit, to invest in various sectors, albeit different sectors from those that interested Comit, i.e., chemicals, sugar refineries and the steel industry. Starting in 1911, this bank performed numerous bailouts on behalf of the steel industry, often operating in close collaboration with the Comit.[126] Its stock listed on the Rome Stock Exchange was relatively stable until the end of the Great War, when starting in 1918 it rose sharply until it reached its peak in the early 1920s at a value of approximately 850 lire (Table 5.2). There are two reasons for this listing: first, the profits of the steel sector, a sector mainly financed by this bank, enabled the latter to generate strong earnings, which reflected positively on the stock listed on the stock exchange; second, the takeover by the Fiat-Snia Viscosa coalition.[127] The takeover engaged in by this coalition had as its main motivation the desire to counter the Ansaldo-Comit concentration and the fear that this concentration could compromise the future development of Fiat.[128] The history of the Italian Banking Company, then known as Banca Italiana di Discount, deserves separate mention. At the behest of the Bank of Italy, this company was saved following the 1907 crisis through the combined intervention of the Comit and Credit. The goal of the Bank of Italy in this intervention was to retain this third important credit institution within the Italian industrial triangle.[129] The bank mainly invested in the steel sector and starting in 1911 was in danger of collapse because of financial transactions by companies in that sector; many of these transactions were considered technically inept and risked bankrupting many banks, including the Italian Banking Company.[130]

The profits of the steel companies, and partly also those of mixed banks, can be explained by the emergence of the Consortium for the Union of Italian steel companies, which, responding primarily to the will of the Bank of Italy, made it possible to halt the production and financial crisis. The merger with the Italian Provincial Credit Society led

[126] Zamagni, 1990, p. 197.

[127] Consob, 2011, p. 19.

[128] *Ibidem.*

[129] Bonelli, 1971, p. 151.

[130] Zamagni, 1990, p. 198.

Table 5.2 Quarterly averages of listed titles (1911–1920)

	1911				*1912*				*1913*			
	1° quarter	*2° quarter*	*3° quarter*	*4° quarter*	*1° quarter*	*2° quarter*	*3° quarter*	*4° quarter*	*1° quarter*	*2° quarter*	*3° quarter*	*4° quarter*
Acqua Pia	1953,46	1955,38	1935,00	1940,17	1992,46	2004,85	2007,38	1996,15	1974,69	1943	1848,85	1832,69
Marcia	1241,62	1205,69	1209,15	1146,58	1221,15	1226,69	1230,85	1195,54	1140,85	1121,38	1029,15	928,62
Anglo Roma Gao												
Ansaldo	272,92	250,08	233,38	250,67	274,85	260,46	295,38	304,15	288,92	285,00	277,69	276,38
Banca Commerciale	936,23	861,38	846,69	823,92	866,69	80,69	850,77	860,62	879,62	849,08	839,15	833,15
Banca d'Italia	1518,15	1468,38	1446,92	1438,50	1479	1390,46	1444,46	1460,23	1475,31	1440,46	1418,38	1435,38
Banco di Roma	108,69	103,08	105	108,92	107,77	102,23	103,46	104,62	105,77	103,62	103,15	104,00
Beni Stabili	341,38	325,54	318,15	313,58	318,15	298,31	309,15	299,38	300,38	292,23	288,77	284,38
Concimi	120,38	113,38	114,85	121,17	133,00	130,00	150,77	150,77	157,46	153,54	152,23	152,23
Roma	596,46	575,38	583,77	595,83	607,15	578,62	573,54	572,85	574,85	549,46	543,31	544,85
Credito Italiano												
imprese fondiarie	124,31	114,92	109,38	113,25	121,09		117,00	114,92	114,77	108	103,38	101,08
Banca italiana di aconto									104,00	99,15	96,15	96,85
S.N.L.A Mediterranea												

(continued)

Table 5.2 (continued)

	1911				*1912*				*1913*			
	1° quarter	*2° quarter*	*3° quarter*	*4° quarter*	*1° quarter*	*2° quarter*	*3° quarter*	*4° quarter*	*1° quarter*	*2° quarter*	*3° quarter*	*4° quarter*
	434,77	424,92	408,92	410,33	414,85	396,31	401,38	386,38	356	325	296,69	256,77
Ilva Acciaieria d'Italia												
Navigarione Runattino	394,46	390,23	364,92	372,25	309	384,62	411,31	411,85	410,31	448,69	436,77	418,38
Obbligarioni ferroviarie	364,31	366,15	361,77	355,75	346,69	339,69	339,31	337,23	333,46	331,38	324,08	321
FIAT												
Renditaitaliana 3,75%	101,52	104,45	103,16	101,86	99,31	96,57	98,03	98,98	98,49	99,14	98,30	99,06
Tram omnibus	292,85	256,31	217	204,42	212,62	196,62	185,31	202,62	177,69	177,46	167,85	152,08
Zuccheri Roma	74,92	73,15	73,08	79,92	79,69	76,85	81,31	82,69	80,62	82,46	80	75,77

	1914		*1918*		*1919*				*1920*			
	1° quarter	*2° quarter*	*July*	*December*	*1° quarter*	*2° quarter*	*3° quarter*	*4° quarter*	*1° quarter*	*2° quarter*	*3° quarter*	*4° quarter*
Acqua Pia	1838,85	1823,69	1790	1956,25	1966,38	1923,46	1889,17	1925	1904,09	1916,15	1848,85	1818,08
Marcia	857,77	826,31	814	908	880,85	843,54	779,33	737,75	670	589,23	1511,62	449,23
Anglo Roma Gao												
Ansaldo	274,15	245,23	222	241,75	251,62	247,77	211,17	212	217,33	184,69	142,85	128,23
Banca Commerciale	835,54	762,23	727	989,5	1099	1220,15	1027,67	1165	1285,83	1088,92	1008	1096
Banca d'Italia	1440,69	1380,23	1343,5	1459,75	1486,15	1476,92	1422,83	1490,50	1512,50	1397,38	1327,23	1361,46

	1914		1918		1919				1920			
	1° quarter	*2° quarter*	*July*	*December*	*1° quarter*	*2° quarter*	*3° quarter*	*4° quarter*	*1° quarter*	*2° quarter*	*3° quarter*	*4° quarter*
Banco di Roma	104,08	94,23	90,75	117,75	117,54	114,38	116	114,75	116,75	112,38	110,69	113,62
Beni Stabili	286	278,46	285,25	265,75	274,92	282,15	279,50	278,75	308,58	308,23	298,69	299,62
Concimi	154,31	138,69	126,5	211	199,54	187,15	178,17	178,5	213,00	210,08	146,15	146,46
Roma Credito Italiano	549,92	523,38	516,5	724,75	734,54	748,15	764,50	811,75	847,25	718,31	667,15	678,54
Imprese fondiarie	97,69	69,46	91	93,25	96,54	93,38	87,83	98,25	108	111,38	100,92	100,31
Banca italiana di aconto	97,69	92,08	90	706,75	681,69	643,62	599,83	618,25	646,00	568,08	551,69	570,31
S.N.L.A				116,75	105	109,08	98,67	98,75	182,33	106	85,62	76,31
Mediterranea	243,08	222	221,75	278	283,85	271,15	235,83	220,75	226,25	206,46	175,38	154,23
Ilva Acciaieria d'Italia				238,5	245	243,92	216,17	215,25	214,83	175,23	128,08	100,69
Navigarione Runattino	402,46	397,62	387,75	757	792,38	859,23	764,17	749,25	818,15	741,69	647,38	656,92
Obbligarioni ferroviarie	321,15	323,92	325,25									
FIAT				447,25	479,08	573,92	335,17	358	393,33	352,46	236,38	231,23
Renditaitaliana 3,75%	97,30	96,83	94,83	83,96	81,88	85,01	86,28	83,28	80,98	76,03	68,86	73,51
Tram omnibus	167,31	154,23	161	197,75	197,69	183,23	170,33	166	170,75	156,38	134,31	139,85
Zuccheri Roma	71,92	68,38	64,25	106,5	102	85,15	69	71	73,69	71,62	65,54	72,77

Source Data processed from by the newspaper *La Tribuna*, several years

the Italian Banking Society to definitively change its name in 1914 to the Italian Discount Bank.[131] Starting from the end of the First World War, the entwinement of the Ansaldo-Italian discount bank with other firms became important, whereby the Ansaldo company, which had grown substantially through war production, was simultaneously a customer and main (controlling) shareholder of the Italian discount bank.[132] The rise in the shares of Ansaldo and the Italian discount bank starting from 1918 was mainly due, in addition to war profits, to the industrial giant's attempt to take over Comit (Table 5.2).[133]

The Comit resisted the takeover by merging its shares into Comofin using loans from the Comit bank itself: consequently, because the debts of Banca Italiana di Sconto at other banks went unexamined, the critical situation of Ansaldo was one reason why the Italian Discount Bank was placed in liquidation in 1921.[134] The listed stock of the Banco di Roma deserves separate consideration as unlike the other three mixed banks it was not considered highly profitable; the reason for its exclusion from the industrial triangle derives from the fact that the bank was the protagonist of only local initiatives.[135] As shown by De Rosa, the Bank's attempts to expand towards areas of Italian international diplomatic interest, such as Libya and part of Ethiopia, were initiated by board member Tittoni Romolo, whose brother was foreign minister until 1909.[136] The Bank's financial circumstances were weakened primarily by losses caused by Italy's effort to colonize these lands, especially in 1911.[137] In this regard, the trend of the value of the share listed on the Rome stock exchange is relevant (Table 5.2); it should be emphasized that the Bank used numerous hedges and rounds to mask its losses.[138] The negative trend of 1914, at the outset of the First World War, is primarily reflected in the resignation of director Tittoni, who until this important point had been

[131] Galli Della Loggia, 1970.

[132] Consob, 2011, p. 19.

[133] Cotula and Spaventa, 1993.

[134] Consob, 2011, p. 19.

[135] Zamagni, 1990, p. 199.

[136] De Rosa, 1982, v. I, chapter V.

[137] Zamagni, 1990, p. 200.

[138] *Ibidem*.

responsible for the Bank's international strategic decisions.[139] The positive trend starting from 1918 can be explained not only by the proceeds deriving from investments, albeit minimal, made in various sectors but also by the bailout performed by the National Credit, a central institution consisting of the Catholic banks of the Vatican, the Banco's most important shareholder.[140]

5.7 The Differences in Absolute and Percentage Terms Between the Rome Stock Exchange and the Milan Stock Exchange in the Period 1911–1920

Having illustrated in detail the composition of the share list of the Rome Stock Exchange and graphically reconstructed the evolution of the exchange's most representative stocks, it is appropriate to look more closely at this period, which opens the interwar period not only nationally but also internationally. This period is one of transition within which the mixed economy model was defined that would play a decisive role following World War II. First, it is useful to rationalize the preceding elaborations not only with respect to the historical period but also, and above all, to the true value in percentage terms of the entire stock market in Italy between 1911 and 1920, starting from total trades in millions of lire. This approach is useful to determe how much, in absolute and percentage terms, the share exchanges of the Rome Stock Exchange affected the total.

In this regard, the data in the appendix to the third chapter of the 2011 Consob publication are highly interesting. These data represent the value of share exchanges on the Italian stock exchanges prior to 1891 and the number of companies listed on the Stock Exchange of Milan broken down by sector. The analysis commences with the processing of the data collected by the Mediobanca Research Area.

The data relating to the 1911–1913 period show that the Rome Stock Exchange represented only 20.8% of the value of all stock exchanges with respect to total trades, equal to approximately 60,600,000,000 lire, unlike the Milan Stock Exchange, which dominated the stock market with

139 *Ibidem.*

140 De Rosa, 1982, v. II, pp. 76–77.

a share that reached nearly 40 percentage points (precisely 38.3%).[141] These data primarily refer to the items settled on average each year in the clearing houses and are estimates made by Da Pozzo and Felloni in 1964. Despite the undoubted superiority of the Milan Stock Exchange to that of Rome, starting in 1911, the data no longer compromise the importance of the latter in Italy; in fact, in the period 1911–1920, the Rome Stock Exchange traded a higher (albeit only slightly) share value than Genoa (20%) and Turin (17.3%).[142]

These data are important because they quantify the share exchanges of the various Italian stock exchanges during the First World War. Again, it is important to consider that the number and quality of these data are based on elaborations by the Mediobanca Research Area, which report, in summary, the total stock value of listed companies divided by sector on the Milan Stock Exchange. One can observe that while approximately 40 different companies were listed on the Rome Commercial Exchange in 1911, primarily distributed across the industrial, construction, banking and transport sectors, on the Milan Stock Exchange for the same year, the total number of listed companies was 158 (four times higher than in Rome), of which 97 companies belonged to the industry sector in the strict sense. This comparison reveals that the most favourable city in which to raise capital useful for war production[143] was certainly Milan, unlike Rome, which hosted in addition to the major companies of the time, such as Ansaldo, only industries belonging to the Roman territory.[144]

Therefore, based on the difference in absolute terms of the two squares, the clear importance prior to the Great War of Milan over Rome emerges. The latter remains a local trading exchange with little possibility of economic and geographical development.

[141] Da Pozzo and Felloni, 1964; Consob 2011, p. 97.

[142] Ibidem.

[143] The winds of war were strengthening. Regarding Italy, in 1911, an exhausting war for the territories of Tripolitania and Cyrenaica in Libya "ended" thanks to the diplomatic support of England, which favoured Italy's expansion into those territories to the detriment of France, its eternal rival.

[144] Consob 2011, p. 98.

References

Acocella, Nicola (ed.). 1985. *Le multinazionali italiane*, Bologna: Il Mulino.

Aleotti, Alessandro. 1990. Borsa e industria. 1861–1989: cento anni di rapporti difficili, Milan: Edizioni di Comunità.

Aquarone, Alberto. 1972, *Alla ricerca dell'Italia liberale*, Naples: Guida Editore.

Artoni, Roberto and Sara Biancini. 2003. *Il debito pubblico dall'Unità ad oggi*, in Pierluigi Ciocca and Gianni Toniolo (eds.), *Storia economica d'Italia*, 3: *Industrie, mercati, istituzioni*, 2: *I vincoli e le opportunità*, Rome-Bari: Laterza, pp. 269–380.

Astraldi, Romolo. 1956, *La Camera di Commercio di Roma nei centoventicinque anni di vita. (1831–1956)*, Rome: Fratelli Palombi Editori.

Atack, Jeremy. 2009. *Financial Innovations and crises: The View Backwars from Nothern Rock*, in Jeremy Atack and Larry Neal (eds.) *The Origin and Development of Financial Markets and Institutions. From the Seventeenth Century to the Present*, Cambridge: Cambridge University Press, 1-31.

Baffigi, Alberto. 2011. Italian National Account, 1861–2011, Banca d'Italia – *Quaderni di Storia economica*, 18.

Baffigi, Alberto. 2015. *Il PIL per la storia d'Italia. Istruzioni per l'uso*, Venoice: Marsilio.

Baia Curioni, Stefano. 1995. *Regolazione e competizione. Storia del mercato azionario in Italia (1808–1938)*, Bologna: Il Mulino.

Baia Curioni Stefano, Luca Fantacci, 2004, *Telegraphy and New Financial Procedures*, in Andrea Giuntini (ed.) *Communication and Its Lines: Telegraphy in the 19th Century Among Economy, Politics and Technology*, Prato: Istituto di Studi Storici Postali.

Bairoch, Paul. 1976. *Commerce extérieur et development économique de l'Europe au XIXe siècle*, Paris: La Haye Mouton.

Balassone, Fabrizio, Maura. Francese and Angelo, Pace. 2013. Public Debt and Economic Growth: Italy's First 150 Years, in Gianni Toniolo (ed.) *Handbook of the Italian Economy Since Unification*, Oxford: Oxford University Press, Ch. 18.

Barbero Maria, Ines. 1991. *Empresas y empresarios italianos en la Argentina, 1900–1930*, in Ostuni Maria. Rosaria (ed.) *Studi sull'emigrazione. Un'analisi comparata*, Milan: Fondazione Sella—Electa, 303–313.

Bava, Umberto. 1926. *I quattro maggiori istituti italiani di credito*, Genoa: Editrice Soc. An. Valugani.

Bernanke, Ben and Mark Gertler. 1990. Financial Fragility and Economic Performance. *The Quarterly Journal of Economics*, 105(1): 87–114.

Berta, Giuseppe. 1990. *Capitali in gioco*, Venezia: Marsilio.

Bezza, Bruno. 1987. L'attività multinazionale della Pirelli (1883–1914). *Società e Storia*, 10(35): 53-80.

Bigazzi, Duccio. 1981. *La Pirelli e la Fiat nel mercato mondiale*, in Cherubini Giovanni, et al. (eds.) *Storia della società italiana. L'Italia di Giolitti*, Milan: Teti Editore, 87–143.

Bocci, Marco. 1999. Banche e edilizia a Roma tra Otto e Novecento. *Roma moderna e contemporanea* n. 1–2: 125-146.

Bonelli, Franco. 1968. *Osservazioni e dati sul finanziamento dell'industria italiana all'inizio del secolo XX*, in Annali della Fondazione Luigi Einaudi, vol. II.

Bonelli, Franco. 1961. *Il commercio estero dello Stato Pontificio nel secolo XIX*, Rome: Archivio Economico dell'Unificazione Italiana", S.I, Vol. XI.

Bonelli, Franco. 1971. *La crisi del 1907. Una tappa dello sviluppo industriale in Italia*, Turin: Fondazione Luigi Einaudi.

Bonelli, Franco. 1982. *The 1907 Financial Crisis in Italy: A Peculiar Case of the Lender of Last Resort in Action*, in Charles P. Kindleberger and Jean-Pierre Laffargue (a cura di) (eds.), *Financial Crises: Theory, History, and Policy*, Cambridge-Paris, Cambridge University Press—Editions de la Maison des Sciences de l'Homme, 51–65.

Bonelli, Franco. 1991. (ed.), *La Banca d'Italia dal 1894 al 1913. Momenti della formazione di una banca centrale*, Rome-Bari: Laterza.

Cafagna, Luciano. 1989. *Dualismo e sviluppo nella storia d'Italia*, Venice: Marsilio.

Cafaro, Pietro. 1993. La Borsa di Milano: origini vicende e sviluppi, in Ezio Antonini (ed.), *La Borsa di Milano. Dalle origini a Palazzo Mezzanotte*, Milan: 24Ore Cultura, 107–134.

Capalbo, Cinzia. 1995. Dal proibizionismo al monopolio. L'istituzione della privativa del tabacco nello Stato pontificio in età moderna, *Roma moderna e contemporanea*, III(1): 173-199.

Capalbo, Cinzia. 1999. *L'economia del vizio. Il tabacco nello Stato pontificio in età moderna fra produzione e consumo*, Naples: Edizioni Scientifiche Italiane.

Caracciolo, Alberto. 1984 (1956 I ed.). *Roma Capitale. Dal Risorgimento alla crisi dello Stato liberale*, Rome: Editori Riuniti.

Cardarelli, Stefano. 1990. *La questione bancaria in Italia dal 1860 al 1892*, in Ricerche per la storia della Banca d'Italia, vol. I, *Rapporti monetari e finanziari internazionali 1860–1914. Le banche di emissione in Italia fino all'inizio del Novecento. Statistiche storiche: il cambio della lira 1861–1979*, pp. 105–180, Collana Storica della Banca d'Italia, Rome-Bari: Laterza.

Cassis Youssef, 2008a. *Crises and Opportunities. The Shaping of Modern Finance*, Oxford: Oxford University Press.

Cassis, Youssef. 2008b. *Le capitali della finanza. Uomini e città protagonisti della storia economica*, Milan, Francesco Brioschi Editore (or. *Capitals of capital: A History of international financial centres, 1780–2005*, Cambridge: Cambridge University Press, 2006).

Cassis, Youssef and Catherine R. Schenk (eds.). 2021. *Remembering and Learning from Financial Crises*, Oxford: Oxford University Press.

Castelli, Alighiero. 1913. *Pagine disperse. Cronache Mondane. Letteratura, Arte di Gabriele D'annunzio, coordinate e Annotate da Alighiero Castelli,* Rome, Bernardo Lux Libraio editore di S.M. La Regina Madre, 1913.

Castronovo, Valerio. 1990. *L'industria italiana dall'Ottocento a oggi*, Nuova edizione aggiornata, Milan: Mondadori.

Castronovo, Valerio. 1995. *Storia economica d'Italia*, Turin: Einaudi.

Cesarano, Filippo, Cifarelli Giulio and Toniolo Gianni. 2012. Exchange Rate Regimes and Reserve Policy: The Italian Lira 1883–1991. *Open Economies Review*, 23(2): 1-23.

Chabod, Federico. 1997. *Storia della politica estera italuana dal 1870 al 1896*, Rome-Bari: Laterza.

Ciampani, Andrea. 1998. Politica nazionale e rappresentanza degli interessi: la legge per Roma del 1881 nell'istruttoria parlamentare della Camera dei deputati. *Rassegna Storica del Risorgimento*, LXXXV, 4: 483-504.

Ciccarelli, Carlo and Stefano Fenoaltea. 2009. *La produzione industriale delle regioni d'Italia, 1861–1913: una ricostruzione quantitativa*, 1, *Le industrie non manifatturiere*, Rome: Banca d'Italia, Roma.

Ciocca, Pierluigi. 2007. *Ricchi per sempre? Una storia economica d'Italia (1796-2005),* Turin: Bollati Boringhieri.

Cohen, Jon. 1967. Financing Industrialization in Italy 1894–1914: The Partial Trasformation of a Late Comer. *The Journal of Economic History,* 27(3): 363-382.

Comune di Roma. 1872. *Rapporto sul censimento dello Stato Romano nel 1871*, Roma: Direzione Comunale di Statistica.

Comune di Roma, 1960. *Popolazione e territorio. 1860–1960. Con la distribuzione territoriale dei risultati dei censimenti*, Rome: Ufficio di statistica e censimento.

Confalonieri, Antonio. 1974. *Banca e industria in Italia, 1894–1906*, 1, *Le premesse. Dall'abolizione del corso forzoso alla caduta del Credito Mobiliare*, Milan: Banca Commerciale Italiana.

Confalonieri, Antonio. 1975. *Banca e Industria in Italia 1894–1906*, vol. 2, *Il Sistema bancario tra le due crisi,* Milan: Banca Commerciale italiana.

Confalonieri, Antonio. 1976. *Banca e Industria in Italia 1894–1906*, vol. 3, *L'esperienza della Banca Commerciale Italiana,* Milan: Banca Commerciale italiana.

Confalonieri, Antonio. 1982, *Banca e industria in Italia della crisi del 1907 all'agosto del 1914*, Milan: Banca Commerciale Italiana.

Confalonieri, Antonio and Gatti E. 1986. *La politica del debito pubblico in Italia 1919–1943*, Bari: Cariplo—Laterza, 2 vv.

Confalonieri, Antonio. 1994. *Banche miste e grande industria in Italia 1914–1933*, I, *Introduzione. L'esperienza della Banca Commerciale Italiana e del Credito Italiano*, Milan: Banca Commerciale Italiana, Milano.

CONSOB. 2011. *Dall'Unità ai giorni nostri: 150 anni di borsa in Italia.* https://www.consob.it/web/area-pubblica/150-unita-d-italia.

Conte, Leandro. Toniolo Gianni and Vecchi Giovanni. 2003. Monetary Union, Institutions and Financial Market Integration: Italy, 1862–1905. *Explorations in Economic History*, 40: 443–461.

Conti Giuseppe, Alberto Cova, Salvatore La Francesca, 2017. *Le crisi bancarie in Italia nell'Ottocento e nel Novecento. Cause e svolgimenti*, Associazione per lo sviluppo degli Studi di Banca e Borsa-Università del Sacro Cuore, Quaderno 291, Milan: Stampato da Grafica Briantea Srl.

Conti, Giuseppe. 1999. *Le banche e il finanziamento industriale*, *Storia d'Italia.* Annali, 15, in Franco. Amatori, Duccio Bigazzi, Renato Giannetti and Luciano Segreto (ed.), *L'industria*, Turin: Einaudi.

Cotula, Franco and Luigi Spaventa. 1993. *La politica monetaria fra le due guerre 1919–1935*, Rome–Bari: Laterza.

Cotula, Franco and Raganelli Tullio. 1996. *Introduzione*, in Franco Cotula (ed.) *I Bilanci delle aziende di credito 1890–1936*, Rome–Bari: Laterza.

Cotula, Franco and Garofalo, Paolo. 1996. *Le aziende di credito nel sistema finanziario italiano. Aggregati monetari e creditizi. Concentrazione e conti economici delle banche*, in Franco Cotula (ed.) *I Bilanci delle aziende di credito 1890–1936*, Rome–Bari, Laterza.

D'Antone, Leandra (ed.). 1996. *Radici storiche ed esperienza dell'intervento straordinario nel Mezzogiorno*, Naples: Bibliopolis.

D'Errico, Rita. 1999. *Una gestione bancaria ottocentesca. La Cassa di risparmio di Roma dal 1836 al 1890*, Naples: Edizioni Scientifiche Italiane.

Da Pozzo, Mario, Giuseppe, Felloni. 1964. *La borsa valori di Genova nel secolo XIX*, Archivio Economico dell'Unificazione Italiana, s II, vol. X, Genoa.

Daniele, Vittorio and Paolo, Malanima. 2011. *Il divario nord-sud in Italia, 1861–2011*, Soveria mannelli (CZ): Rubbettino editore.

De Cecco, Marcello. 1990. *Introduzione*, in Marcello De Cecco (ed.) *La Banca d'Italia e il sistema finanziario internazionale*, Rome–Bari: Laterza.

De Luca, Giuseppe. 2002. *Le società quotate alla borsa valori di Milano dal 1861 al 2000. Profili storici e titoli azionari*, Milan: Libri Scheiwiller.

De Rosa, Luigi. 1982. *Storia del banco di Roma*, voll. I e II: Rome: Banco di Roma.

De' Gennaro, Maso. 1934. *I debiti dello Stato nel Regno d'Italia, (1861–1932)*, Naples: Tipomeccanica.

Della Seta, P. 1954. Un problema tipico della capitale: la speculazione edilizia, *Critica economica* August; 78–93.

Deslex, Gustavo. 1914. *La questione della Mediterranea,* Turin: Società Tipofrafico Editrice Nazionale.

Dunning, John. H. 1983. Changes in the Level and Structure of International Production: The Last One Under Years, in Casson Mark. (ed.), *The Growth of International Business*, London: Unwin Hyman.

Elmendorf, Douglas W. and N. Gregory Mankiw. 1999. *Government Debt.* In Joh B. Taylor and Michael Woodford (eds.) *Handbook of Macroeconomics*, IC, Amsterdam: Elsevier, 1627–1640.

Falchero, Anna Maria. 1990. *La Banca Italiana di Sconto, 1914–1921. Sette anni di guerra*, Milano: Franco Angeli.

Fauri, Francesca. 2015. Storia *economica delle* migrazioni *italiane*, Bologna: Il Mulino.

Felice, Emanuele. 2007. *Divari regionali e intervento pubblico. Per una rilettura dello sviluppo in Italia*, Bologna: Il Mulino.

Fenoaltea, Stefano. 1987. Le costruzioni in Italia 1861-1913. *Rivista di Storia economica*, IV: 1-34, 2011

Fenoaltea, Stefano. 2006, *L'economia italiana dall'Unità alla Grande guerr*a, Rome-Bari: Laterza.

Fenoaltea, Stefano. 2011. *The Reinterpretation of Italian Economic History from Unification to the Great War*, Cambridge: Cambridge University Press.

Fohlin, Caroline and Reinhold, Steffen. 2010. Common Stock Returns in the pre-WWI Berlin stock exchange. *Cliometrica*, 4: 75–96.

Fohlin, Caroline. 2008. Does Civil Law Tradition (or Universal Banking) Crowd Out Security Markets? Pre-World War I Germany as a Counter—Example. *Enterprise & Society*, 8: 602–641.

Formica, Marina 2021. *Roma Capitale. La città laica, la città religiosa (1870–1915),* Rome: Viella.

Forsyth, Douglass. J. 1993. *The Crisis of Liberal Italy: Monetary and Financial Policy, 1914–1922*, Cambridge, UK: Cambridge University Press

Fortunato, Giustino. 1911. *Il Mezzogiorno e lo Stato italiano,* Bari: Ed. Gius. Laterza & Figli.

Francese, Maura and Angelo Pacc. 2008, Italian Public Debt since National Unification: A Recostruction of the Time Series, Banca d'Italia – *Questioni di economia e finanza*, 31.

Fratianni, Michele. and Spinelli Franco. 1997. *A Monetary History of Italy*, Cambridge: Cambridge University Press.

Frascani, Paolo. 1975. *Politica economica e finanza pubblica in Italia nel primo dopoguerra (1918–1922*), Naples: Giannini ed.

Friz, Giuliano. 1972. *La popolazione di Roma dal 1770 al 1900*, "Archivio dell'unificazione italiana", serie II, volume XIX, Rome.

Friz, Giuliano. 1980. *Consumi, tenore di vita e prezzi a Roma dal 1770 al 1900*, Rome: Edindustria.

Galasso, Giuseppe. 1970. *La capitale inevitabile*, in Pietro Piovani (ed.) *Un secolo da Porta Pia,* Naples: Guida Editore, 71–92.

Galli della Loggia, Ernesto. 1970. Problemi di sviluppo industriale e nuovi equilibri politici alla vigilia della Prima guerra mondiale. La fondazione della Banca Italiana di Sconto. *Rivista Storica Italiana*, 82(4).

Gehering, Thomas and Fohlin, Caroline. 2006. Trading Costs in Early Security Markets: The Case of the Berlin Stock Exchange. *Review of finance*, 10: 587–612.

Gerschenkron, Alexander. 1965. *Il problema storico dell'arretratezza in Italia*, Turin: Einaudi.

Graziani, Ersilia. 1995. *La Banca Romana (1834-1870),* in *Gli Archivi degli Istituti di Credito e le fonti d'archivio per la storia delle banche, Rome*: Ministero per I beni culturali e ambientali. Ufficio centrale per i beni archivistici. 463-492.

http://www.lombardiabeniculturali.it/archivi/soggetti-produttori/ente/MIDB000D10/?.

Insolera, Italo. 1995, *Le città nella Storia d'Italia: Roma*, Rome-Bari: Laterza editori.

Izzo, Luigi 1962, La finanza pubblica nel primo decennio dell'unità italiana, Milan: Giuffrè Editore.

Jacini, Stefano. 1867. *L'amministrazione dei lavori pubblici in Italia dal 1860 al 1867*, Florence: Heredi Botta.

James, Harold and O'Rourke Kevin H. 2013. *La prima globalizzazione e I suoi contraccolpi*, in Gianni Toniolo (ed.) *L'Italia e l'economia mondiale dall'unità a oggi,* Venice: Marsilio Editori, 53–96.

La Francesca, Salvatore. 1965. La statalizzazione delle ferrovie e lo sviluppo dell'industria elettrica in Italia, *Clio,* I, 2: 275-306.

La Francesca, Salvatore. 2006. *La crisi del 1907*, in Paolo PECORARI (ed.) *Crisi e scandali bancari nella storia d'Italia*, Venezia: Istituto Veneto di Lettere Scienze ed Arti.

La Francesca, Salvatore, 2009. *Le crisi finanziarie nell'Italia del primo Novecento,* in *Credito e nazione in Francia e in Italia (XIX–XX secolo),* a cura di G. Conti, P. Feiertag e R. Scatamacchia, Pisa: Plus.

Martinelli, Franco. 1964. *Ricerche sulla struttura sociale della popolazione di Roma: 1871–1961,* Pisa: Libreria Goliardica.

Nardozzi, Giangiacomo and Piluso Giandomenico. 2010. *Il sistema finanziario e la Borsa*, Rome–Bari: Laterza.

Neal, Larry. 2009. *Lessons from History for the Twenty-First Century*, in Jeremy Atack and Larry Neal (eds.) *The Origin and Development of Financial Markets and Institutions. From the Seventeenth Century to the Present,* Cambridge: Cambridge University Press, 450-464.

Negri, Guglielmo (ed.). 1989. *Giolitti e la nascita della Banca d'Italia nel 1893*, Rome-Bari: Laterza, vol. III.

Nitti, Francesco Saverio. 1900. *Nord e Sud: prime linee di una inchiesta sulla ripartizione territoriale delle entrate e delle spese dello Stato in Italia*, Turin: Roux and Viarengo.

Palermo, Stefano. 2006. *La Banca Tiberina. Finanza ed edilizia tra Roma, Napoli e Torino 1869–1895*, Naples: Editoriale Scientifica Italiana.

Pecorari, Paolo (ed.). 2006. *Crisi e scandali bancari nella Sttoria d'Italia*, Verona: Istituto Veneteo di Scienze Lettere ed Arti.

Piccialuti, Caprioli, Maura. 1991. *Amministrazione pubblica ed istituzioni assistenziali dal 1871 al 1911*, in Alberto Caracciolo (ed.), *Storia d'Italia. Le regioni, Il Lazio*, Turin: Utet, 368–369.

Pollard, John F. 2005. *Money and the Rise of the Modern Papacy, Financing the Vatican, 1850-1950*, Cambridge: Cambridge University Press.

Pollard, Sydney. 1981. *Peaceful Conquest: The Industrialization of Europe 1760-1970*, Oxford: Oxford Universiuty Press.

Postigliola, Michele and Donatella Strangio. 2017. Il debito pubblico italiano. Una serie storica dal 1861 al 2012. *Storia economica*, XX(1): 313–330.

Riva, Angelo, 2018. *La crisi del 1907 e l'organizzazione delle borse: cause e conseguenze*. In De Luca, Giuseppe, Lorenzini Marcella, Romano Roberto (eds.) *Banche e banchieri in Italia e in Svizzer. Attività, istituzioni e dinamiche finanziarie tra XVI e XXI secolo*, Bologna, Il Mulino, 317–348.

Romeo, Rosario. 1984. *Cavour e il suo tempo, III. (1854–1861)*, Rome-Bari: Editori Laterza.

Sanna Randaccio, Francesca. 1985. *L'Evoluzione nel tempo dell'investimento diretto italiano: 1900–1981*. In Nicola Acocella (ed.) *Le multinazionali italiane*, Bologna: Il Mulino: 25–50.

Servén, Luis. 1997. Uncertainty, Instability and Irreversible Investment: Theory, Evidence, and Lessons from Africa. *World Bank Policy Research Working Papers*, 1722.

Siciliano, Giovanni. 2001. *Cento anni di borsa in Italia. Mercato, imprese e rendimenti azionari nel ventesimo secolo*, Bologna: Il Mulino.

Sori, Ercole. 1979 and 1984 (new edition). *L'emigrazione italiana dall'Unità alla seconda guerra mondiale*, Bologna: Il Mulino.

Strangio, Donatella. 1997. *L'economia dello Stato pontificio tra il 1860–1870*, in Fiorella Bartoccini and Donatella Strangio (eds.), *Lo Stato del Lazio. 1860–1870*, Rome: Istituto Nazionale di Studi Romani: 147–187.

Toniolo Gianni, Conte Leandro, Vecchi Giovanni, 2003. Monetary Union, Institutions and Financial Market Integration: Italy, 1862–1905. *Explorations in Economic History*, 40(4): 443-461.

Toniolo, Gianni (ed.). 1989. *La banca d'Italia e l'economia di guerra 1914–1919*, Rome–Bari, Laterza.

Toniolo, Gianni. 1990. *An Economic History of Liberal Italy, 1850–1918*, London: Routledge.

Toniolo, Gianni. 1992. *Storia dell'Italia liberale 1850–1918*, Bologna: Il Mulino.

Toniolo, Gianni. 1993. *Il profilo economico*, in Giuseppe Guarino and Gianni Toniolo *La Banca d'Italia e il sistema bancario 1919–1936*, Rome–Bari: Laterza.

Toniolo, Gianni. 2013. *La crescita economica italiana, 1861–2011,* in Gianni Toniolo (ed.) *L'Italia e l'economia mondiale dall'unità a oggi*, Venice: Marsilio Editori: 5–52.

Viarengo, Adriano. 2010. *Cavour*, Rome: Salerno editrice.

Vidotto, Vittorio, 1997. Roma: una capitale per la nazione, in *Mélanges de l'école française de Rome,* 109–111: 7-20.

Volpi, Alessandro. 2002. *Breve storia del mercato finanziario Italiano*, Roma: Carocci.

Warglien, Massimo. 1985. Nota sull'investimento industriale in macchinari e altre attrezzature meccaniche: Italia 1881–1913. *Rivista di storia economica*, 2(1): 126–146.

Warglien, Massimo. 1987. Investimenti industriali e instabilità finanziaria in Italia 1878–1913. *Rivista di storia economica*, n.s., 4, 3: 384–439.

Zamagni, Vera. 1990. (1993 II ed.). *Dalla periferia al centro. La seconda rinascita economica dell'Italia (1861–1990)*, Bologna: Il Mulino.

Zamagni, Vera. 1998. Il debito pubblico italiano 1861–1946: Ricostruzione della serie storica. *Rivista di storia economica*, n.s. 14: 207–242.

Sources

State Archive of Rome (SAR)

Tribunale del Commercio di Roma, Atti di società, bb. 404–426.

Ministero dei Lavori pubblici Segretariato generale Inventario 30/3, b. 178. fasc. 480; b. 179, fasc. 482.

Capitolino Archive

Contratti Atti pubblici Marotti & Frontini & Geisser, 2 giugno 1886.

Contratti Atti Pubblici, Marotti GB Botta & altri 22 april 1899.

Historical Archive of the Bank of Italy

Liquidazioni, Pratt., c.13, fasc. 1.

Liquidazioni, Ufficio Legale Pratt., c. 209, fasc. 1.

Liquidazioni Cpl c 131–140; c. 9, fasc.1.

Liquidazioni Banca Tiberina Pratt. C. 84 fasc. 3.

Liquidazioni Compagnia Fondiaria Cpl c. 6.

Liquidazioni Geisser Pratt c. 71, fasc.1 sfac 1.

Liquidazioni Impresa Esquilino Cpl. Cc. 659–695.

Edited Sources

Atti parlamentari Camera dei Deputati, Legislazione XIV sessione 1880

Bollettino delle strade ferrate. 27,35,40,54 (4 april, 2 and 29 may, 13 june and 8 july 1880).

Giordano, Felice 1871. *Cenni sulle condizioni fisico-economiche di Roma e del suo territorio,* Florence: G. Civelli.

L'Opinione (roman newspaper from 1880 to 1890)

La Tribuna (daily roman newspaper) Giorn. 104, Library of the Senate of the Italian Republic "Giovanni Spadolini", several years.

Ministero di agricoltura industria e commercio, 1889 Direzione generale della statistica, Notizie sulle condizioni edilizie e demografiche della città di Roma e di alcune alter grandi città italiane ed estere del 1888, Rome: Tipografia Eredi Botta.

Ministero di agricoltura industria e commercio, 1893 Direzione generale della statistica, Notizie sulle condizioni edilizie e demografiche della città di Roma e di alcune alter grandi città italiane ed estere del 1891, Rome: Tipografia Naz Bertero.

CHAPTER 6

The 1920s and the Great Depression

The industrialization process that commenced in Italy in the early twentieth century had positive effects, especially on the list of the Rome Stock Exchange. Reflecting Italy's economic progress, the list came to include the stocks of firms operating in the new sectors of chemicals, machinery, electricity and transportation.

Because it was linked to the economic progress of northern Italy, the Milan Stock Exchange had long represented the centre of trading in the country. Its list included numerous securities of primary importance. As shown by our analysis of the Rome Stock Exchange list, the role played by the exchange evolved after the issuance of national regulations for stock exchanges, for example, those issued during the Giolitti period (1893–1914).

During the two-year period, 1921–1922, the Rome Stock Exchange listed numerous industrial companies, unlike the previous century, when only local companies were present.

It is interesting to note that these years were turbulent from an industrial perspective. There was rapid substitution and acquisition of companies in this area of the economy. The turbulence occurred for

D. Strangio, *The Roman Stock Exchange between the 19th and 20th Centuries*, Palgrave Studies in the History of Finance,
https://doi.org/10.1007/978-3-031-00359-2_6

reasons that have been repeatedly discussed, including the excessive exposure of the banks through the industries to which they were connected, which eventually caused the collapse of this fragile system.

The depression of 1929 that hit the United States also affected Europe to a large extent: it was communicated from country to country (and also affected the Rome Stock Exchange) in part by rapidly changing capital movements, in part by a collapse in the prices of goods treated internationally.

Compared to that of the late nineteenth century, change in the list of the Rome Stock Exchange during the period addressed here is also evident in the presence of numerous securities relating to the most important banks in arrangements that characterized the Italian economy in the first half of the 1900s.

6.1 The Rise of Fascism and the 1929 Crisis: The Stock Market in Italy

In this chapter, we address the historical period 1921 to the early 1930s, a delicate period for the world stock market. We approach the events that characterized the Italian stock market from a global perspective, with particular emphasis on the Stock Exchange and the city of Rome. As observed in the previous chapter, in Italy, the ambivalent role assumed by the mixed banks forced the state to adopt targeted interventions to save most of the industrial and banking companies as early as the period immediately following the First World War. Following the political events that shaped Italy in the first twenty years of the twentieth century, the rise of the fascist party commenced, and Benito Mussolini became head of state. In the wake of subsequent events in the rest of Europe, the fascist regime soon became totalitarian and dictatorial.

Although this topic (fascism regime and its policy) is not discussed in this work, the authoritarian regime of the fascist government had inevitable repercussions for the country's economy and stock market.

The largest problem the new fascist government inherited was the public budget deficit, which in 1922 accounted for 1/3 of expenditure, equal to 12.1% of GDP.[1]

[1] Zamagni, 1990, p. 308.

The government undertook to achieve a balanced budget over time by containing public spending. During the two-year period, 1924–1925, cuts were made that stabilized the balance of payments. Among the economic policies implemented by the fascist government, one above all appears to be of particular importance for the analysis of the stock market: the decision to revalue the lira to 90 (i.e., 90 lire per pound).[2] In line with this decision, the government determined to impose the mandatory consolidation of ordinary public debt securities through the issue of the so-called "Loan of the Littorio". This political manoeuvre amounted to a transformation of short-term public debt into a long-term debt, termed consolidation, with a yield set at 3.5% per annum. Until this time, the primary public debt instrument, present on the stock exchange, had been the *Italian 5% Rendita*, as previously discussed.

The set of policies implemented by Mussolini, including protectionism, autarchy, the lira's revaluation and the war in Libya, would amplify the effects of the financial crisis of 1929.[3]

In 1922, a new phase of development for the movable market commenced, driven above all by the electricity sector and the sectors open to export, i.e., machinery and textiles. Overall, considering the stock market price list, between 1920 and 1925, there was an increase in share capital (135%) and overall capitalization (303%).[4]

In 1925, the stock exchange was again reorganized through regulatory provisions, which also addressed stockbroker discipline. In fact, the bullish phase of the stock exchanges worried Bank of Italy Governor Stringher and Minister of Finance De Stefani, who developed an intervention aimed at controlling speculation. Of particular note is the Royal Decree of 26 February 1925, n. 176, which prohibited stockbrokers from accepting or executing forward purchase orders for securities except against payment by the clients of 25% of the relative current price (Article 4).[5]

[2] This provision was harshly criticized by various banking institutions which, although in favor of the stabilization of the currency, were at the time strongly opposed to a revaluation deemed excessive, in fact, according to the top management of the Commercial, a revaluation deemed adequate should have been no less than 120 lire per pound (Toniolo, 1994).

[3] In this regard, see in the substantial relevant bibliography (Bof, 2015, pp. 119–156 and 157.185).

[4] Baia Curioni, 1995, p. 321.

[5] Galanti et al., 2012, p. 284.

A few days later, on March 7, the government ruled as follows:

- The stockbroker is a public official appointed by the Ministry of Finance and must act in absolute independence from any banking or commissioning activity;
- The deposit is raised to one million, and the number of stockbrokers is strictly limited;
- No one other than the agents may bargain at shouting;
- All previous agent appointments are considered invalid, and all the agents up to the required number must be re-elected in three successive rounds.[6]

The government therefore emphasized several points previously introduced by the 1913 law: the incompatibility between intermediation activities and other functions of the stockbrokers and their exclusive access to the so-called shouts, precluding the participation of anyone else.

The reforms created tension above all regarding the decree's retroactivity, which annulled a previous right: the appointment of agents.

In fact, however, the government had done nothing but controlled the ever-increasing number of agent registrations, which occurred in response to rising stock market prices (Fig. 6.1).

At the end of 1924 and the beginning of 1925, the Italian securities market exhibited the effects of the demographic instability of intermediaries combined with the inability of local governments to guarantee adequate discipline as well as the devaluation of the lira and the exchange crisis. These phenomena were another reason for the fascist government to revalue the lira in 1926; in 1927, the lira was again anchored to gold at 92.46 lire per pound, thus introducing the "gold exchange standard".[7]

The Italian economy from 1922 to 1925 was driven by a boom in exports. However, the boom was predominantly in agricultural and textile products. Furthermore, Mussolini's Italy was forced to negotiate

[6] Baia Curioni, 1995, p. 333.

[7] Bof, 2015, pp. 122–126.

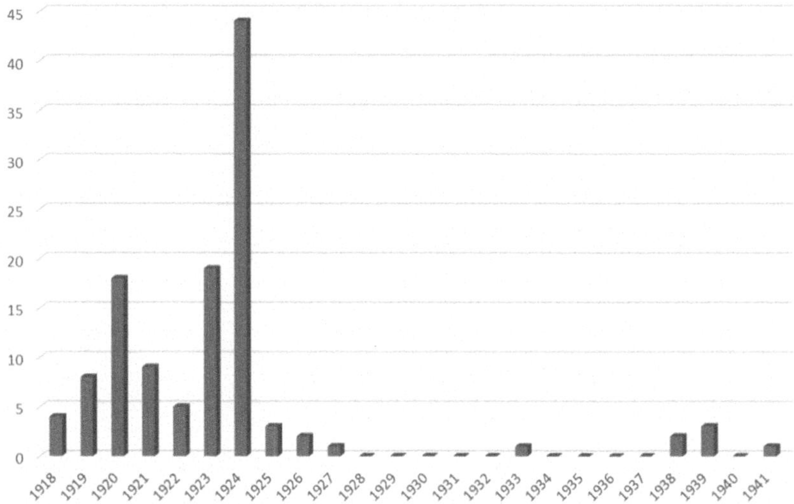

Fig. 6.1 Stockbrokers' inscriptions (*Source* Data mining by Baia Curioni, 1995, p. 328)

with the United States, whose government had prohibited private investment in countries that had not agreed regarding the payment of war debts.[8] In this way, Italy received approximately 316 million dollars from America, divided between public and private entities. The electricity sector absorbed 2/3 of this capital, while the remainder flowed into companies of substantial importance in Italy's economy, such as Fiat, Pirelli, Snia and a few others.

However, given the subsequent stock market crisis in the US financial market, the relief provided for the Italian economy did not last long. Similarly, the Italian balance of payments was strongly negative (Table 6.1).

Table 6.1 shows a clear improvement in exports over the considered decade. The improvement, however, occurred by virtue of an increase in imports, which made the trade balance always negative. The circumstances worsened in the aftermath of lira revaluation, at a time—the

[8] Zamagni, 1990, p. 336.

Table 6.1 Imports, exports and balances—Summary data—1921–1930 (values in thousands of current euros)

Year	*Imports*	*Exports*	*Balances*	*Normalized balance (a)*
1921	8.735	4.154	−4.581	−35,5
1922	8.130	4.731	−3.399	−26,4
1923	8.861	5.655	−3.206	−22,1
1924	10.005	7.370	−2.635	−15,2
1925	13.531	9.384	−4.147	−18,1
1926	13.365	9.577	−3.788	−16,5
1927	10.523	8.015	−2.508	−13,5
1928	11.321	7.460	−3.861	−20,6
1929	11.002	7.627	−3.376	−18,1
1930	8.959	6.259	−2.700	−17,7

Source Data processing by "L'Italia in 150 anni. Sommario di statistiche storiche 1861–2010", in www.istat.it

1930s—when many nations abandoned the gold standard and international trade decreased dramatically.

In industry, between 1923 and 1929, average annual growth was over 5%. The boom also affected companies, driven by the mixed banks that the Bank of Italy saved through the Grants on *Industrial Values Consortium* (established by the Bank of Italy in 1914, the program had the task of creating alternatives to mixed banks for corporate financing in industry). The 1920s marked an evolution of industry towards the new sectors that were emerging in the new century. Progress was being achieved in several areas: from textiles and manufacturing to the electricity, chemicals and machinery.

Contrary to what certain researchers have argued, the fascist period was not one of stagnating industrial development. It is clear that international events required delicate and questionable decisions.

Against this general backdrop of developments in the Italian economy, the securities market was affected by the intertwined bank industry characteristic of the peninsula's economy. The 1920s, therefore, initiated a cycle of transformation in the banking system that included the following important aspects:

1. The multiplication of special lenders;
2. The banking law of 1926;
3. The transformation of ordinary credit companies from mixed banks to holding banks.[9]

Regarding the first point, the special credit institutions were *Crediop* (1919) and the Grants on Industrial Values Consortium. These institutions were unusual in that they specialized in long-term credit to support major construction projects. *Crediop* was founded, thanks to the role played by Alberto Beneduce, who headed large companies during the Fascist period. He viewed in these institutions the solution to the banking crises, as they specialized in long-term credit. Beneduce also conceived the foundation of a new institute, the Credit Institute for public utility companies, in 1924, of which he became president and which had the aim of financing the rapidly expanding electricity companies over the long-term.[10]

Of substantial importance was the establishment of the Italian Mobiliar Institutes in 1931 for the rehabilitation of the banking system. These institutes referred to as "Beneduce institutes" shared the characteristic of being under direct control of the state. They also expanded the funding channel, which was no longer just the Bank of Italy and the Treasury, but also the *Cassa Depositi e Prestiti*, the National Insurance Institute and the National Insurance Fund (later named The National Institute of Social Security—in Italian INPS).[11] These institutions placed bonds on the market to remedy the financial unavailability of individual stocks.

[9] Zamagni, 1990, p. 371.

[10] Ibidem.

[11] The *Cassa* went through all the institutional political regimes of Italy: the constitution of the Kingdom of Italy in 1861; the monarchical period; the fascist period; the republican period; affected in the various periods of greater or lesser autonomy with respect to the central state. It has always survived. Its business was never closed. In the credit market it was the promoter of financial instruments—very often innovative—such as the first interest-bearing postal bonds. The *Cassa Depositi e Prestiti* was born with a law of the Sardinian Parliament of 18 November 1850, having the purpose of mobilizing capital for public utility works. The important reform of 1898 transformed the *Cassa* into the Directorate General of the Treasury, as a policy tool of the Treasury.

Regarding the second point, the banking law of 1926 decreed the uniqueness of the Bank of Italy as the sole issuing institution, downgrading *Banco di Sicilia* and *Banco di Napoli* to public law institutions.[12] This was the first step towards the elimination of the Bank of Italy's involvement in the industry, which was completed with the banking law of 12 March 1936, n. 375. With this law, the Bank of Italy became a public law institution with supervisory obligations towards other banking institutions while also configuring itself as a lender of last resort. The bank was prohibited from granting loans to individuals.[13]

Finally, regarding the final point (i.e., the replacement of the mixed bank model by that of the holding company through the establishment of the Industrial Reconstruction Institute in 1932), it is first appropriate to retrace the stages of the severe stock market crisis of 1929.

In Italy, during the 1920s, the securities market did not undergo major changes in institutional character. From 1920 to 1929, there were 97 entries on the stock exchange and 46 exits; in 1925, half of the capital of all banks and the mining and metallurgical sector was listed, three-quarters of that of the electricity sector and 56–57% of that

In the Fascist period there was a strong push towards organizational centralization aimed at tighter control: Ministry of the Treasury was absorbed by the Ministry of Finance; the minister of Finance directly assumed the presidency of the Board of Directors of the *Cassa*. In 1931, IMI (Italian Mobiliar Institute) was established, half of which was capital participated by the *Cassa*. The *Cassa* also participated in the constitution of IRI in 1933. On 22 June 1944, the Ministry of the Treasury (separate from that of Finance) was reconstituted and the Minister of the Treasury continued to chair the Board of Directors. A 1947 decree definitively separated the *Cassa* from the social security institutions, which became autonomous and separate Directorates General (De Cecco and Toniolo, 2001, 2014; Bricco, 2021).

In 1898, social security took its first steps with the foundation of the national pension fund for the invalidity and old age of workers. It is a voluntary association supplemented by a state contribution and a contribution from entrepreneurs. In 1919 it became compulsory through the decree law of 21 April 1919, n. 603, presented to the Chamber on 28 November 1918; the decree was issued on 21 April 1919. It was converted only in 1923 with a decree that gave the measure the value of law, taking the name of the National Fund for Social Insurance. The Mussolini government, with royal decree law n. 371, transforms the National Fund into a Fascist National Institute of Social Security as a public law entity with legal personality and autonomous management with the aim of guaranteeing social security.

In 1943, with article 3 of the Royal Decree Law 2 August 1943 n.704, the name became that of the National Institute of Social Security.

[12] Zamagni, 1990, p. 373.

[13] De Cecco, 1990; Cardarelli, 1990; Bonelli, 1991; Gigliobianco, 2006.

of the mechanical and textile sector.[14] *Pirelli, Snia Viscosa, Fiat, Sme-Meridionale di elettricità* and other companies entered the Milan stock exchange. It was a remarkable decade: at first highly turbulent, quite positive from 1925 and disastrous after 1929.[15]

On the stock exchange, inherent speculation far exceeded private investment. Moreover, as the great financial crisis approached, the price of money increased, reducing stock market operations. Following the events relating to the lira's revaluation to 90, the Italian banks confronted the great world crisis, which had already weakened them.

Circumstances changed when in the United States a serious stock market crisis occurred following an expansive credit policy introduced by the American government. The famous "Black Thursday" of 24 October 1929, when prices collapsed on the Wall Street Stock Exchange, is emblematic of a crisis of previously unexperienced dimensions.[16] The primary cause was the ease with which private individuals were able to acquire low-interest bank loans based on the credit expansion policy initiated by the US government during the so-called "roaring years". This policy provoked speculation on the stock exchange that had repercussions for the real economy, as the crash on the stock exchange caused a run on deposits by savers, resulting in a liquidity crisis in the banks and related industries. The widespread panic is dramatically described by J. K. Galbraith, who writes of individuals left holding near-zero-value securities and seeing their dreams shattered.[17] Subsequently, President Roosevelt issued a series of laws that guaranteed the solidity of the banking system. These laws were part of a program of economic and social reform: the New Deal, in which the state would play a regulatory role in the economy. The United States would not fully emerge from the crisis until after World War II. The consequences of the crisis were not long in manifesting themselves even outside the United States, whose withdrawal of loans to war-affected nations serious damaged the real economy of nearly all of Europe, in particular in Germany and the United Kingdom. The consequences were stock market crashes, bankruptcies, unemployment and banking and industrial crises.

[14] Coltorti, 2011, p. 83.

[15] De Luca, 2002.

[16] Eichengreen, 1994, pp. 95–144. See also Kindleberger, 1987, pp. 495–520.

[17] Galbraith, 2003, p. 93.

For Italy, the effects of the American crisis first manifested themselves in the early 1930s, and the country was much less affected by the world crisis than other European countries more directly exposed to the influence of the United States. However, the fragile condition of the Italian banking system after the revaluation of the lira to 90 clearly worsened in the aftermath of the global crisis.

The three large mixed banks (i.e., *Credit*, *Comit* and *Banco di Roma*) suffered a depreciation of the securities in their portfolios. Generally, 74 exits from the stock exchange list occurred versus 21 new registrations. In 1929, the list counted 12 credit institutions, while by the end of 1936, all these institutions had disappeared. The situation remained this way for many years out of a fear that a fall in the exchange rates could cause a run at the branches.

A solution was reached by establishing the Institute for Industrial Reconstruction based on a decision to adopt a bailout policy.[18] This decision was dictated both by events in the Italian economy, as the State replaced private individuals in the management of companies in difficulty, and a need to resolve the stock market crisis. Through the control of the large mixed banks that went into difficulty, the Institute for Industrial Reconstruction also controlled the industries connected to them, overall accumulating capital equal to 42% of the total capital of Italian joint-stock companies. Specifically, the Institute for Industrial Reconstruction controlled 100% of the war steel industry, artillery manufacturing and coal mining, 90% of shipyards, 40% of steel, 30% of electricity, all telephony and smaller shares of other sectors.[19]

The Institute for Industrial Reconstruction became a permanent institution in 1937. The demobilization section was abolished, the financing section merged with IMI and Alberto Beneduce was appointed to the presidency. The crisis of the mixed bank model, following the international crisis, required rescue efforts, and these efforts proceeded along a path established in the early 1920s by Beneduce.

The financial and industrial restructuring of the peninsula involved separating the banks from industry, the specialization of credit and credit exchanges between commercial banks and special credit institutions. The Institute for Industrial Reconstruction resembled a holding company,

[18] Castronovo, 2012 (6 volls.).

[19] Zamagni, 1990, p. 379.

and the companies under its control had the legal form of joint-stock companies. These companies belonged to the finance sector: originally the *Turin company telephone businesses* (1934); *Finmare, Maritime Finance Company* (1934) and *Finsider, Steel Finance Company* (1937), to which, after the war, *Finmeccanica, Meccanica Finance Company* (1948) and *Finelettrica, National Electric Finance Company* (1952) were added, also under control of the Institute for Industrial Reconstruction.[20]

6.2 An Analysis of Securities and Prices on the Rome Stock Exchange (1921–1930)

Following the proclamation of the Kingdom of Italy, the Italian stock market underwent profound changes, which had repercussions for the Rome Stock Exchange. The Roman exchange adapted to the national regulations regarding stock exchanges, which concerned the commercial code and stockbrokers, and was integrated (a phenomenon also due to the transfer of the national capital to Rome) into the national and international context. However, one element that remained unchanged, which invisibly connected the new Rome and the territory that ultimately became part of united Italy, concerned the listing of the public debt securities of the Italian state (albeit in a discontinuous way). These securities were subsequently not only always present on the Roman list but also represented its strong point.

For a long period during the twentieth century, the Roman stock exchange was the second-most important exchange in Italy after Milan. It maintained this status until the privatization that merged all the national stock exchanges into one: the Milan stock exchange.[21]

Table 6.2 confirms the importance of the Rome Stock Exchange in the twentieth century.

With the birth of the Kingdom of Italy, the nation's new capital also became attractive to foreign investors. This effect is demonstrated by the list of the Roman stock exchange, which at the end of the nineteenth century featured numerous banking securities, as mentioned. However,

[20] www.archiviostoricoiri.it.

[21] Following the privatization of the stock exchange markets, which took place in 1998, the ten local stock exchanges present in Italy—Milan, Rome, Trieste, Venice, Naples, Turin, Genoa, Florence, Bologna and Palermo—were closed and merged in a single entity: Borsa Italiana.

Table 6.2 Number of companies listed on Italian stock exchanges (1921–1981)

Years	*Turin*	*Rome*	*Genoa*	*Florence*	*Naples*	*Trieste*	*Bologna*	*Venice*	*Palermo*
1921	37	36	30	17	12	34	–	–	–
1931	56	46	58	31	24	28	22	23	–
1941	53	46	56	24	21	18	11	9	–
1951	61	61	60	30	19	16	–	11	–
1961	67	70	72	33	22	26	10	16	–
1971	77	76	64	43	28	26	14	17	22
1981	77	68	62	34	21	20	12	13	14

Source Data processing from CONSOB, 2011, p. 103

the investments and negotiations in the Roman square were not so numerous as to guarantee the presence of large companies. The industrialization process that commenced in Italy in the early twentieth century had positive effects, especially on the list of the Rome Stock Exchange. Reflecting Italy's economic progress, the list came to include the stocks of firms operating in the new sectors of chemicals, machinery, electricity and transportation.

Because it was linked to the economic progress of northern Italy, the Milan Stock Exchange had long represented the centre of trading in the country. Its list included numerous securities of primary importance. In contrast, in the period prior to Italian unification, the Rome Stock Exchange remained isolated, playing a marginal role.

As shown by our analysis of the Rome Stock Exchange list, the role played by the exchange evolved after the issuance of national regulations for stock exchanges, for example, those issued during the Giolitti period (1893–1914).

During the two-year period, 1921–1922, the Rome Stock Exchange listed numerous industrial companies, unlike the previous century, when only local companies were present. Several listed firms were of substantial importance on the national scene, such as *Fiat, Ansaldo, Ilva* and *Snia*. Others were local firms, whose names nevertheless still deserve a mention, for example, *Tramways Omnibus Roma* and *Acqua Marcia*. Certain of these companies will persist into the future and even exist today. Others were acquired by larger companies, while others disappeared altogether.

It is interesting to note that these years were turbulent from an industrial perspective. There was rapid substitution and acquisition of companies in this area of the economy. The turbulence occurred for reasons that have been repeatedly discussed, including the excessive exposure of the banks through the industries to which they were connected, which eventually caused the collapse of this fragile system.

Compared to that of the late nineteenth century, change in the list of the Rome Stock Exchange during the period addressed here is also evident in the presence of numerous securities relating to the most important banks in arrangements that characterized the Italian economy in the first half of the 1900s.

In the two-year period, 1921–1922, we find quotations of the securities of seven banking institutions, although the Italian Discount Bank was delisted in 1922.

During the three-year period, 1928–1930, a further evolution of the list occurred with the entry of new securities, especially bank and government securities. There were eleven bank securities on the list at the decade's end, while four other government securities were added to the Italian *Rendita and Consolidato.*

Tables 6.3, 6.4 and 6.5 describe this evolution, showing the large number of listed securities compared to the late nineteenth century. The presented prices were found in the newspaper "La Tribuna" and revised by calculating the quarterly averages for each recorded year so as to better analyse the performance of individual stocks.

As noted at the chapter's outset, the examined years include the decade 1921–1930, a particularly complex period at the international and national levels due to important economic and political events (such as the advent of fascism and National Socialism in Europe and the crisis of 1929) that had a disruptive effect on the political and social circumstances of the European continent.

Within this decade, it was considered appropriate to restrict the analysis of the stock exchange to the early 1920s (i.e., 1921–1922) and to the years preceding and following the 1929 crisis (i.e., 1928, 1929 and 1930) so as to better interpret the period, including the changes that occurred and how these changes affected the listed companies.

Table 6.3 Securities listed on the Rome Stock Exchange and their quarterly trends in 1921

	1° quarter	*2°quarter*	*3°quarter*	*4°quarter*
Rendita Italiana 3.5%	73.56	74.18	71.34	71.78
Banca d'Italia	1465.69	1352.23	1342.64	1383.60
Istituto Fondiario	437.50	436.31	392.20	
Banca Com. Italiana	1101.15	952.46	856.27	927.83
Credito Italiano	665.08	612.83	613.55	630.36
Banca Italiana di Sconto	586.77	568.08	549.00	538.82
Banco di Roma	116.10	111.27	111.71	114.08
Banca Com.Triestina	604.54	585.00	536.18	551.11
Meridionali	310.23	284.23	301.36	336.09
Mediterranee	148.62	137.85	140.22	170.20
Rubattino	597.69	496.08	499.18	537.00
S.N.I.A	51.87	31.19	27.86	30.50
Tramway Roma	126.23	93.46	111.41	76.56
Acqua Marcia	1781.15	1715.38	1685.50	1630.50
Gas Roma	450.31	437.15	421.60	444.50
Condotte d'Acqua	275.77	223.77	218.09	270.25
Acciaierie Terni	621.08	514.23	519.64	509.90
ILVA	86.42	48.98	33.05	21.68
Ansaldo	121.42	136.12	109.50	90.40
Metallurgica	83.73	79.42	87.91	92.35
Miniere Elba	120.62	66.37	87.91	60.83
Miniere Antimonio	49.76	40.69	54.63	39.35
Kerka	502.46	396.31	308.91	291.20
Viscosa di Pavia	102.00	72.88	84.70	116.95
Miniere Montecatini	144.69	124.31	124.21	140.25
Immobiliari	438.38	447.38	451.48	484.8
Beni Stabili	308.92	328.38	331.2	312.85
Fondi Rustici	230.77	225.08	218	246.4
Carburo	720.27	616.38	530.45	576.9
Azoto	272.08	219.15	165.27	209.5
Elettrochimica	85.27	73.12	69.6	68.61
Forni Elettrici	62.88	48.04	32	24.15
Zuccheri Roma	65.23	59.25	59.28	65.725
Eridania	306.08	262.08	290.36	323.36
Molini Pantanella	131.19	132.92	120.63	164.8
Marconi	197.31	188.77	173.02	160.55
F.I.A.T	190.12	160.42	147.7	171.85
Cotoniere Meridionali	114.00	84.75	82.6	90.63
Cosulich	464.23	361.25	344.3	333.7
Consolidato 5%	74.66	78.8	75.9	76.93

Source *"La Tribuna"*, Quotidiano, 1921, Giorn. 104, Biblioteca del Senato "Giovanni Spadolini"

Table 6.4 Securities listed on the Rome Stock Exchange and their quarterly trends in 1922

	1° quarter	*2°quarter*	*3°quarter*	*4°quarter*
Rendita Italiana 3.5%	72.67	72.05	71.97	75.53
Banca d'Italia	1335.00	1289.00	1318.31	1392.67
Istituto Fondiario				
Banca Com. Italiana	832.50	832.75	861.23	905.00
Credito Italiano	617.30	609.13	592.58	690.00
Banca Italiana di Sconto				
Banco di Roma	110.70	104.90	104.33	104.16
Banca Com.Triestina	569.00	547.27	531.54	500.73
Meridionali	288.75	291.25	288.08	306.00
Mediterranee	134.70	141.75	150.54	207.25
Rubattino	487.90	476.33	516.62	552.33
S.N.I.A	25.40	24.94	50.77	62.29
Tramway Roma	79.15	72.13	105.54	122.08
Acqua Marcia	1578.33	1426.61	1428.85	1516.58
Gas Roma	411.40	424.08	539.19	597.33
Condotte d'Acqua	270.45	244.42	240.92	293.27
Acciaierie Terni	404.60	394.33	443.23	476.00
ILVA	14.85	12.73	11.31	12.48
Ansaldo	33.70	17.54	19.12	22.75
Metallurgica	85.00	91.92	105.06	120.63
Miniere Elba	44.95	39.04	49.33	61.17
Miniere Antimonio	34.43	35.33	35.21	31.81
Kerka	258.50	290.92	314.46	308.00
Viscosa di Pavia	106.00	144.96	105.96	106.00
Miniere Montecatini	141.20	136.48	142.85	167.71
Immobiliari	470.6	443.54	491.85	542.42
Beni Stabili	282.7	269.58	316.77	365.91
Fondi Rustici	227.65	213.41	231.92	257.83
Carburo	548.9	495.16	600.00	634.00
Azoto	168.4	148.41	169.62	183.36
Elettrochimica	59.15	58.3	60.38	65.92
Forni Elettrici	18.7	18.9	21.69	22.71
Zuccheri Roma	54.45	60.45	66.12	73.46
Eridania	297.9	320.8	331.54	381.04
Molini Pantanella	139.3	147.08	146.77	196.18
Marconi	159.65	209.9	214.00	227.08
F.I.A.T	165.75	191.9	233.04	252.71
Cotoniere Meridionali	69.33	71.6	65.67	72.25
Cosulich	283.36	279.8	314.77	354.00
Consolidato 5%	76.994	79.17	80.34	84.06

Source "*La Tribuna*", Quotidiano, 1921, Giorn. 104, Biblioteca del Senato "Giovanni Spadolini"

Table 6.5 Securities listed on the Rome Stock Exchange and their quarterly trends in 1928

	1° quarter	*2°quarter*	*3°quarter*	*4°quarter*
Littorio	84.23	86.56	82.87	0.00
Rendita 3.5%	74.72	75.32	72.96	74.47
Consolidato 5%	84.59	86.75	82.27	85.17
Venezie 3.5%	74.38	77.67	75.41	76.64
Buoni del tesoro novennali 1931	94.88	96.68	95.80	0.00
Buoni del tesoro novennali 1934	94.25	96.52	76.25	0.00
Banca d'Italia	2414.08	2600.15	2444.64	2508.64
Istituto di credito fondiario	450.00	478.69	462.18	467.00
Banca Comm. Italiana	1284.77	1392.92	1324.27	1324.93
Credito Italiano	835.85	842.92	817.45	833.29
Banco di Roma	112.38	116.79	113.59	115.43
Istituto credito marittimo	527.62	515.96	519.73	526.68
Banca Comm. Triestina	565.92	559.38	553.00	564.50
Banca Nazionale di credito	557.19	572.50	552.77	568.14
Consorzio Mob. Fin	678.67	857.15	742.55	740.92
Meridionali	731.38	837.31	754.82	780.36
Tramways	446.38	398.75	400.45	396.29
Navigazione	537.00	556.85	543.70	538.43
Libera Triestina	335.46	280.88	279.27	289.57
Cosulich	189.15	197.54	179.27	189.18
Cotoniere	43.92	49.02	55.05	45.70
Snia Viscosa	159.64	181.31	157.91	149.45
Soie de Chatillon	146.00	247.92	180.91	187.11
Varedo	58.85	77.02	58.64	63.91
Elba	45.87	366.77	44.84	45.18
Metallurgica	136.08	151.88	141.45	144.73
Ilva	143.00	160.42	146.45	161.46
Montecatini	231.75	262.50	233.68	254.23
Monte amiata	339.62	340.92	330.18	321.54
Antimonio	191.85	199.42	191.36	198.79
Ansaldo	96.92	99.08	96.36	95.14
F.I.A.T	386.50	438.65	405.23	434.18
Valdarno	145.96	163.15	155.27	151.82
Seso	126.50	138.90	126.00	134.96
Terni	425.88	447.08	458.40	428.54
Sip	149.69	174.62	155.80	158.29
Tirso	278.23	244.75	235.45	235.29
Gas di Roma	755.31	809.00	760.55	736.50
Unes	113.19	129.19	118.15	119.18
Azoto	227.08	235.46	199.20	235.57

(continued)

Table 6.5 (continued)

	1° quarter	*2°quarter*	*3°quarter*	*4°quarter*
Elettrochimica	88.54	95.77	0.00	0.00
Forni elettrici	103.65	98.08	95.90	99.89
Distillerie	147.08	152.92	147.35	148.89
Zuccheri Romani	140.15	128.50	133.36	131.86
Molini pantanella	297.15	323.04	257.55	253.39
Bonifiche ferraresi	468.69	495.38	481.68	490.68
Fondi rustici	207.46	215.31	212.91	199.00
Immobiliari	801.38	924.46	826.86	849.93
Beni stabili	613.54	743.77	668.18	689.86
Imprese fondiarie	128.31	119.40	110.18	112.55
C.F. Regionale	112.69	133.50	231.65	121.46
Aedes	9.11	9.41	8.15	8.25
Risanamento	1085.69	1358.77	1191.27	1229.07
Acqua Marcia	2223.23	2957.31	2685.00	2573.36
Condotte d'acqua	719.15	1068.38	820.18	838.00
Serino	634.08	742.08	645.82	689.86
Palermo	563.38	524.15	519.55	557.61
Spalato	262.92	250.92	252.50	249.73
Isonzo	93.54	88.96	89.09	90.36
Marconi's Wireless	252.31	280.69	265.91	309.86
Assicurazioni vita	903.08	995.15	902.91	910.07
Eridania	862.17	833.85	675.90	794.36
Banca d'America			144.23	124.79
Banca Italo-Britannica			512.25	530.04

Source "*La Tribuna*", Quotidiano, 1928, Giorn. 104, Biblioteca del Senato "Giovanni Spadolini"

6.3 Annual and Quarterly Trends of Securities on the Rome Stock Exchange (1921–1922; 1928–1930)

The preceding discussion is supported by our analyses of the securities on the Rome Stock Exchange performed.

Based on the quarterly averages calculated for the securities recorded in the two-year period, 1921–1922, and in the three-year period, 1928–1930, it is clear that the Roman square was fully inserted in the national context. Support for this statement is furnished by the different prices of securities relating to the banks and industrial companies that were most important nationally: *Fiat, Ansaldo, Ilva and Snia.*

However, unlike the Milan stock exchange, the Roman exchange still featured purely local company securities on its list: Tramways Roma, *Gas*

Roma (a gas distribution company located in the capital) and *Acqua Marcia*.

In fact, as has been stated several times, the speciality of the Roman stock market remained public debt securities. In the studied years, these securities were 3.5% return and 5% consolidated income.

In early 1920s, the Rome Stock Exchange emerged from the marginal role it had played in the past and came to represent a highly important institution for both local and national economic development.

Tables 6.3 and 6.4 present the quarterly averages of the securities listed on the Rome Stock Exchange and highlight its expansion phase.

The Italian securities market had undergone considerable development, thanks to companies operating in the electricity, machinery and textile sectors, recording an increase in the share capital of such companies and in their overall capitalization.

The tables enable one to better appreciate the change that the Rome Stock Exchange underwent over the years, with a considerable increase in listed securities and the number of companies present compared to the end of the nineteenth century.

In fact, despite its reputation as a peripheral stock exchange, the presence of titles of primary importance on the national scene indicate the true significance of the Roman stock exchange.

The two-year period considered here (i.e., 1921/1922) was also a volatile historical period characterized by banking events of considerable importance.

Tables 6.3 and 6.4 show the number of securities of the most important banking institutions in the considered two-year period: the Bank of Italy, the Italian Commercial Bank, the Italian Credit, the Italian Discount Bank, the *Banco di Roma* and the *Banca Commerciale Triestina*. Among the company shares, the following firms are most important: *Fiat*, *Ansaldo*, *Snia*, *Ilva*, *Acciaierie Terni*, *Eridania*, *Southern Railways*, *Gas Roma*, *Rubattino*, *Tramway Rome* and others. In addition to these companies, the Rome Stock Exchange listed small and medium-sized companies that persist for a good part of the twentieth century, such as *Marconi*, *Molini Pantanella* and *Zuccheri Romani*.

The collection and processing of these data facilitate examining the trends of the most important titles during the early 1920s and the three years prior to the decade's end. Tables 6.5, 6.6 and 6.7 present the securities listed on the Rome Stock Exchange and the related quarterly trends for the three-year period, 1928–1930.

Table 6.6 Securities listed on the Rome Stock Exchange and their quarterly trends in 1929

	1° quarter	*2°quarter*	*3°quarter*	*4°quarter*
Littorio	0.00	0.00	0.00	0.00
Rendita 3.5%	71.02	70.07	68.11	67.27
Consolidato 5%	81.91	81.92	79.40	80.43
Venezie 3.5%	74.45	73.45	73.05	72.28
Buoni del tesoro novennali 1931	0.00	0.00	0.00	0.00
Buoni del tesoro novennali 1934	0.00	0.00	0.00	0.00
Banca d'Italia	2210.23	1912.77	1766.82	1894.64
Istituto di credito fondiario	483.83	467.85	455.18	456.82
Banca Comm. Italiana	1455.15	1371.81	1379.05	1343.86
Credito Italiano	848.08	760.85	809.82	786.23
Banco di Roma	117.33	113.30	118.32	117.50
Istituto credito marittimo	528.85	501.15	501.18	509.73
Banca Comm. Triestina	542.92	491.46	461.05	464.14
Banca Nazionale di credito	584.85	543.69	549.73	552.09
Consorzio Mob. Fin	888.92	836.92	842.50	771.32
Meridionali	882.77	898.00	1101.64	1210.73
Tramways	263.50	274.73	275.23	246.27
Navigazione	524.35	501.96	510.77	510.39
Libera Triestina	160.85	128.77	136.41	124.86
Cosulich	152.04	104.73	98.91	84.78
Cotoniere	42.57	30.73	30.39	27.91
Snia Viscosa	119.92	96.50	86.16	69.16
Soie de Chatillon	236.62	222.62	231.20	204.55
Varedo	53.08	42.10	45.57	38.86
Elba	50.00	44.31	49.23	49.36
Metallurgica	173.96	186.19	199.41	209.55
Ilva	205.81	206.62	227.23	216.55
Montecatini	282.13	251.79	258.27	249.82
Monte amiata	307.58	289.88	269.77	260.95
Antimonio	219.54	235.23	249.18	206.82
Ansaldo	116.15	136.65	140.70	110.95
F.I.A.T	582.85	525.46	544.05	404.86
Valdarno	181.04	185.75	190.14	193.95
Seso	134.27	126.65	124.95	128.82
Terni	431.38	394.81	404.64	396.30
Sip	174.12	159.38	148.91	146.64
Tirso	241.65	216.15	216.00	204.40
Gas di Roma	823.38	709.15	723.73	776.45
Unes	128.13	118.35	116.73	108.61
Azoto	185.83	170.38	156.64	147.23

(continued)

Table 6.6 (continued)

	1° quarter	*2°quarter*	*3°quarter*	*4°quarter*
Elettrochimica	0.00	0.00	0.00	0.00
Forni elettrici	74.08	52.00	51.18	61.00
Distillerie	155.27	136.38	144.91	150.02
Zuccheri Romani	112.85	108.77	111.61	114.00
Molini pantanella	255.62	222.08	209.09	206.50
Bonifiche ferraresi	528.46	482.27	478.55	434.86
Fondi rustici	210.42	196.62	195.27	192.32
Immobiliari	956.15	904.46	936.83	951.82
Beni stabili	743.77	647.42	648.05	620.73
Imprese fondiarie	130.85	131.69	137.27	141.77
C.F. Regionale	121.27	109.12	105.89	97.50
Aedes	5.94	5.83	5.74	5.34
Risanamento	1198.85	1120.62	1169.64	1226.55
Acqua Marcia	2537.08	1585.23	1499.82	1491.45
Condotte d'acqua	839.17	1090.38	771.82	740.00
Serino	603.92	553.62	557.90	522.27
Palermo	534.00	474.15	472.36	481.50
Spalato	234.54	228.08	215.91	214.50
Isonzo	90.31	86.77	78.10	67.82
Marconi's Wireless	397.77	372.08	376.18	270.27
Assicurazioni vita	877.77	737.88	768.27	741.91
Eridania	497.00	472.96	476.14	464.91
Banca d'America	117.73	101.31	100.45	99.61
Banca Italo-Britannica	498.92	480.33	506.18	502.09

Source "*La Tribuna*", Quotidiano, 1929, Giorn. 104, Biblioteca del Senato "Giovanni Spadolini"

The tables enable one to quickly comprehend what has been argued thus far. That is, an exponential increase occurred in the number of listed securities.

We temporarily leave aside the data that will be used to analyse the share performance of the securities in the next section. For now, it is important to highlight the composition of the stock market (1922 and 1930) (Fig. 6.2 and 6.3).

The evolution of the stock exchange list was primarily influenced by the presence of many banking institutions. Specifically, in addition to *Credit, Comit, Banco di Roma*, Bank of Italy and *Banca Commerciale Triestina*, the Rome Stock Exchange listed the following institutions: the *Istituto di Credito Fondiario*, the *Istituto di Credito Marittimo*, the *Banca Nazionale*

Table 6.7 Securities listed on the Rome Stock Exchange and their quarterly trends in 1930

	1° quarter	*2° quarter*	*3° quarter*	*4° quarter*
Littorio	0.00	0.00	0.00	0.00
Rendita 3.5%	67.17	69.42	68.40	68.85
Consolidato 5%	79.81	83.85	81.22	82.04
Venezie 3.5%	73.57	74.08	75.69	76.34
Buoni del tesoro novennali 1931	0.00	0.00	0.00	0.00
Buoni del tesoro novennali 1934	0.00	0.00	0.00	0.00
Banca d'Italia	1925.23	1971.08	1791.50	1678.33
Istituto di credito fondiario	479.88	470.15	479.60	453.83
Banca Comm. Italiana	1428.35	1422.81	1414.70	1410.00
Credito Italiano	745.85	785.96	791.05	699.63
Banco di Roma	117.62	113.29	109.85	108.60
Istituto credito marittimo	524.15	502.46	500.85	503.67
Banca Comm. Triestina	407.15	405.00	405.00	0.00
Banca Nazionale di credito	573.04	390.35	100.41	100.31
Consorzio Mob. Fin	813.58	825.04	805.25	740.58
Meridionali	1188.46	1289.38	1083.80	935.54
Tramways	248.00	227.38	241.90	149.00
Navigazione	495.23	474.62	378.30	329.04
Libera Triestina	114.27	103.17	88.80	75.13
Cosulich	90.12	88.72	86.18	87.39
Cotoniere	31.37	25.72	31.03	18.67
Snia Viscosa	62.67	64.65	46.23	38.63
Soie de Chatillon	182.83	253.27	239.55	235.04
Varedo	40.02	42.06	36.53	29.67
Elba	63.13	48.41	62.65	45.21
Metallurgica	185.92	174.69	167.33	166.58
Ilva	223.81	205.38	207.17	214.19
Montecatini	254.69	242.08	212.25	199.00
Monte amiata	279.35	296.73	203.48	147.25
Antimonio	172.38	161.92	158.50	155.67
Ansaldo	108.23	110.71	95.90	83.63
F.I.A.T	367.96	376.46	290.95	234.54
Valdarno	189.92	176.96	183.33	157.54
Seso	187.37	109.56	84.43	78.50
Terni	402.54	377.92	364.20	384.48
Sip	148.73	163.29	130.30	192.63
Tirso	200.23	232.00	186.30	174.17
Gas di Roma	767.62	789.38	766.50	727.75
Unes	107.85	108.08	149.15	74.94
Azoto	140.12	151.04	127.30	110.13

(continued)

Table 6.7 (continued)

	1° quarter	*2° quarter*	*3° quarter*	*4° quarter*
Elettrochimica	0.00	0.00	0.00	0.00
Forni elettrici	72.23	64.29	64.05	59.46
Distillerie	152.62	141.68	127.20	110.83
Zuccheri Romani	109.50	105.73	114.48	92.58
Molini pantanella	207.69	181.65	166.40	168.04
Bonifiche ferraresi	455.04	410.19	129.83	15.81
Fondi rustici	185.40	160.85	139.15	81.71
Immobiliari	981.81	935.04	661.60	675.00
Beni stabili	638.00	642.15	589.10	507.92
Imprese fondiarie	164.77	159.85	152.10	145.83
C.F. Regionale	85.85	80.38	55.78	30.02
Aedes	3.66	44.44	132.60	202.83
Risanamento	1212.69	1242.69	1023.10	1036.40
Acqua Marcia	1513.27	1473.46	905.00	638.75
Condotte d'acqua	749.54	749.85	664.60	476.33
Serino	510.62	466.85	378.00	347.42
Palermo	549.92	510.92	458.60	421.17
Spalato	206.52	194.48	177.00	136.92
Isonzo	78.69	71.38	67.40	44.79
Marconi's Wireless	247.31	205.23	150.00	155.00
Assicurazioni vita	551.00	645.62	566.30	506.67
Eridania	451.65	471.92	388.70	350.50
Banca d'America	100.10	89.60	92.05	79.00
Banca Italo-Britannica	480.23	476.85	471.00	376.50

Source "*La Tribuna*", Quotidiano, 1930, Giorn. 104, Biblioteca del Senato "Giovanni Spadolini"

di Credito, the Financial Mobiliar Consortium (Comofin), the Bank of America and the Italo-British Bank (both entered the Roman list in the third quarter of 1928).

Additionally, with the listing of the "Littorio", the Venezie Obligations and the nine-year Treasury Bills (1931 and 1934), the Rome Stock Exchange evolved considerably in terms of public debt securities. However, as indicated by Table 6.5, the "Prestito del Littorio" and Treasury bills exited the list in 1928.

In terms of corporate securities, all the securities of the companies presented above remained firmly listed on the Roman stock exchange. To these were added companies operating in the microfibres sector (Soie

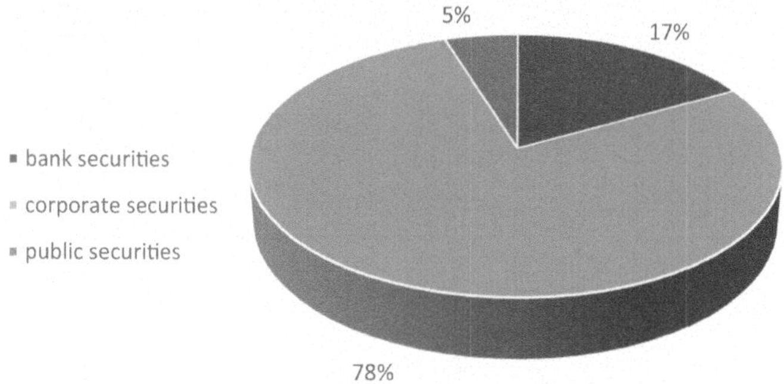

Fig. 6.2 Percentage composition of securities listed on the Rome Stock Exchange in 1922

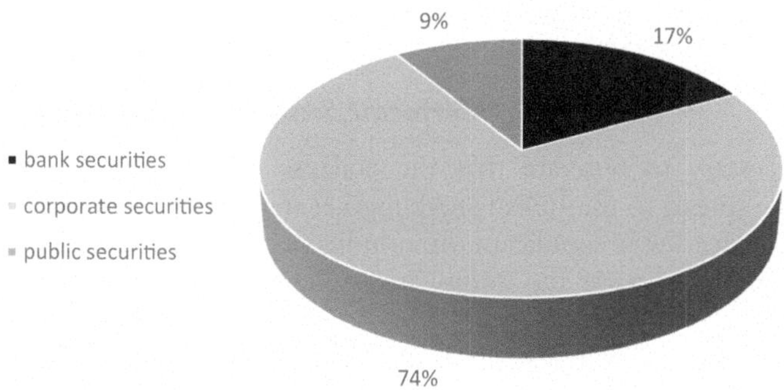

Fig. 6.3 Percentage composition of securities listed on the Rome Stock Exchange in 1930

de Chatillon), railways (C. F Regionale, Palermo), electricity (Sip) and the previously mentioned booming sectors.

In the following, we examine in greater detail the trend of the most important securities through graphic representation. We group the listed securities into three types: corporate securities, bank securities and public debt securities.

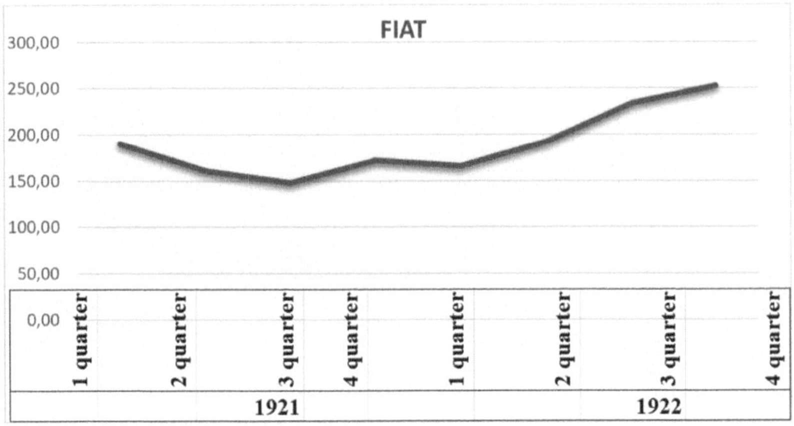

Fig. 6.4 Quarterly trend of Fiat shares (1921–1922)

6.3.1 *Corporate Securities*

It is necessary to reiterate that the collapse of the Wall Street Stock Exchange spread to the Italian stock market starting in 1930. The decline in share prices was significant in nominal terms, but the decrease in consumer prices made the equity investment loss less dramatic in real terms.[22]

The recession that began in 1929 placed the Italian mixed banks in difficulty, which can also be deduced from the performance of their shares on the Rome Stock Exchange. However, starting with the corporate stocks, it is interesting to compare the share trends of the most important companies listed on the Roman exchange based on data relating to securities quotations.

One of the most important national-level industrial companies listed on the Roman exchange was Fiat. Founded in Turin on 1 July 1899, Fiat expanded considerably in the early years of the twentieth century. As shown in Fig. 6.4, Fiat shares on the capital's stock exchange listing exhibit a constant trend for the early 1920s.

Starting in 1922, the average quarterly value of Fiat shares on the Rome Stock Exchange increased until the end of the same year, reaching

[22] Siciliano, 2001, p. 28.

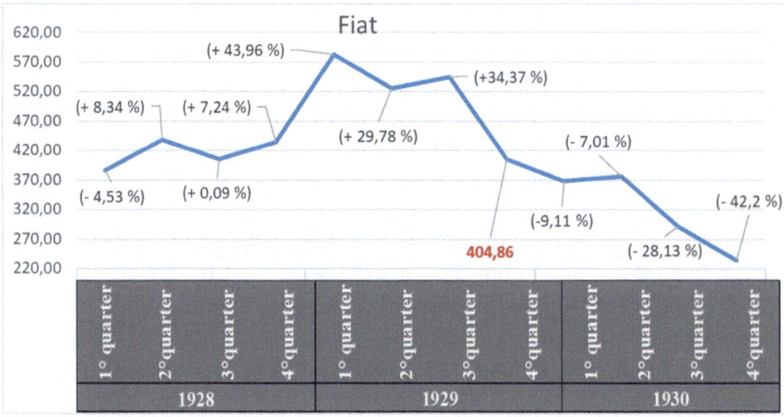

Fig. 6.5 Quarterly trend of Fiat shares (1928–1930)

an average value of approximately 252.71 lire in the fourth quarter (Table 6.4).

Fiat was clearly an Italian corporate giant that despite autocratic fascist policy managed to grow during the 1920s; thanks to domestic demand and the firm's specialization in sectors in addition to automobile manufacturing, such as the production of war material.[23] During the 1920s, numerous Fiat subsidiaries were founded headed by anonymous companies, and by 1928, Fiat was responsible for 80% of car production and controlled numerous companies.[24]

Fiat also listed its shares on other stock exchanges on the peninsula, and in the aftermath of the 1929 stock market crash, it was not particularly affected by the global crisis. According to an analysis of the data related to Fiat shares on the Rome Stock Exchange during the three-year period, 1928–1930, the average value of Fiat shares increased considerably towards the decade's end (Fig. 6.5). In fact, the price of the shares

[23] The choice of autarchy, which would have characterized the fascist economy from 1935 to 1940, could appear as an immediate reaction to the sanctions suffered; in reality, this economic policy approach had already had its embryo in the interventions following the 1929 crisis through the replacement of imports of raw materials with national products in order to achieve a level of self-sufficiency that would allow Italy to be autonomous in food and productive in case of war (Bof, 2015).

[24] Zamagni, 1993, p. 514.

stood at 400 lire against an average of approximately 200 lire during the two-year period, 1921–1922.

The positive performance of Fiat shares during the two-year period, 1928–1929, is explained by the firm's highly effective managerial policy and its numerous exports abroad. However, as shown in Fig. 6.5, a progressive decline in the stock's value following the 1929 crisis can be noted.

Fiat had foreign subsidiaries in the United States and was financed by large banks, especially Comit. The firm was affected by the crisis due to such interconnections. Nevertheless, the company overcame the phase of turbulence.

Another important industry listed on the Roman exchange was the Italian-American Navigation Company. Founded in Turin in 1917, the firm was involved in sea transport between Italy and the United States. However, the company soon changed its business focus to the production of textile and synthetic fibres.[25] The Italo-American Navigation Company absorbed the Viscosa di Pavia company, also present on the Rome Stock Exchange (Tables 6.4 and 6.5).

The company's shares were listed on all national stock exchanges as well as in London and New York. It was a strong company and one that reflected the technological progress that had been achieved in the Italian chemicals and machinery sectors.

The shares of the Italian-American Navigation Company on the Roman square exhibit an ever-increasing trend during the two-year period, 1921–1922, although their value was low.

Figure 6.6 shows the trend in the value of the company's shares of and reveals how they differ considerably from those of Fiat, which during this decade saw its stock at the centre of intense trading and with significantly higher share value.

The Italian-American Navigation Company, however, remained on a growth path throughout the decade and into the early 1930s, as shown by the share price data presented in Table 6.5. Because the company operated in an emerging sector with ample room for expansion, the value of its shares on the Rome Stock Exchange increased significantly.

[25] www.ilsole24ore.com.

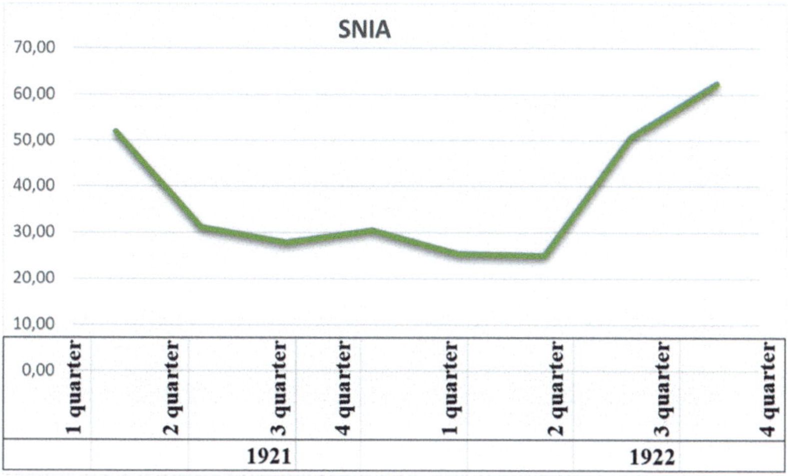

Fig. 6.6 Quarterly trend of the shares of *Società di Navigazione Italo-Americana* (1921–1922)

The yield on the shares of the *Società di Navigazione Italo-Americana* remained stable for one year: from the second quarter of 1921 to the second quarter of 1922, when the yield improved.

Nevertheless, as shown in Fig. 6.7, the firm's shares on the Roman stock exchange underwent an obvious change, and although they earned a higher return than in the early 1920s, they experienced a progressive decline starting in the fourth quarter of 1928.

In the aftermath of the world financial crisis, the Italian-American Shipping Company did not experience major problems and was able to continue to develop while making other acquisitions. However, the crisis eventually struck all listed company more or less directly, affecting stock exchanges worldwide.

The turbulent phase on the stock exchanges of the period is also highlighted in Fig. 6.7. However, despite a sharp depreciation of its stock to a value of approximately 40 lire at the end of the decade, the Italian-American Navigation Company Viscosa remained stable during the period following the stock collapse.

In sharp contrast to these two industrial firms is the fate of another large Italian company established in those years: Ilva. The largest Italian

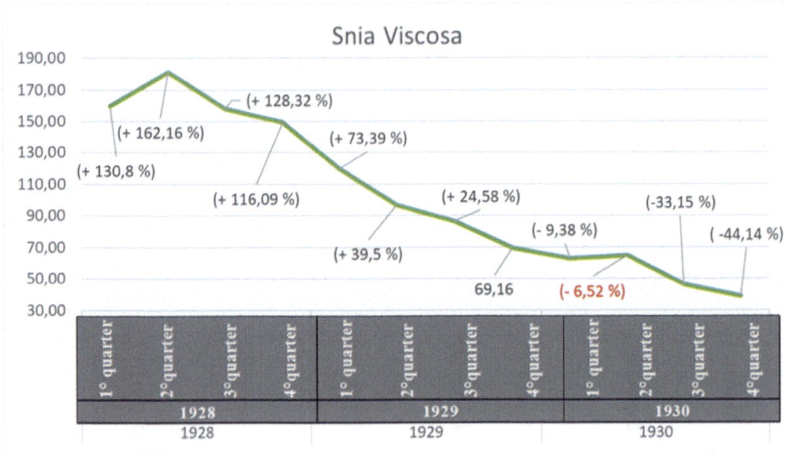

Fig. 6.7 Quarterly trend of the shares of *Società di Navigazione Italo-Americana* (1928–1930)

steel company, Ilva was founded in 1905 and subsequently controlled numerous smaller companies. In 1911, the Ilva Consortium was formed after a merger between *Ilva, Alti Forni* and *Ilva Acciaierie d'Italia*. The consortium also listed its shares in the Roman square. Ilva confronted many problems during the postwar phase, although the previous years were vital for the company because it manufactured steel products needed in the war. The company ran into difficulties when demand decreased dramatically in the postwar period, forcing *Banca Commerciale Italiana*, the firm's largest creditor, to assume ownership in 1921.[26]

Figure 6.8 analyses the performance of Ilva shares listed on the Roman stock exchange and reflects the drastic depreciation that occurred at the end of 1922. The figure also shows that the price of Ilva shares reached a maximum value at the beginning of 1921 of approximately 90 lire and a minimum value of approximately 10 lire at the end of 1922.

It is evident that certain industrial companies were particularly affected by war events, fascist policies and the world stock market crisis of 1929.

The depreciation phase of Ilva shares on the Roman stock exchange represents a further symptom of the company's difficulty in addressing

[26] www.gruppoilva.com.

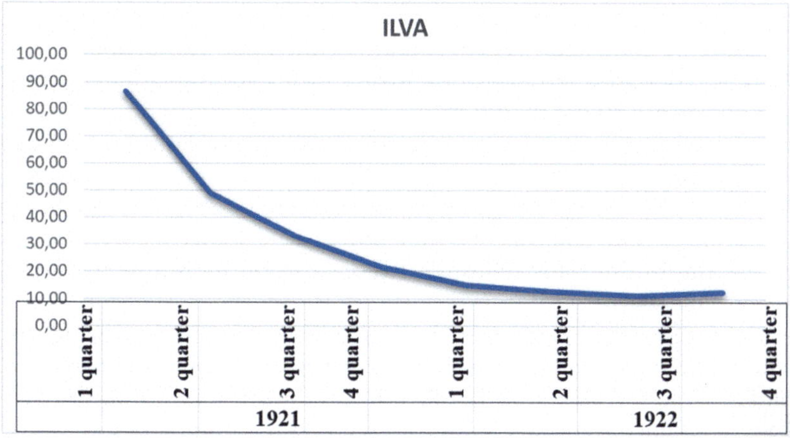

Fig. 6.8 Quarterly trend of ILVA shares (1921–1922)

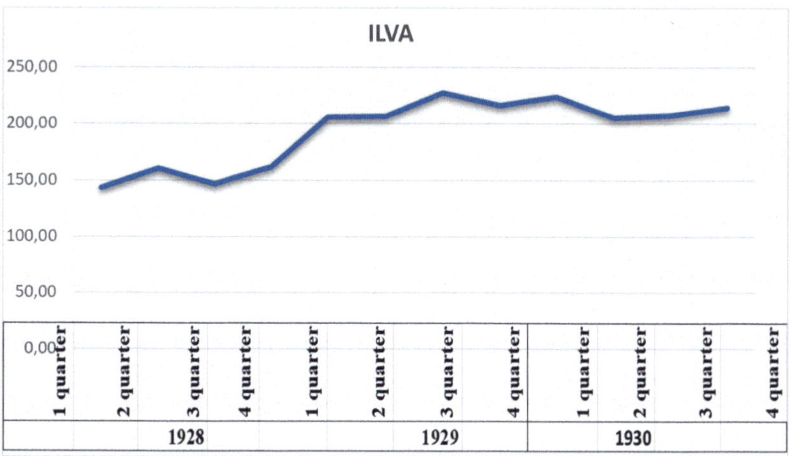

Fig. 6.9 Quarterly trend of ILVA shares (1928–1930)

a demand that contracted considerably at the end of the war. However, as in the case of the Italian-American Shipping Company, the share price had a higher value towards the end of the decade (Fig. 6.9).

Additionally, in this case, Ilva shares on the Rome Stock Exchange do not exhibit a completely negative trend for the three-year period, 1928–1930. In contrast, the value of the shares increased from a minimum of approximately 150 lire to 200 lire.

The explanation for this positive trend can be attributed to the fact that the global crisis hit Italy *after* 1929. In addition, one must not forget that Ilva was purchased by Comit, its largest creditor, before being placed under state control. The situation worsened after the 1929 crisis, forcing the Institute for Industrial Reconstruction to assume the firm's ownership.

These events had negative effects for those companies heavily dependent on creditor banks, such as Ilva, which was kept alive, thanks to funding from the Comit. Most likely, it was for this very reason that Ilva shares continued to exhibit a positive trend on the Rome stock exchange at the end of the decade. However, when the banks went into crisis, failure became inevitable. In this book, the interconnection between banks and industry in the Italian economic framework has been continually emphasized, and the case of Ilva is representative of such interconnection. Furthermore, because Ilva benefited from the First World War, it managed to recover from the difficult phase it experienced at the beginning of the decade, as can be appreciated from the share performance of the stock on the Rome Stock Exchange (Fig. 6.8).

Another industry listed on the Rome Stock Exchange that benefited from the war and that experienced difficulty after the 1929 crisis was *Ansaldo*. As previously mentioned, *Ansaldo* was a large manufacturer of ships and other machinery. The firm exhibits fluctuating share trends after the First World War. Although the company underwent substantial development during the war, when the war ended, it found it difficult to convert to industrial production that no longer served war aims.

The analysis of the *Ansaldo* share prices on the Rome Stock Exchange (Fig. 6.10) confirms the previous thesis: *Ansaldo's* shares on the Rome Stock Exchange suffered a decline from the second quarter of 1921 until they collapsed at the end of 1922. *Ansaldo* was strongly linked to the Italian Discount Bank, which owned 40% of the firm. Thus, it is appropriate to compare the two companies with the aid of Figs. 6.11 and 6.12.

The negative performance of *Ansaldo* shares at the beginning of the decade coincided with the delisting of the *Banca Italiana di Valore* from the stock exchange when the firm entered liquidation. Despite

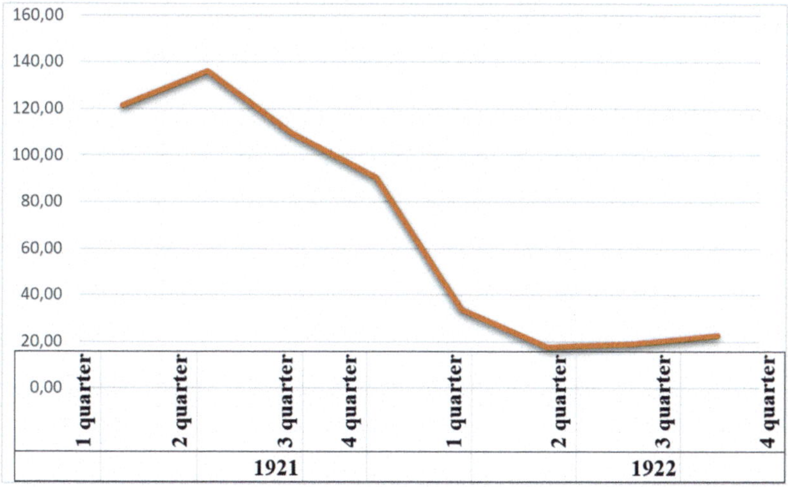

Fig. 6.10 Quarterly trend of Ansaldo shares (1921–1922)

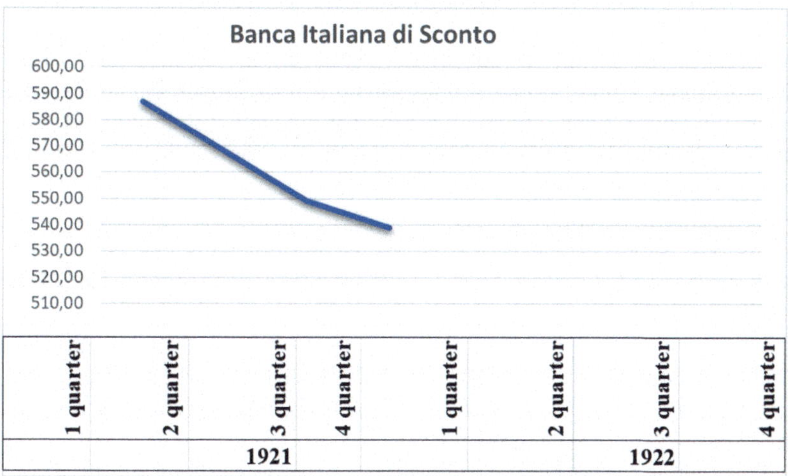

Fig. 6.11 Quarterly trend of the shares of the Italian Discount Bank (1921–1922)

Fig. 6.12 Quarterly trend of Ansaldo shares (1928–1930)

the creation of a support consortium between the issuing institutions and the large banks, promoted by Stringher in November 1921, the Italian Discount Bank obtained a moratorium and was liquidated with the intervention of the special autonomous section of the Consortium for Subsidies on Industrial Values.[27] The government also guaranteed the reimbursement of approximately 60% of the firm's capital to investors. Figure 6.12 reflects the exit of the Italian Discount Bank from the Italian stock market and therefore from the Rome Stock Exchange in 1922 (see also Table 6.4).

The years 1925 to 1930 represent a period of uncertainty for *Ansaldo*, which was controlled by the Bank of Italy until 1925, when it was transferred to the *Banca Nazionale di Credito* (becoming *Ansaldo* SA), to finally pass into public hands in 1933.[28]

As shown in Fig. 6.12, the performance of *Ansaldo* shares on the Rome Stock Exchange remained constant during the three-year period, 1928–1930.

[27] Galanti et al., 2012, p. 63.

[28] Zamagni, 1993, p. 514.

The shares suffered a decline starting in the second quarter of 1930, a prelude to a complicated situation that resulted in the firm's bankruptcy in 1932, when *Ansaldo's* shares collapsed because of the company's difficulties in meeting demand.

The company was subsequently revived and managed by the Institute for Industrial Reconstruction and experienced new growth in its shares when it increased production to support the policy of Mussolini, who was preparing for the Second World War.

From 1921 to 1930, the list of the Rome Stock Exchange clearly reflects the Italian economy of the period, with corporate upheavals, acquisitions, bailouts and industries belonging to the new sectors.

Alongside these large companies, however, it is also appropriate to analyse several little-known companies that are also important in the history of the Rome Stock Exchange.

Among these, the company *Acqua Pia Marcia* deserves mention, as it was listed on the stock exchange at the end of the nineteenth century. The Acqua Marcia company was established with the aim of supplying water in the city of Rome through a project to redevelop the Marciano aqueduct.

Figure 6.13 shows the quarterly trend of the company's shares during the two-year period, 1921–1922.

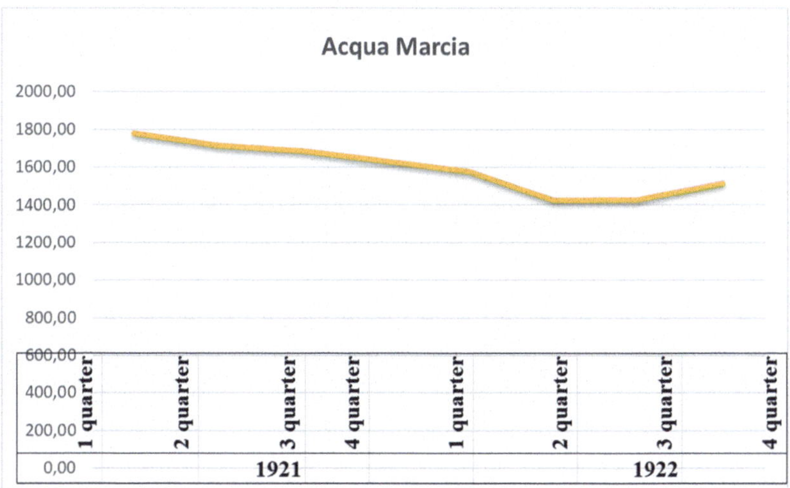

Fig. 6.13 Quarterly trend of Acqua Marcia shares (1921–1922)

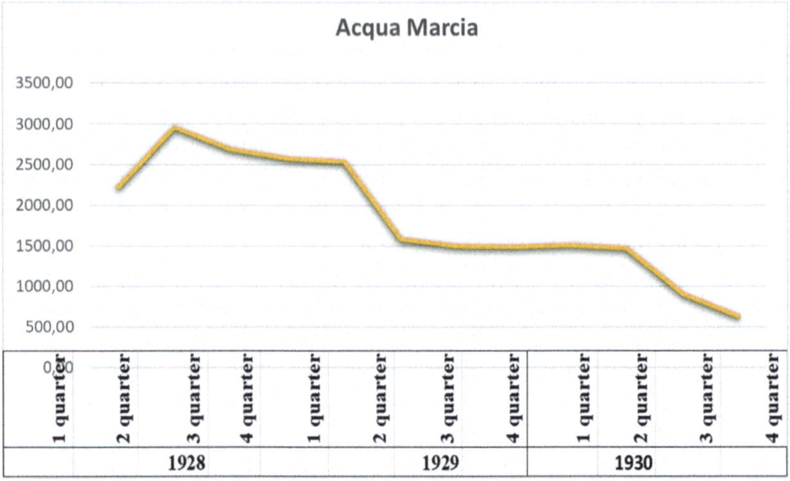

Fig. 6.14 Quarterly trend of Acqua Marcia shares (1928/1930)

The shares of the *Acqua Marcia* company exhibit a continuous and stable trend for the entire two-year period. In the list of the Rome Stock Exchange, shares in the "aqueducts" have always been at the centre of lively trading.[29] Even the shares of *Condotteacqua*, also present in the Roman list (Tables 6.3, 6.4, 6.5, 6.6 and 6.7), always generated a lively interest in investors. Interest did not wane even at the end of the decade, despite a depreciation in the shares.

During the two-year period, 1921–1922, the fluctuations of Acqua Marcia stock were relatively modest, with values ranging from a maximum of 1,800 to a minimum of 1,400 lire.

The situation is different at the end of the decade, when significant fluctuations in the stock occur during the three-year period, 1928–1930.

As shown in Fig. 6.14, after a period of stability in the company's stock prices in the early 1920s, a progressive depreciation commenced in the first quarter of 1929, with a further fall in the second quarter of 1930. Most likely, the stock's depreciation was due to the lower interest

[29] "La Tribuna", Quotidiano, 1922, Biblioteca del Senato "Giovanni Spadolini".

of capital holders in investing in the stock market. The tense atmosphere that reigned following the events of 1929 intensified investor scepticism, causing a sharp decline in stock market trading.

Another historically important company on the Rome Stock Exchange was the Romana Tramways Omnibus company, which operated in the public transport services sector. The company was founded in the mid-nineteenth century, and after experiencing opposition related to concerns over a transport monopoly in the capital, it was able to obtain a concession from the municipality to operate a transport service.

The service was initially provided through horse-drawn omnibuses on the streets of the capital. Subsequently, however, in the wake of innovations related to electricity in the late nineteenth century, the company introduced electric trams.

The company's shares on the Rome Stock Exchange were a constant focus of intense trading. The establishment of the Tramways Omnibus company was clearly one of the many concessions the state granted to individuals to construct and operate railways. In Fig. 6.15, the positive trend of the share price during the two-year period, 1921–1922, is evident.

Figure 6.15 presents the quarterly trend of the shares of Tramways Roma and, more precisely, underlines the lack of significant fluctuations

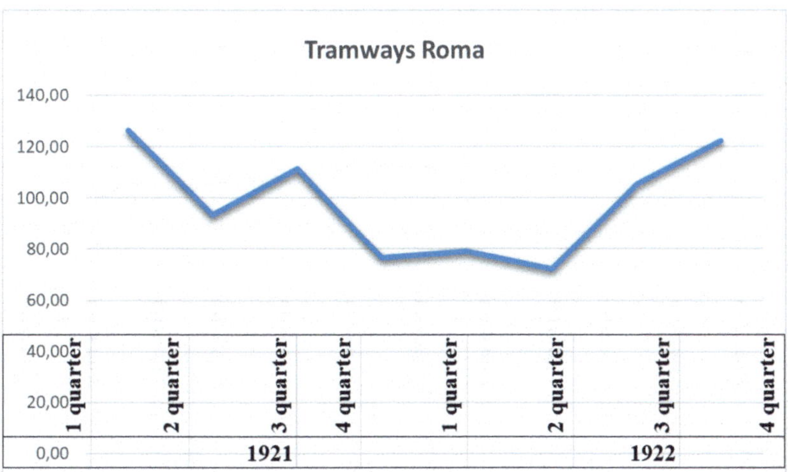

Fig. 6.15 Quarterly trend of Tramways Omnibus shares (1921–1922)

in the stock during the considered two-year period, with a minimum price ranging from 80 lire to a maximum of 130 lire.

In particular, one can note improvement in the trading volume of the stock, with an increasing share value starting in the second quarter of 1922. As shown in Fig. 6.16, these circumstances changed towards the end of the decade, when the volume of trading of the stock increased. Nevertheless, the trend was one of depreciation of the value of the shares, as with all the titles examined to this point. Additionally, in this case, the 1929 crisis evidently represented a disincentive with respect to the share exchanges of all the companies on the list, including Tramways Omnibus.

Figure 6.16 depicts a return to the past in the sense that the value of the shares at the end of the decade reached that of the early 1920s after a highly positive trend in previous years.

Following transport sector reforms, Tramways Omnibus was forced to sell its business to Rome's municipal government. Subsequently, in 1935, the company merged with the Italian Electric Railway Company (SEFI), which was also listed on the capital's stock exchange.

In sum, regarding the corporate securities on the Rome Stock Exchange, it can be stated that the decade from 1920 to 1930 clearly

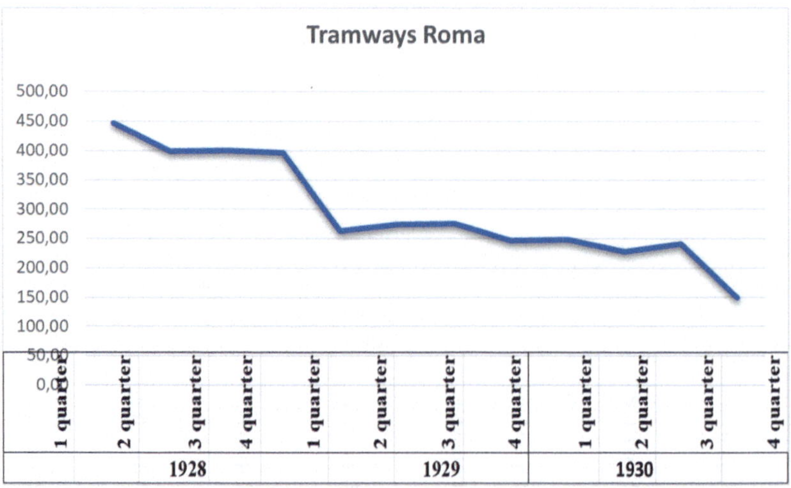

Fig. 6.16 Quarterly trend of Tramways Omnibus shares (1928–1930)

reflects the influence of the industry-bank model that characterized the Italian stock market.

For the entire decade of 1920–1930, the Rome Stock Exchange did not experience any major shocks in terms of corporate stocks, and the performance of these shares was relatively stable. The banks, in fact, nourished the financial resources of the companies with which they were linked, which enabled these companies to survive. One element that all the corporate stocks on the Rome Stock Exchange shared was the depreciation in share value they experienced at the decade's end, with values similar to those of the two-year period, 1921–1922. Exceptions to this depreciation include Fiat, whose shares on the Rome Stock Exchange were always in demand and comparable to those of the banks.

However, all the analysed corporate stocks began depreciating in 1930 in response to the crisis of 1929.

The depreciation can be traced to two causes: the crisis of the banks and investor distrust in the stock market. Having accumulated fixed assets, the banks were sorely afflicted by the international crisis (as we will examine shortly) and dragged down with them nearly all the companies that had benefited from their support.

For their part, investors lost faith in the stock market and initiated a bank run. The experience of the Rome Stock Exchange represents what also occurred in other stock exchanges, that is, depreciation of securities in the aftermath of the crisis and the takeover of nearly all corporate property by the state.

6.4 Bank Securities

In addition to corporate securities, the Rome Stock Exchange listed the securities of numerous banking institutions. These institutions contributed importantly to the country's industrialization.

We have noted that the early 1920s were the years in which the mixed banks began a process of decline that culminated in the aftermath of the 1929 crisis. These banks were of course listed on all Italian stock exchanges and at the centre of events related to Italian industry. The most important banking institution was clearly the Bank of Italy, as much for its fundamental role in state monetary policy as for its role as creditor for many companies and as the coordinator of various bailouts. In this regard, we recall the numerous interventions through consortia on behalf of companies in crisis, such as *Ilva* and *Acciaierie Terni*, both listed on the Roman price list.

Figure 6.17 indicates the stability of the Bank of Italy's shares in the square of Rome, although in those years the bank was engaged on several fronts, placing the Discount Banking Company into liquidation on the one hand while saving the *Banco di Roma* from bankruptcy on the other.

During the decade 1921–1930, the Bank of Italy guaranteed the monetary stability necessary to overcome the banking crisis, especially because with the banking law of 1926 it became the only issuing institution. With the subsequent banking law of 1936, in the same year, the Bank of Italy exited the stock exchange. It was transformed into a supervisory institution, and because it was declared a "public law institution", its private shareholders were expropriated of their shares.

Prior to this development and despite the decrease they experienced in the third quarter of 1929, Bank of Italy shares were fairly stable on the Rome Stock Exchange. They subsequently rose again, albeit slightly, then fell once more (Fig. 6.18).

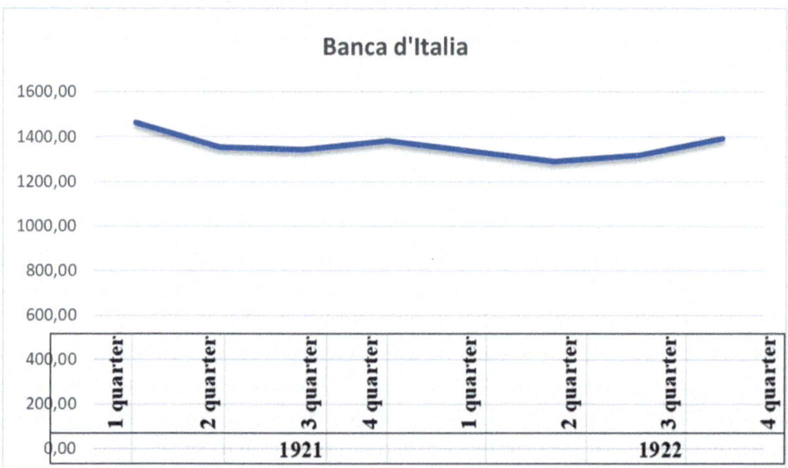

Fig. 6.17 Quarterly trend of the shares of the Bank of Italy (1921–1922)

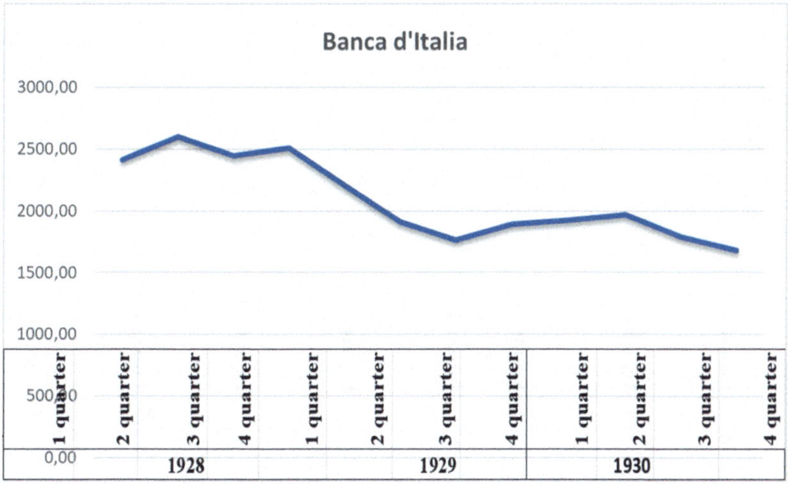

Fig. 6.18 Quarterly trend of the shares of the Bank of Italy (1928–1930)

Obviously, this was an institution that together with the government played a part in many manoeuvres on the stock market and ensured the survival of numerous banks affected by the crisis.

After the issuance of the banking law of 1926, the Bank of Italy was the guarantor of correct monetary policy, a responsibility that became difficult to fulfil when the lira was revalued by Mussolini.

With the exception of the Italian Discount Bank, which was placed into liquidation in 1921, the analysis of the mixed banks of the time is more intriguing. In particular, it is interesting to compare the performance of the shares of the *Banca Commerciale Italiana* and the *Credito Italiano* to highlight their differences (as done previously for an earlier period).

Based on an analysis of the data relating to the shares of Credit and Comit on the Rome Stock Exchange, Figs. 6.19 and 6.20 show the share performance of the two banks over the two-year period, 1921–1922.

Comit shares had greater stability, with a maximum value of nearly 1,200 and a minimum of 800 lire. Comit shares were at the centre of lively trading on the Rome Stock Exchange since their initial listing.

Similarly, Credit experienced highly stable share performance in the early 1920s although its shares had a lower value than those of Comit, with a minimum value of 600 and a maximum of 700 lire.

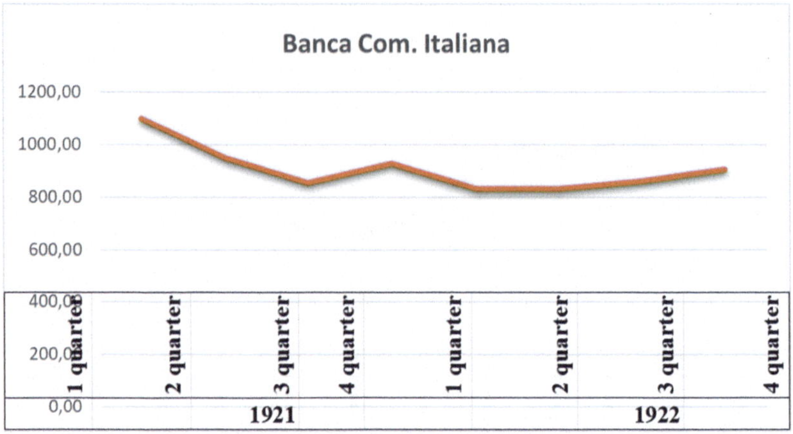

Fig. 6.19 Quarterly trend of Comit shares (1921–1922)

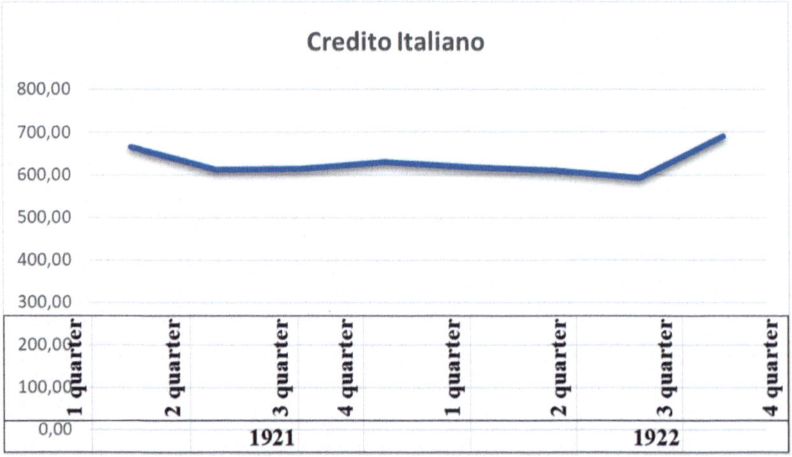

Fig. 6.20 Quarterly trend of Credit shares (1921–1922)

Comit controlled numerous Italian industries, such as *Ilva*, *Acciaierie Terni* or Italgas, and became highly exposed to the Bank of Italy by accumulating substantial debts.

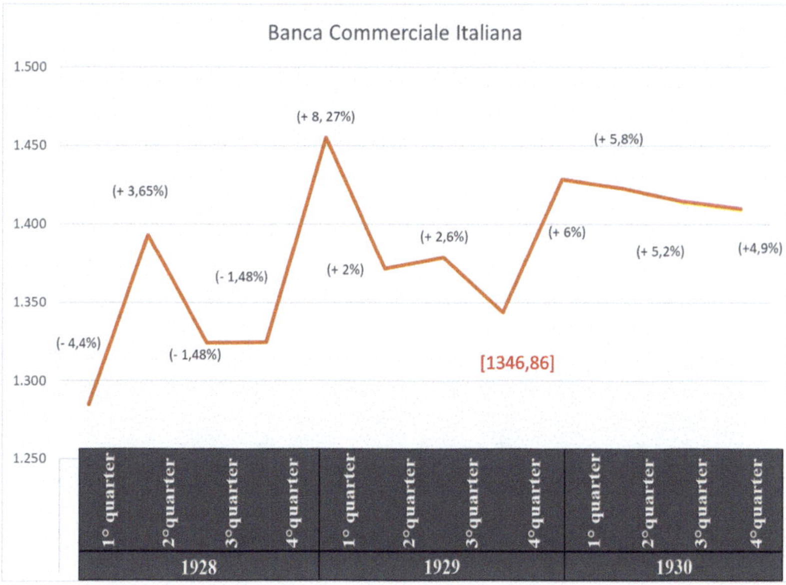

Fig. 6.21 Quarterly trend of Comit shares (1928–1930)

Its behaviour in the development of the companies it financed and owned has been mentioned several times. However, a paradox characteristic of the firm was the cause of a profound crisis after the events of the 1929 crisis. Although in the 1920s the return on Comit shares was stable, Comit's tangled ownership structure and its eventual dependence on state intervention to ensure its survival were representative of the situation of many banks.

Figure 6.21 shows the performance of Comit shares on the Rome Stock Exchange, which at the end of the decade appear to fluctuate somewhat.

After the crisis of 1929, Comit found itself in a disastrous condition as the industrial firms it financed (and owned) depleted its resources. When Comit went into insolvency in 1932, it held stakes in listed companies representing 10% of the stock market's capitalization and approximately

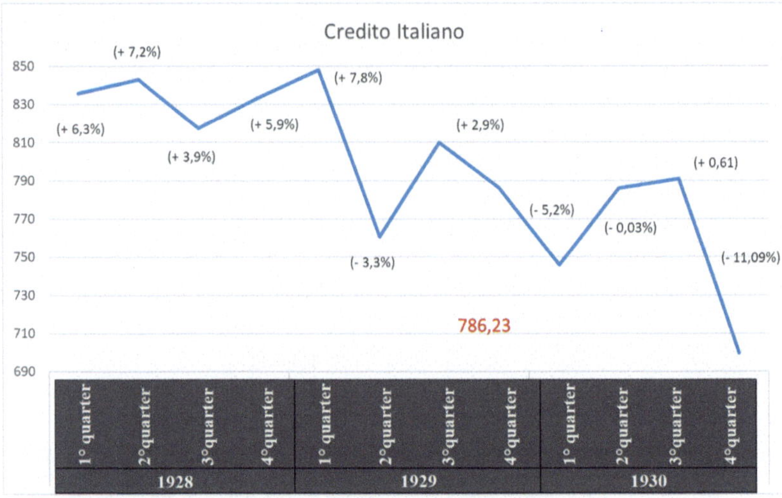

Fig. 6.22 Quarterly trend of credit shares (1928–1930)

one-quarter of the total number of Italian limited companies.[30] Therefore, in 1933, Comit joined the Institute for Industrial Reconstruction, and its shares were delisted.

Figure 6.22 shows the share price trend on the Rome Stock Exchange of *Credito Italiano* during the three-year period, 1928–1930. The trend remained stable until the end of 1930 when a decline began in the third quarter. *Credito Italiano* was forced to avail itself of the Bank of Italy's last resort credit, an emergency operation characterized by speed and secrecy that enabled the crisis to be limited temporarily.[31]

The 1929 crisis caused a credit crisis that affected the Institute of Industrial Reconstruction in 1933, with the consequent delisting of its stock.

In addition to the two largest Italian mixed banks of the time, the *Banco di Roma* was also listed on the Rome Stock Exchange. As previously mentioned, this banking institution was also at the centre of numerous unfortunate events,

[30] Siciliano, 2001, Bologna, p. 29.

[31] Galanti et al., 2012, p. 77.

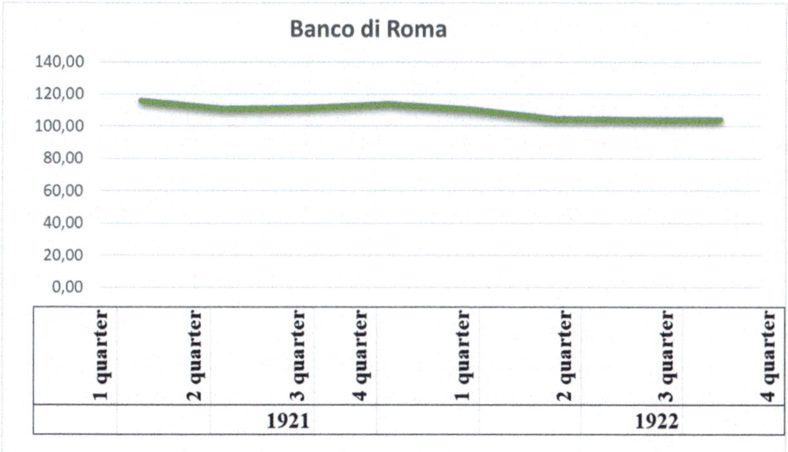

Fig. 6.23 Quarterly performance of Banco di Roma shares (1921–1922)

The *Banco di Roma* shares data that display a certain homogeneity over time. Figure 6.23 shows how the share price reached a maximum value of 116 lire at the beginning of 1921 and a minimum value of 104 lire for the entire fourth quarter of 1922. The analysis of *Banco di Roma*'s share performance focusses on a delicate period for the banking institution during which it was heavily indebted to the Bank of Italy.

Banco di Roma steadily accumulated fixed assets, eventually forcing a government bailout in 1923. The bailout extended to Comit and Credit, which were also unable to sell their portfolios on the market within a reasonable period.

For this reason, a need was felt for a financing institution disconnected from companies that could provide capital without involving rescued banks.[32]

Banco di Roma primarily differed from the other two mixed banks (Comit and Credit) with respect to the dynamics of the crisis. The latter two showed positive returns and equity trends for the entire considered decade and entered into crisis after 1930 as a result of proprietary

[32] Zamagni, 1993, p. 384.

intertwining with industries. In contrast, *Banco di Roma* repeatedly experienced difficulties during the early years of the twentieth century, a symptom of a lack of prudence in its capital management.

As shown in Fig. 6.24, *Banco di Roma's* shares maintained a trend highly similar to that of the early 1920s during the three-year period, 1928–1930.

Although *Banco di Roma* was the third-most important banking institution, the trading volume of its stock was negligible and the bank experienced great difficulties during these years. *Banco di Roma* was subsequently absorbed by IRI, resulting in the cancellation of its shares on the stock exchange lists.

The share price trends on the Roman list of the *Banco di Roma* and the other mixed banks were not entirely negative. Our analyses do not indicate a drastic change in the performance of bank shares when the crisis of 1929 occurred. The crisis of the Italian banks was already an intrinsic problem of the Italian economic system, and in this context, the fascist totalitarian regime played a fundamental role in avoiding disasters by centralizing the ownership of banks and other companies through holding companies.

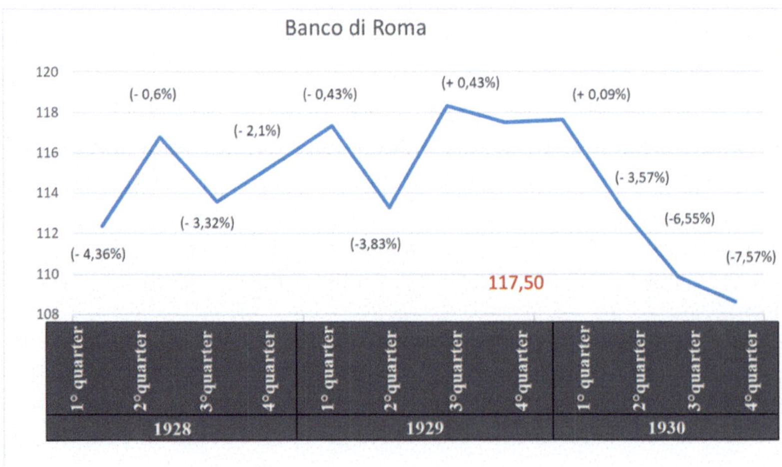

Fig. 6.24 Quarterly performance of Banco di Roma's shares (1928–1930)

Furthermore, the decline in stock prices in late 1929 was caused by an increase in the cost of money, which reduced trading, with significant depreciation of share values. In addition to the large mixed banks, at the decade's end, the Rome Stock Exchange also listed banking companies that did not exist in the early 1920s, such as the Bank of America, the Italo-British Bank, the *Consorzio Mobiliare Finanziario* (*Comofin*), maritime credit and the National Credit Bank. Among these institutions, it is interesting to analyse two that played an important role during this historical phase: *Comofin* and *Banca Nazionale di Credito*. *Comofin* was founded in 1925 by *Comit* to defend itself from takeover attempts by the Perrone brothers, owners of *Ansaldo*.

Figure 6.25 shows the performance of *Comofin* shares on the Rome Stock Exchange at the end of the decade.

Comofin was officially controlled by a group of companies close to *Comit* that held the majority of *Comit* shares and controlled *Comofin* through a holding company (Sofindit).

In such a context, it is complicated to offer a precise overview of the share performance of these companies. Figure 6.25 shows a positive trend in Comofin shares on the Roman stock exchange during the three-year period in question, with a slight decline that began in the third quarter of 1930.

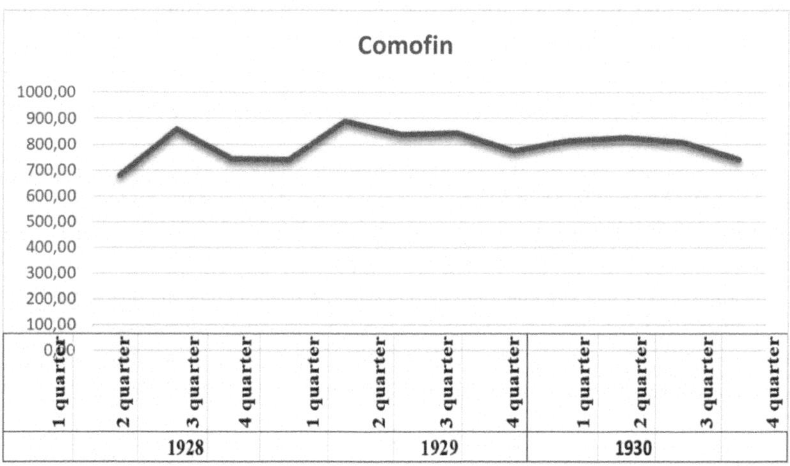

Fig. 6.25 Quarterly trend of Comofin shares (1928–1930)

One should emphasize that Comofin indirectly controlled the share packages of numerous industrial companies financed by Comit, such as Ilva, Breda, Terni and many others. Therefore, Comit's collapse following the crisis of 1929 dragged all chain-controlled companies with it. Generally, all the mixed banks had similar experiences. For example, Breda, which specialized in the construction of locomotives, agricultural machinery and war material, was for a long time 49% owned by *Comit*, but in 1928, its thirty-year partnership with the bank collapsed, and *Banco di Roma* took over.[33]

Another important banking institution of the decade that was listed on the Rome Stock Exchange was the *Banca Nazionale di Credito*, whose foundation dates to 1921 when it was created to manage the liquidation of the Italian Discount Bank. It can, therefore, be considered to all intents and purposes a continuation of the Italian Discount Bank because it oversaw that bank's management. The equity framework of the National Credit Bank represents yet another example of the previously described pattern: a collapse of the stock trend in the aftermath of the 1929 crisis (Fig. 6.26).

Furthermore, in 1930, Credit incorporated the *Banca Nazionale di Credito* due to the difficulties in which this bank found itself. Through the foundation of the Italian financial company, the industrial shareholdings of the two banks were taken over so they could be disinvested, something possible, thanks to a 1931 agreement with the Bank of Italy and using the financing of the liquidation institute.[34]

In sum, the banking stocks on the Rome Stock Exchange were affected by the 1929 crisis only starting in 1930, when the fascist government had to implement a regulatory economic policy.

However, all the banks on the Rome Stock Exchange that were analysed exhibited solid stability in share performance with few share fluctuations. This stability probably reflects the fact that the 1929 crisis had yet to exert its full effect, having spread to Italy in 1930.

Unlike corporate bonds, however, bank bonds disappeared completely. This phenomenon was a common element among the mixed banks of the time (i.e., *Comit, Credit* and *Banco di Roma*), that is, their merger with the Institute for the Industrial Reconstruction following the 1929

[33] Zamagni, 1993, p. 504.

[34] Ibidem, p. 383.

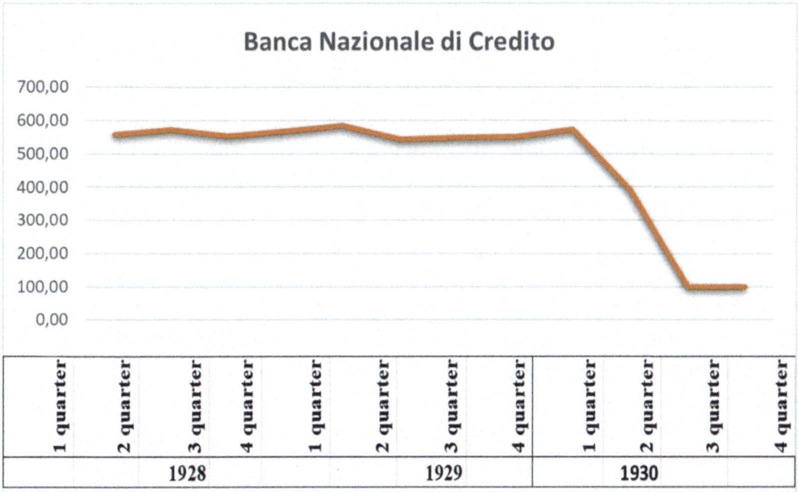

Fig. 6.26 Quarterly trend of the shares of the National Credit Bank (1928–1930)

crisis and the delisting of the related securities. The shares of the three banks were reregistered in 1970 when Mediobanca performed placement operations for them.

6.5 Government Bonds: The Annuity and the Consolidated (la rendita e il Consolidato)

The stock market in Italy, including in Rome, was characterized not only by corporate and banking securities but also, and above all, by the presence of public debt securities. During the nineteenth century, the states of the Italian Peninsula used these securities to raise capital to support their economic policies.[35]

The Papal State used the Rome Stock Exchange as a source of financing through the Roman Consolidation. Subsequently, with the founding of the Kingdom of Italy, the public debt securities of the individual states

[35] Sabatini, 2004; Postigliola-Strangio, 2017; Teodolti-Volpi, 2021.

disappeared as they were merged into a single security, the Italian Rendita, with an interest rate of 5%. Between 1921 and 1930, the Rome Stock Exchange listed public debt securities that reflected national economic and monetary policy.

In the period preceding the outbreak of the First World War, the Rendita represented approximately 60% of the total public debt. Subsequently, on 1 January 1907, the 5% yield was converted into a 3.75% net yield and on 1 January 1912 into a 3.5% net yield.[36]

As mentioned in the previous chapter, these measures represented exceptional manoeuvres by the Giolitti government, whose conversion of public debt securities from a yield of 5% to one of 3.5% meant considerable savings for state coffers. In 1917, six consolidated national loans were issued to finance war expenses. Among these, the Rome Stock Exchange listed the fifth consolidated national loan of 1918 in the early 1920s.

Alongside the Rendita and Consolidato, in 1928, the so-called "Prestito del Littorio", irredeemable and with a 5% coupon, was listed together with other public debt securities as it was perfectly fungible. This manoeuvre was intended to prevent the repayment of capital to avoid a further increase in public debt by stipulating repayment would begin in 1937. The public debt securities listed on the stock exchange between 1920 and 1930 represented approximately 80% of medium/long-term public debt.

In 1922, the issuance of government bonds absorbed approximately 36% of national savings, and in this context, the banks continued to grant loans to businesses. Here, the stock market played a relatively small role on the equity side.

Public debt securities could assume various forms based on the type of credit the state wished to obtain. It is important to realize that the state changed the structure of public debt securities according to its budget. Thus, for example, thanks to the budget surpluses of the early twentieth century, Giolitti could perform the previously mentioned conversion of the Rendita. When the state budget was in the red, the state was forced to issue long-term consolidated debt securities, which were configured as a real annuity, i.e., with the payment of coupon interest only and without a precise repayment date.

[36] Siciliano, 2001, p. 186.

Therefore, in the decade 1921–1930, the Rome Stock Exchange listed the Italian Rendita at 3.5%, and the Consolidation relating to war loans, issued until 1918 by the State, was listed at a rate of 5%.

We can analyse the trend of the 3.5% Italian annuity income on the Rome Stock Exchange in the early 1920s and at the decade's end.

However, let us first note an important fact: the Italian Rendita was also issued on the Paris stock exchange, other European markets and the Italian stock exchanges. Therefore, it is difficult to separate the foreign from the domestic component.

Figure 6.27 reveals a certain stability of the annuities on the Rome Stock Exchange during the two-year period, 1921–1922. The minimum value is approximately 71 lire, while the maximum is approximately 75.5 lire.

The decade in question was characterized by various government interventions to limit the burden of the public debt arising from the First World War, especially because the support for the lira desired by Mussolini required sacrifices. Through the consolidation of floating debt, of which

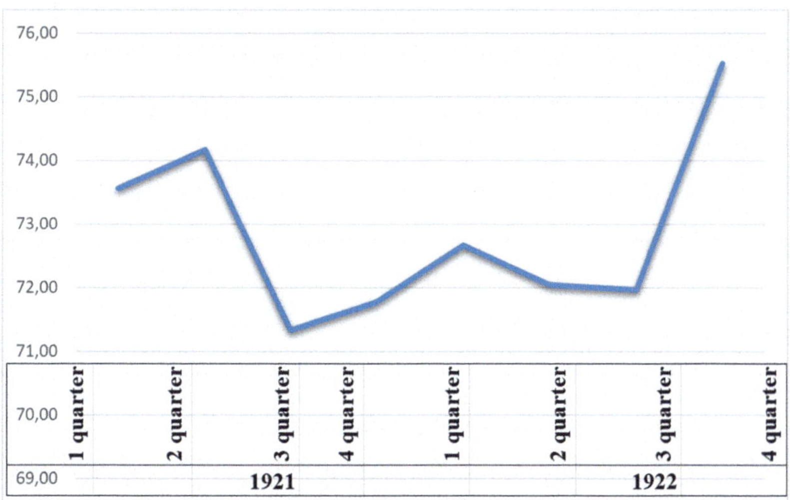

Fig. 6.27 Quarterly trend of the Italian annuity (Rendita Italiana) 3.5% (1921–1922)

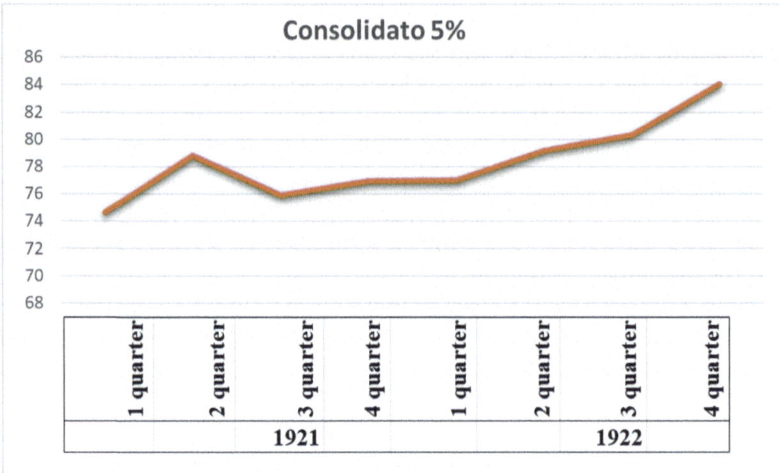

Fig. 6.28 Consolidation trend 5% (1921–1922)

the "Littorio" was the implementation instrument, the value of the short-term debt held by the public and the banking system was reduced from 27 to 6 billion lire.[37]

In addition to the Rendita, for the two-year period, 1921–1922, we also find in the list of the Rome Stock Exchange another public debt security: the Consolidato.

Based on our research, the security was referred to "Consolidato 5% 1918" (Fig. 6.28). Thus, consolidated public debt securities were evidently issued to finance war expenses. Of particular note was the fifth national loan for war expenses, issued in December 1917 and signed beginning in 1918.

The loan was configured as an annuity at a rate of 5% per annum, payable in two annual coupons and tax exempt, with an issue price to the public of 86.50 lire for every 100 of nominal capital.[38]

During the war period, as many as six national loans were issued, of which the last three were configured as a consolidated annuity.

[37] Toniolo, 1980, p. 112.

[38] Manifesto ufficiale per il prestito, 1918.

These loans overlapped because the state guaranteed better treatment for underwriters whenever it issued a loan. In this case, it was possible to subscribe the new bonds through payment by means of other bonds held, including ordinary, three-year and five-year Treasury bills and government bonds. The latter included 3.5% Italian Rendita bonds, 5% Blount Loan bonds, railway bonds, 4.5% National Loan bonds of 1915 and 5% National Loan bonds of 1916.[39]

As shown in Figs. 6.27 and 6.28, the performances of the annuity and consolidation on the Roman stock exchange appear positive. However, it is difficult to establish a global estimate, especially with regard to the Rendita, which, as previously mentioned, was also quoted outside the peninsula, where the price was fixed. Nevertheless, many economists believe the economic manoeuvres of those years were important with respect to public debt securities. Following the conversion of the Giolitti government, there was in 1926 a forced consolidation of short-term securities into Littorio securities, with a thirty-year maturity at a rate of 3.75%.

Subsequently, however, in 1928, the Littorio securities became irredeemable, and their rate became 5%, taking the form of a consolidated income. Forced consolidation caused a fall in the price of the consolidated and difficulty obtaining liquidity for the underwriters. The National Consolidated Loan 5% (Littorio) left the list of the Rome Stock Exchange at the end of 1928 (Table 6.5).

In addition to the Littorio securities, the Rome Stock Exchange also saw the nine-year Treasury Bills issued in 1931 and 1934 disappear from its list. Figures 6.29, 6.30 and 6.31 show the securities trends up to the third quarter of 1928.

The fall in the rate of the Consolidated in the aftermath of the mandatory consolidation of short-term securities is also evident from the quotations on the Roman stock exchange. In fact, starting in the fourth quarter of 1928, a depreciation of the stock began that continued until it reached a minimum in the third quarter of 1929. As shown in Fig. 6.32, the trend appears to fluctuate.

In contrast, regarding the Italian annuity, Fig. 6.33 shows how at the end of the decade, the stock's trend was in sharp decline compared to

[39] Ibidem, p. 29.

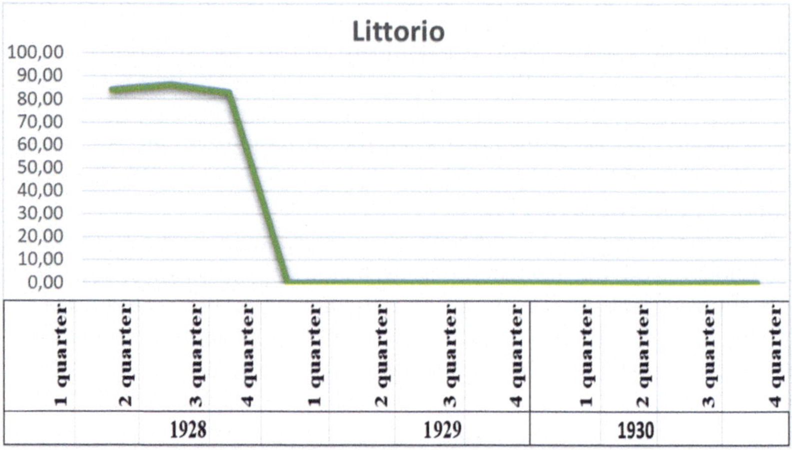

Fig. 6.29 Quarterly trend of the "Littorio" (1928–1930)

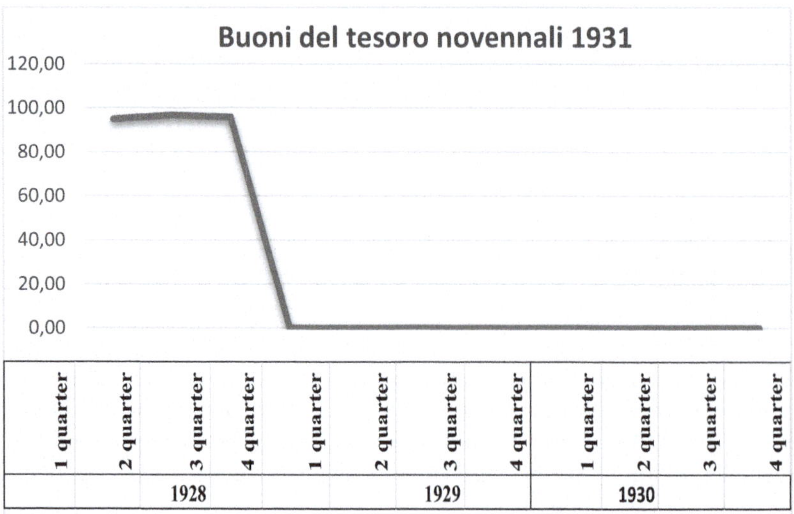

Fig. 6.30 Quarterly trend of nine-year Treasury Bills of 1931 (1928–1930)

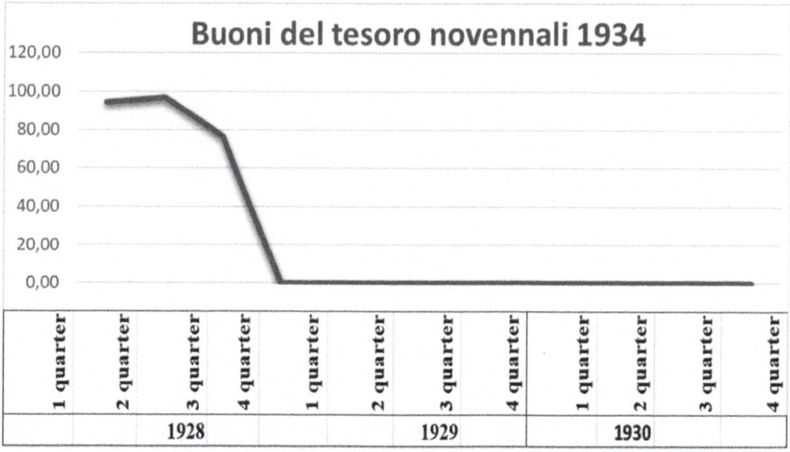

Fig. 6.31 Quarterly trend of nine-year Treasury Bills of 1934 (1928–1930)

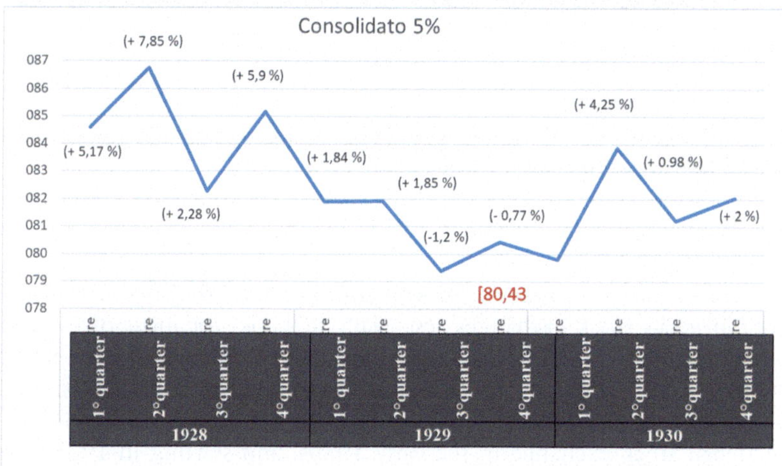

Fig. 6.32 Quarterly trend of the consolidated 5% (1928–1930)

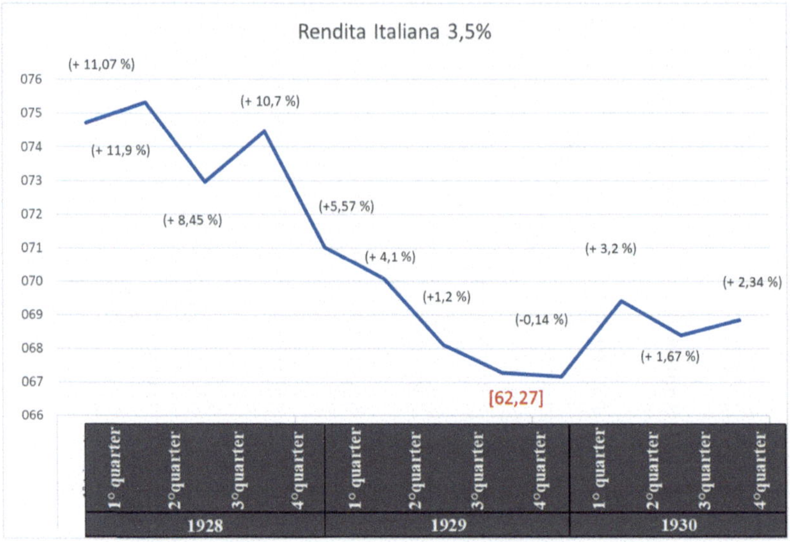

Fig. 6.33 Trend of the 3.5% Italian annuity (1928–1930)

the early 1920s. The decline is probably attributable to the decrease in trading following the onset of the world economic crisis.

In addition to the Rendita and Consolidato, the Rome Stock Exchange also listed another government bond, the "*Venezie Bonds*", with an interest rate of 3.5%.

According to our research, these securities were listed on all national and European stock exchanges (especially in Paris) for most of the last century, with the exception of the Consolidated 5%, which as a result of subsequent economic interventions by the Italian government was subject to continuous conversions. In fact, the 5% Treasury Bills entered the Italian stock exchange in the early 1930s, and starting in 1935, the 5% Italian Rendita was listed following the conversion of a redeemable loan.[40]

[40] Gazzetta ufficiale del Regno d'Italia, 1935, in www.augusto.agid.gov.it.

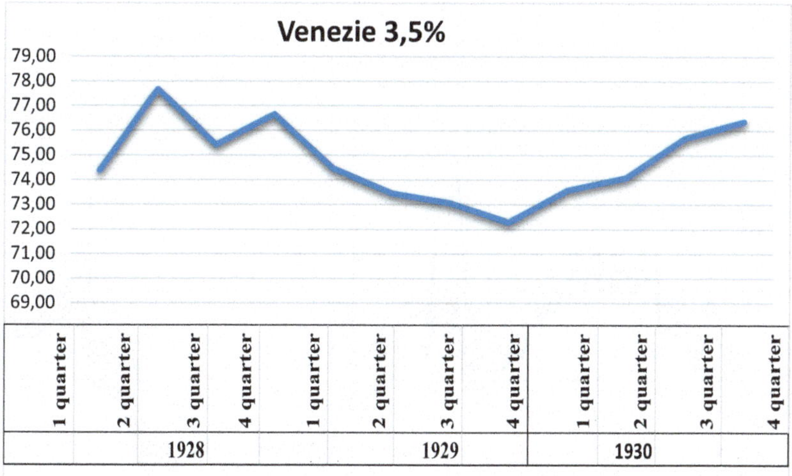

Fig. 6.34 Quarterly trend of the 3.5% Venezie bonds (1928–1930)

Figure 6.34 shows the performance of the "*Obbligazioni Venezie*" (Venezie Bonds) stock on the Rome Stock Exchange during the three-year period, 1928–1930. The figure reflects how the stock declined from the end of 1928–1929, with a turning point in the early 1930s.

Public debt securities have always represented an important instrument in state financing, especially in Italy, where their yield has always been higher than that of shares, to the detriment of a real development of the stock market.

Figure 6.35 shows the composition of the public debt based on the instruments used in relation to GDP. Long-term securities have always distinguished the Italian stock market.

In the period 1921–1930, there were many short-term securities on the Rome Stock Exchange. However, at the end of the decade, they were transformed into long-term securities.

Following the establishment of the Institute of Industrial Reconstruction, nearly all industrial companies were controlled by the state through special institutions, and the role of the stock exchange was limited.

The 1929 crisis left a legacy of large banking imbalances and a greater awareness of the importance of state regulation in the national economy. This legacy resulted in the configuration of the stock exchange in subsequent years as a mere tool for raising capital through public debt securities.

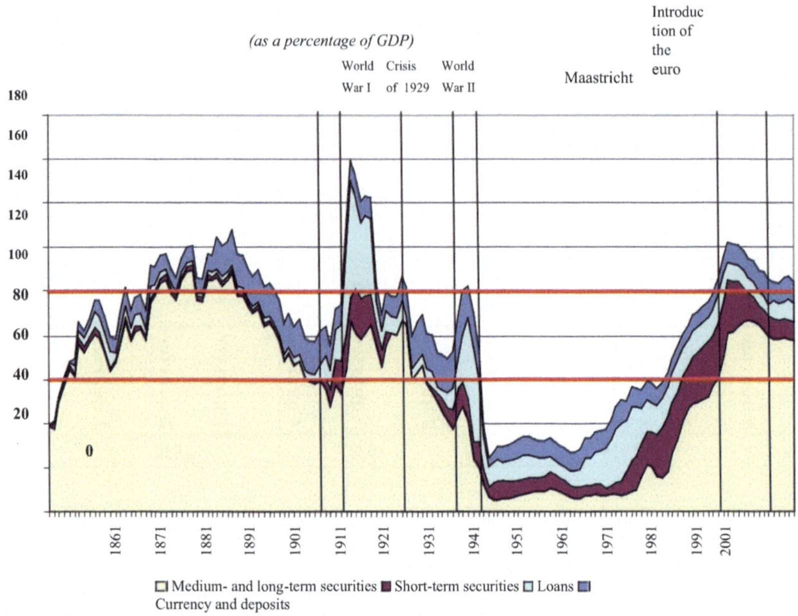

Fig. 6.35 Public Administration Debt: breakdown by instrument (*Source* Questioni di economia e finanza, Il *debito pubblico italiano dall'Unità an oggi. Una ricostruzione della serie storica*, Maura Francese e Angelo Pace, Pubblicazioni Banca d'Italia, 2008, p. 22, in www.bancaditalia.it)

References

Baia Curioni, Stefano. 1995. *Regolazione e competizione. Storia del mercato azionario in Italia (1808–1938)*, Bologna: Il Mulino.

Bof, Frediano. 2015. Economia e politica economica in tà fascista, in Paolo Pecorari (ed.) *L'Italia economica. Tempi e fenomeni del cambiamento (1861–2000)*, Padoa: Cedam, 119–156 and 157–185.

Bonelli, Franco (ed.). 1991. *La Banca d'Italia dal 1894 al 1913. Momenti della formazione di una banca centrale*, Rome-Bari: Laterza.

Bricco, Paolo. 2021. *Cassa Depositi e Prestiti. Storia di un capitale dinamico e paziente. Da 170 anni*, Bologna, Il Mulino.

Cardarelli, Sergio. 1990. *La questione bancaria in Italia dal 1860 al 1892*, in Ricerche per la storia della Banca d'Italia, vol. I, Rome-Bari: Laterza.

Castronovo, Valerio (ed.). AA VV, 2012. *Storia dell'IRI*, Rome-Bari, Laterza (6 volls.)

Coltorti, Fulvio. 2011. Il ruolo dell'Industria. Grandi e medie Imprese, in Luca Paolazzi (ed.) *Libertà e benessere in Italia*, Rome-Bari: Laterza.

CONSOB. 2011. *Dall'Unità ai giorni nostri: 150 anni di borsa in Italia*. https://www.consob.it/web/area-pubblica/150-unita-d-italia.

De Cecco, Marcello (ed.). 1990. *L'Italia e il sistema finanziario internazionale 1861–1914*, Rome-Bari: Laterza.

De Cecco, Marcello and Gianni Toniolo. 2001. *Storia della Cassa Depositi e Prestiti*, Rome-Bari: Editori Laterza.

De Cecco, Marcello and Gianni Toniolo. 2014. *Storia della Cassa depositi e prestiti. Un nuovo corso: la società per azioni*, Rome-Bari: Editori Laterza.

De Luca, Giuseppe. 2002. *Dall'economia industrial all'industria della finanza: le società quotate al listino azionario della Borsa di Milano dal 1861 al 2000*, a cura di Giuseppe De Luca, *Le società quotate alla borsa valori di Milabo dal 1861 al 2000. Profili storici e titoli azionari*, Milano: Libri Scheiwiller, 25–86.

Eichengreen Barry. 1994. *Gabbie D'Oro. Il "gold standard" e la grande depressiozn 1919–1939*, Rome-Bari: Cariplo Laterza.

Galanti, Enrico, Raffaele D'Ambrosio, and Alessandro V. Guccione. 2012. *Storia della legislazione bancaria, finanziaria e assicurativa. Dall'Unità d'Italia al 2011*, Venice: Marsilio.

Galbraith, John Kenneth. 2003. *Il grande crollo*, Hoepli: Che cosa ci ha insegnato sul capitalismo la Grande Depressione, Milan.

Gazzetta ufficiale del Regno d'Italia. 1935, in www.augusto.agid.gov.it.

Gigliobianco, Alfredo. 2006. *Via Nazionale. Banca d'Italia e classe dirigente. Cento anni di storia*, Rome: Donzelli.

Kindleberger Charles, P. 1987. *La depressione del 1929*, in *Storia della finanza nell'Europa occidentale*, Milano: Cariplo Laterza, 495–520.

"L'Italia in 150 anni. Sommario di statistiche storiche 1861–2010", in www.istat.it.

Manifesto ufficiale per il prestito. 1918. http://www.museibologna.it/risorgimento/percorsi/52273/luogo/47752/id/48244/oggetto/48848/

Postigliola, Michele and Donatella Strangio. 2017. *Il debito pubblico italiano. Una serie storica dal 1861 al 2012*, *Storia economica*, XX(1): 313–330.

Sabatini, Gaetano. 2003. La storiografia più recente sulla finanza italiana dell'età moderna: Gli studi sul debito pubblico. *Rivista di storia finanziaria* 10: 79–128.

Sabatini, Gaetano. 2004. Il debito pubblico in età moderna, in Angelo Moioli and Fausto Piola Caselli (eds.) *La storiografia finanziaria italiana. Un bilancio degli studi più recenti sull'età moderna e contemporanea*, Cassino: Edizioni dell'Università degli Studi di Cassino, 89–145.

Siciliano, Giovanni. 2001. *Cento anni di borsa in Italia. Mercato, imprese e rendimenti azionari nel ventesimo secolo*, Bologna: Il Mulino.

Teodolti, Leonida and Alessandro Volpi. 2021. *Storia del debito pubblico in Italia. Dall'Unità a oggi*, Rome-Bari: Editori Laterza.

Toniolo, Gianni. 1980. *L'economia dell'Italia fascista*, Rome-Bari: Editori Laterza.

Toniolo, Gianni. 1994. *Cent'anni 1894–1994. La Banca Commerciale e l'economia italiana*, Milan: Nardini-Banca Commerciale Italiana.

www.archiviostoricoiri.it.

www.gruppoilva.com.

www.ilsole24ore.com.

Zamagni, Vera. 1990. (1993 II ed.). *Dalla periferia al centro. La seconda rinascita economica dell'Italia (1861–1990)*, Bologna: Il Mulino.

Sources

"La Tribuna", (roman daily newspaper), Biblioteca del Senato "Giovanni Spadolini" various years.

Conclusion

During this century of analysis of the stock exchange, the city has grown in demographic terms, passing from approximately 226,022 inhabitants in 1870 to 945,621 in the early 1930s (where the analysis of this book stops) and in terms of territory, acquiring new areas and constructing new buildings and neighbourhoods and integrating into the complex new Italian national system. The particular angle through which we proceeded to indirectly analyze the city, the Rome Stock Exchange, made it possible to understand these changes together with those of finance and the economy: in fact, it is undeniable that the portfolio of stock market securities reflected the main financial and economic attitudes of the capital city.[1]

As Marina Formica wrote, the rupture of relations between the State and the Church would have appeared to everyone as incurable. Only time, history could have shown that the "breach of Porta Pia", the denial of the pope's temporal authority, the nationalization of ecclesiastical assets would have been rather positive factors for the Church itself and for her spiritual life.[2] As for Rome, if the secularization imposed from above favoured the civil growth of its inhabitants and accelerated the process of adapting the city to other urban realities, its universal and cosmopolitan

[1] Comune di Roma, 1960.

[2] Formica, 2019, p. 237.

D. Strangio, *The Roman Stock Exchange between the 19th and 20th Centuries*, Palgrave Studies in the History of Finance,
https://doi.org/10.1007/978-3-031-00359-2

nature, favoured and produced by the presence of the Church, would have guaranteed that openness and the receptivity necessary for the affirmation of a new and great capital. Her alleged weak identity which, according to her detractors, made her unsuitable for governing (multiethnicity, the absence of a consolidated dynasty), turned out, on the contrary, to be a strong point.[3]

Certainly the papal court had always determined over the years a significant influx of French, Belgian, English, Israelite capital (three quarters of the public debt were in foreign hands) from which the capital of a young Kingdom, animated by ambitions of integration in the European scenarios, could only benefit.[4]

The advance of the capitalist system in Europe during the nineteenth century is enriched with the growth of anonymous companies, with the circulation of share and bond certificates. As Sapelli wrote, the Stock Exchange is an observatory through which it is possible to understand the evolution of companies, in this case Italian: the Stock Exchange tells the different evolutionary forms of companies in the markets and, in the Italian case, more specific than that of Roman, the patrimonial enterprise appears, typical of pre-industrial capitalism, which sees the family at the centre, which creates this economic association to maximize the return on the capital invested.[5]

From this social construct emerges the large financial enterprise, the result of the credit differentiation that occurs on a large scale for the analysis of industrial capitalism. The prototype of this type of enterprise is the "mixed bank". It is characterized by the hierarchical power it exercises over the investment decisions of companies of any kind to a greater or lesser extent, giving rise to financial capitalism, that is to say the inseparable link between bank and company.

This system spread in particular in the second half of the nineteenth century up to the early nineties and had a certain importance for the industrial and commercial growth of continental and Asian Europe. After that, everything begins to change in the world of economy due to the transformations that take place in the world political and military system.

[3] Ibidem.

[4] Gille, 1968.

[5] Sapelli, 2002, p. 17; see also Kindlebergher, 1987.

A city between cities, the City, with its marked rural aspect, also favours a lively, if sometimes disordered, urban development. In an international panorama on which the advance of the workers' forces was considered a threat to Europe, the rarity of factories and industries in Rome was synonymous with the absence of an industrial proletariat and this was judged as a source of guarantee for the entrepreneurial and industrialists of the North, terrified by the Communist danger.[6] Even thirty or forty years after 20 September 1870, no large industries were established in Rome.[7] Rome increasingly differs in its economic structure from the large industrial and developed metropolises of the main European countries and other Italian regions: the city moves and arranges itself around the survivals of the tradition of tourist city and religious centre and, in particular, around the increased administrative activities of the capital of the unitary state.

In the light of this examination of the city of Rome, made starting from a particular angle such as that of a financial stock exchange, within a few particular decades, one might wonder if it was Italy that "deromanized" the city or if it was rather the latter to Romanize Italy.[8]

What is certain is that the charm of this city and the main challenge of examining the economic and social aspects through the study of a stock exchange (perhaps considered narrow and not very exhaustive at first sight) has revealed a tiring and fluctuating path that has seen it. "To transform itself" from the "capital" of a particular and two-faced state, such as the papal one, to the capital of a Kingdom, which was trying to consolidate and build its own identity, just like Rome, which was called upon to meet a new challenge.

[6] Formica, 2019, p. 239; Caracciolo, 1984, pp. 244–268.

[7] Caracciolo, 1984, p. 244.

[8] Formica, 2019, p. 239.

References

Bertrand Gille, *Les investissements francais en Italie* in «Archivio Economico dell'Unificazione Italiana», serie II, vol. XVI, Roma 1968.

Caracciolo, Alberto. 1984 (1956 I ed.). *Roma Capitale. Dal Risorgimento alla crisi dello Stato liberale*, Rome: Editori Riuniti.

Comune di Roma. Roma. 1960. *Popolazione e territorio dal 1860 al 1960. Con la distribuzione territoriale dei censimenti*, Roma: Ufficio di Statistica e censimento.

Formica, Marina. 2019. *Roma, Romae. Una capitale in Età moderna*, Rome-Bari: Laterza.

Kindlebergher, Charles P. 1987. *Storia della finanza nell'Europa occidentale*, Milan: Cariplo-Laterza.

Sapelli, Giulio. 2002, *Premessa*, in Giuseppe De Luca (ed.), *Le società quotate alla borsa valori di Milano dal 1861 al 2000. Profili storici e titoli azionari*, Milan: Libri Scheiwiller.

Index

D. Strangio, *The Roman Stock Exchange between the 19th and 20th Centuries*, Palgrave Studies in the History of Finance,
https://doi.org/10.1007/978-3-031-00359-2

The manufacturer's authorised representative in the EU is Springer Nature Customer Service Centre GmbH, Europaplatz 3, 69115 Heidelberg, Germany. If you have any concerns regarding our products, please contact ProductSafety@springernature.com

Printed and bound by CPI Group (UK) Ltd, Croydon, CR0 4YY
30/09/2026
02225492-0003